JOAN ROBINSON

Recent Titles in
Bio-Bibliographies in Economics

William J. Fellner: A Bio-Bibliography
James N. Marshall

JOAN ROBINSON

A Bio-Bibliography

JAMES CICARELLI
AND JULIANNE CICARELLI

Bio-Bibliographies in Economics, Number 2

GP

GREENWOOD PRESS
Westport, Connecticut • London

Library of Congress Cataloging-in-Publication Data

Cicarelli, James.
Joan Robinson : a bio-bibliography / by James Cicarelli and Julianne Cicarelli.
p. cm.—(Bio-bibliographies in economics, ISSN 1063-3197 ; no. 2)
Includes bibliographical references and index.
ISBN 0-313-25844-9 (alk. paper)
1. Robinson, Joan, 1903– . 2. Economists—Great Britain—Biography. I. Title. II. Series.
HB103.R63C53 1996
330′.092—dc20 96-23236

British Library Cataloguing in Publication Data is available.

Library of Congress Catalog Card Number: 96-23236
ISBN: 0-313-25844-9
ISSN: 1063-3197

First published in 1996

Greenwood Press, 88 Post Road West, Westport, CT 06881
An imprint of Greenwood Publishing Group, Inc.

Printed in the United States of America

The paper used in this book complies with the Permanent Paper Standard issued by the National Information Standards Organization (Z39.48–1984).

10 9 8 7 6 5 4 3 2

Copyright Acknowledgments

The authors and publisher gratefully acknowledge permission for use of the following material:

Marjorie Turner. *Joan Robinson and the Americans*. Armonk, NY: M. E. Sharpe, 1989.

for jill and david

Contents

Preface ix

Acknowledgments xiii

Chronology xvii

1. Biographical Sketch 1

    Family Values 1

    The Quaking Discipline 5

    Robinson after Marx 9

    The War between the Cambridges 13

    Afflicting the Comfortable 19

    Questions without Answers 22

    Assessing a Life 27

2. Works by Joan Robinson 33

    A User's Guide 33

3. Works about Joan Robinson and Her Writings 133

Index 165

Preface

As L. L. Pasinetti points out in his biographical essay [477], in 1975, the year the United Nations proclaimed the International Year of the Woman, virtually everyone in the economics profession thought Joan Robinson would be chosen for the Nobel Prize in Economics.[1] Indeed, expecting Robinson to win the award, "The American magazine *Business Week*, after sounding out the American economics profession, felt so sure of the choice as to anticipate the event by publishing a long article on her, presenting her explicitly as being on everyone's list for this year's Nobel Prize in Economics" [477:212]. Characterizing her as a "socialist who sounds like a conservative," the *Business Week* article noted that her views on wages and prices "are what American businessmen talk about at board meetings," even though among American economists "she has been more ignored than adored" [440:80]. Still, the magazine, citing "her work on the relationship between capital accumulation and growth, as well as her 1933 classic *The Economics of Imperfect Competition*," considered her a prime candidate for a Nobel Prize.

Prime candidate or not, she did not receive the award then or in any subsequent year. The 1975 prize was shared by Tjalling C. Koopmans, a pioneer in the mathematical technique of linear programming, and Leonid Kantorovich, a

[1] Initiated in 1901, the Nobel Prize was originally limited to physics, chemistry, medicine or physiology, literature, and peace. In 1968, in conjunction with its tercentenary celebration, the Central Bank of Sweden instituted "The Central Bank of Sweden Prize in Economic Science in the Memory of Alfred Nobel." Announced each October when the other Nobels are awarded, this prize is given "according to the same principles and rules as the original Nobel prizes." Technically however, it is not a Nobel Prize despite being commonly referred to as such [472].

Russian economist virtually unknown outside the then Soviet Union. Not winning the award had a perverse effect on Robinson's reputation: "Ever since, in shoptalk among economists all over the world, Joan Robinson has become the greatest Nobel Prize winner that never was" [477:212].

That the royal Swedish Academy of Science--the awarding authority for the prizes in physics, chemistry, and economics--missed a golden opportunity to recognize one of the truly great economists of the twentieth century in no way diminishes Joan Robinson and her significance to the discipline. In compiling this bio-bibliography, we pay homage to one of the intellectual giants of modern economics and seek to extend the knowledge of her contributions to a new generation of economics students and scholars who, for whatever reasons, may be unfamiliar with Joan Robinson's work or influence. This is not, however, a valentine. As Marjorie Turner points out, the diamond that was Joan Robinson had many facets, some of which reflected more light than others:

> Joan Robinson the economist is inseparable from the complex person that she was. A strong woman, who as a teacher could make her men students cry themselves to sleep in despair, who as a colleague could cause some of the world's leading economists to tremble with rage, she was never a feminist. An admirer and critic of Marx, she was never a Marxist. She approved of the communist social experiments, particularly those in China and North Korea, but was not a communist. She expressed deep sympathy for the working class, but she was sometimes a critic of the Labour Party. She was a tender mother and grandmother, and a devoted and popular teacher. She never yielded a point until she could see it plainly. Joan Robinson's family background, her education in economics at Cambridge, and the changing times through which she lived were important factors in molding her views and personality. [481:9]

Joan Violet Robinson had her faults; she also had an abundance of strengths and virtues. The purpose of this book is to reflect the whole Joan Robinson, to project a hologram that shows the warts as well as the beauty marks and, in so doing, captures the essence of a life that had a profound effect on the nature of economic thinking as we in the Western world know it.

The book begins with a chronological history of Joan Robinson. This is followed with a biographical sketch that is divided into seven parts, each covering a distinct portion of her life. "Family Values" is a description of her early life, with particular emphasis on the family environment in which she grew up. We believe that it is absolutely essential to understand her heritage and the atmosphere which nurtured her, if one wants to know why Joan Robinson turned out the way she did.

The second section of the biographical essay--"The Quaking Discipline"--is about Joan Robinson in the 1930s, a period in which Western economics was literally reinvented and in which Robinson made her greatest contributions to the field according to some economic historians. That period of intense activity was followed by one in which Joan Robinson was, by comparison, dormant. In the 1940s, Robinson's writing, if not her life, changed direction, and that change is chronicled in "Robinson After Marx."

"The War Between the Cambridges" is the portion of the biographical essay devoted to one of the most turbulent times in Joan Robinson's intellectual life. Always at odds with main-stream thinking, Joan Robinson became especially disenchanted with orthodox economics in the 1950s. The so-called war between Cambridge (UK) and Cambridge (USA) that began in the 1950s lasted through the 1960s, and the story of the second half of that protracted conflict is the topic of "Afflicting the Comfortable."

In the 1970s and until the end of her life in 1983, Joan Robinson spent a great deal of time and energy pondering where her economics had taken her and the discipline of which she was an integral part for nearly half a century. That period is the focus of "Questions Without Answers." The last section of the biographical essay--"Assessing a Life"--tries to make sense of the complicated and controversial person who was Joan Robinson.

The biographical sketch is followed by the second portion of the book, an annotated bibliography of Joan Robinson's published works. This section of the book begins with a brief introduction on how to use the annotated bibliography, and then lists, in chronological order by year, the annotated works of Joan Robinson. The third part of the book is an annotated bibliography of selected works about Joan Robinson and her writings. This material is listed in chronological order by decade and is preceded by a short description on how to use this portion of the bibliography. The book concludes with an index of names and subjects.

All references to works annotated in this book are framed by brackets. Thus, the earlier reference--[472]--indicates that information about the Nobel Prize in Economics can be found in the entry of that number. The reference to [481:9] means that the quotation cited can be found on page 9 of item [481]. The number of entries in the entire annotated bibliography of works by and about Joan Robinson is sequential, beginning with [001] and ending with [488]. Entries [001] through [347] refer to works by Joan Robinson, while entries [348] through [488] refer to works about Joan Robinson and/or her writings.

Acknowledgments

All books are the product of a collaborative effort for which the authors of record take a disproportionate share of the credit. This book is no exception. Indeed, we want to make it abundantly clear that our contribution is primarily one of arranging the good works of others.

Of the many persons we wish to recognize, Joan Robinson is first and foremost. We never met Joan Robinson, so what we know of her we have gleaned from her writings, the writings about her and her work, and the anecdotes those who did know her were willing to share with us. Even though we have no personal knowledge of Joan Robinson, we do believe that reading works by or about her provided us with the insights necessary to write this book. Joan Robinson was a writer who revealed through the written word her soul as well as her mind, and we are grateful for that.

Three scholars that we want to single out for special recognition are Marjorie S. Turner, Ingrid H. Rima, and Maria Cristina Marcuzzo. The biographical sketch in this book owes much to Turner and Rima, two writers who knew Robinson well and admired her greatly. Marjorie Turner's book [481] is the closest thing to an official biography of Joan Robinson currently available, and a must read for anyone who wants to know the details of Robinson's personal and professional life. The book is thorough and comprehensive, and we followed its architecture in designing our biographical sketch.

Ingrid Rima's anthology [482] provided us with many of the parts necessary to make our biographical sketch whole. Of particular significance were the essays by Hans E. Jensen [482:20-33] and Krishna Bharadwaj [482:80-103]. The former furnished much of the inspiration and material used in the "Family Values" portion of our biographical sketch, and the latter did likewise for the section of the biographical essay titled "Robinson After Marx."

We also owe a considerable debt to Maria Cristina Marcuzzo. Early on in this project, she graciously provided us with a mimeograph of her bibliography [470], then a work in progress. Elements of her biographical essay can be found in our own, and her comprehensive and well cross-referenced bibliographic listing made the task of tracing and annotating the writings of Joan Robinson far easier than would otherwise have been the case.

Among the other scholars whose fingerprints can be found on our work are: George Feiwel, whose publications about Joan Robinson [479 and 480] and especially [475], influenced the "Questions Without Answers" portion of the biographical sketch; Geoffrey Harcourt, whose essays [473, 474 and 483] formed the backbone of "The War Between the Cambridges" segment of the biographical sketch; and Harvey Gram and Vivian Walsh, whose perceptive article [463] helped us put Robinson's economics in perspective. Other authors whose works we relied on heavily include Joseph Schumpeter [354], Gerald Shove [368], Ronald Findlay [390], Kenneth Boulding [397], G. L. S. Shackle [406], John Gurley [421 and 436], James Tobin [432], Alfred Eichner and J. A. Kregel [441], F. Mahloudji [442], Phylis Deane [446], Paul Davidson [453], A. Asimakopulos [469 and 478], and Gerald Danford [476].

A special thanks is in order to A. Asimakopulos, Ernest Dale, George Dawson, George Feiwel, Claire Friedland, G. C. Harcourt, Maria Cristina Marcuzzo, D. E. Moggridge, Chris O'Brien, Luigi Pasinetti, Marjorie Turner, Juliet Schor, and Lee Sheng-Yi for taking the time to pen personal letters expressing support for our efforts, offering assistance with this book, or recollecting an anecdote involving Joan Robinson.

In many respects, those who helped us track down the works by and about Joan Robinson were as important to this project as the authors of the books, articles, essays, notes, and reviews we annotated. Most of the annotated bibliography was completed when the authors were at Youngstown State University, where we made extensive use of the Maag Library, especially its human resources. We acknowledge and appreciate the many fine efforts of Bob Ault, Debbie Beronja, Brian Brennan, Tracy Horst, Dorothy Notarnicola, Lisa Rohrbaugh, Jean Romeo, Jan Schnall, Hildegard Schnuttgen, and Valsa Varma for their tireless efforts in locating even the most obscure writing by or about Joan Robinson.

This project also benefited from several research grants from the Graduate School at Youngstown State University, and we are grateful for that support. Adrian Jones and the library staff at the Murray-Green Library of Roosevelt University are acknowledged for their assistance in finding and/or acquiring many of the materials used in the writing of the biographical sketch.

Like an unfocused picture, our writing would lack clarity and definition if not for the image-sharpening work of Bill Rowe, an editor par excellence. The contributions of Professor Gary Langer, who teaches economics at Roosevelt University, improved the annotated bibliography, and the critical comments of

Professor Samuel Rosenberg, also an economist teaching at Roosevelt University, did the same for the biographical sketch. Mary Anne Burgess, Connie Clayborne, Faye Costarell, Helen Costas and Stacy Glover prepared the manuscript with good-humored patience and professionalism. Marilyn Nance compiled the index and worked her computer magic preparing the camera-ready manuscript.

This book is the joint effort of two people, each of whom brought different skills and talents to the project. Julianne developed the chronology of Joan Robinson's life and outlined the biographical sketch. James was responsible for the annotated bibliography and integrating Joan Robinson's intellectual contributions into the fabric of her personal life as described in the biographical essay. Working together, the authors have written a book that neither could have created individually.

Chronology

1903 Born Joan Violet Maurice on October 31, in Camberley, Surrey, England.

1921 Enters Girton College of Cambridge University to study economics.

1924 Takes her economics Tripos. That same year, Alfred Marshall dies, ending his leadership of the Cambridge economics tradition and opening the way for the ascendancy of John Maynard Keynes and his approach to economics.

1925 Graduates from Girton College with second-class honors, a personal disappointment for she was by some accounts the best economics student graduating from Cambridge University that year.

1926 Marries Austin Robinson, a junior fellow at Corpus Christi College of Cambridge University. Two months later, the Robinsons move to India, where Austin serves as a tutor to the Maharajah of Gwailor.

1929 The Robinsons return from India to Cambridge University, where Austin begins a long career as a faculty member in economics.

1930 Her first professional publication, a book review [001], appears in print.

1931 Becomes an assistant lecturer in economics at Cambridge University. Is an active participant in the "Circus," an informal seminar at which prominent economists at Cambridge meet to discuss John Maynard Keynes's *Treatise on Money* (1930).

1932 *Economics Is a Serious Subject* [002] appears, the first of many pamphlets Robinson would publish during her career.

1933 Publishes *The Economics of Imperfect Competition* [005], which mainstream economists consider her most important work.

1934 First daughter, Ann, is born on May 25. Publishes "Euler's Theorem and the Problem of Distribution" [015], in which she questions the Neoclassical notions of income distribution.

1936 Second daughter, Barbara, is born on October 9. Michal Kalecki writes a letter of introduction to Joan Robinson. He is motivated to do so after reading her essay "Disguised Unemployment" [024].

1937 Becomes lecturer in economics at Cambridge University. Publishes *Introduction to the Theory of Employment* [033].

1942 Publishes *An Essay on Marxian Economics* [049].

1944 Selected to serve on a government commission reviewing Britain's Patent and Design Acts.

1946 John Maynard Keynes dies, leaving her as one of the preeminent economists at Cambridge University.

1949 Made a reader in economics at Cambridge. Appointed as a part-time member to a government commission reviewing Monopolies and Restrictive Practices in British industry.

1951 Publishes the first volume of the five-volume set of her *Collected Economic Papers* [086].

1952 Visits several Eastern European countries, including for the first time, the then Soviet Union.

1953 Publishes "The Production Function and the Theory of Capital" [099], an article some consider to be the first shot fired in the war between the Cambridges. Visits several Mideastern and Asian countries, including China for the first time.

1954 Publishes *Letters from a Visitor to China* [104].

1956 Publishes *The Accumulation of Capital* [111], which Post-Keynesian economists consider to be her most important work.

1957 Visits Ceylon (now Sri Lanka) as an invited guest of the government to advise the National Planning Council on the broad issues of economic growth and development.

1960 Publishes *Collected Economic Papers*, Volume 2 [143].

1961 Visits the United States, Canada, and Cuba.

1962 Publishes *Economic Philosophy* [158], a book that, unlike many of her other works, was well received in the United States.

1965 Made a Professor at Cambridge University. Husband Austin retires from teaching. Publishes *Collected Economic Papers*, Volume 3 [195].

1971 Retires from her chair at Cambridge. On the invitation of her good friend John Kenneth Galbraith, President of the American Economics Association in 1971, delivers the Richard T. Ely Lecture at the Association's annual meeting, held that year in New Orleans.

1973 Publishes *Collected Economic Papers*, Volume 4 [263].

1975 Delivers the commencement address [311] at the University of Maine at Orono.

1976 Appointed a Virginia C. Gildersleeve Lecturer at Barnard College. Publishes her Gildersleeve Lecture [291].

1978 Pens an article [312] in the inaugural issue of the American periodical *Journal of Post Keynesian Economics*.

1979 Publishes final volume of *Collected Economic Papers*, Volume 5 [317]. Delivers the David Kinley Lecture [332] at the University of Illinois, Urbana/Champaign.

1980 Receives an honorary Doctor of Laws from Harvard University. The Massachusetts Institute of Technology Press republishes her *Collected Economic Papers*, along with a General Index [335], thus completing the project.

1981 Delivers the Tanner Lecture on Human Values [341] at the University of Utah.

1983 Dies in Cambridge, England, on August 5 after several months in a coma.

1985 Her last writing on economics, a mimeographed work crafted in 1983 under the title "Spring Cleaning," is published posthumously [346].

Chapter 1
Biographical Sketch

> I was brought up in an old liberal tradition, believing in progress and rationality of human behavior.
>
> Joan Robinson [470:5]

FAMILY VALUES

Joan Violet Maurice was born in Camberly, Surrey, England, on October 31, 1903, to Helen Margaret Marsh and Major General Sir Frederick Maurice. One of four girls in a family of five children, Joan grew up in a distinguished and prominent upper-middle-class English family "characterized by vigorous dissent and independence of mind" [449:663]. At the time of her birth, Joan's father had already established himself as one of the ablest officers in the British Army. In 1918, when Joan was fourteen years old, Sir Frederick Maurice became involved in what is referred to in British history as the Maurice debate.

The crux of the debate was an unprecedented letter Frederick Maurice, then Director of Military Operations, wrote to the London *Times* "accusing Prime Minister Lloyd George's government of deceiving Parliament and the country about the strength of the British army on the western front" [481:11]. Maurice alleged that the deception left Britain unprepared to handle the Germans, who in March 1918 "broke through the British lines and drove them almost to the Channel ports ..." [481:11]. The letter precipitated a parliamentary debate about the government's handling of the war, and, as often happens to whistle blowers, resulted in the abrupt end of Frederick Maurice's military career. Even though he fully realized what might happen, Maurice published his criticism of government policy anyway, explaining in a letter to his daughter Nancy, then seventeen, "I am persuaded that I am doing what is right and once that is so, nothing else matters to a man" [481:11].

This incident, which undoubtedly had a profound effect in shaping Robinson's view that "one must act on conscience" [481:11], was not an isolated case of dissent in the history of her family. Robinson's paternal great-grandfather, Frederick Denison Maurice (1805-1872), was a Christian Socialist who often engaged in fundamental controversies over religious questions. The Knightbridge Professor of Moral Philosophy in Cambridge University, he "was expelled by King's College for casting doubts on the plausibility of eternal damnation" [470:4]. In *The Dictionary of National Biography*, the headstrong F. D. Maurice was described as having "an even excessively scrupulous sense of honor, and throughout his life was devoted exclusively to setting forth what he held to be the truth. He was at times moved to vehement indignation, and could be very sharp in controversy; some natural irritability joined with his keen sense of the importance of certain truths, and with the consciousness that, from whatever cause, his meaning was very liable to be misconceived" (Quoted in [481:11]). This description so fit Joan Robinson, it caused one biographer to write: "How like him his great-granddaughter Joan Robinson was!" [481:11].

Though not nearly so cantankerous as her father's ancestors, Robinson's family tree on her mother's side was equally distinguished. Joan's maternal great-great-grandfather was Spencer Perceval (1762-1812), who "distinguished himself in politics by becoming Prime Minister, only to be assassinated by a bankrupt madman while in office" [481:10]. Her maternal grandfather, Frederick Howard Marsh, was a professor of surgery and Master of Downing College at Cambridge University; her knighted uncle, Sir Edward Marsh, was a respected art collector and civil servant; and her grandmother, Jane Perceval Marsh, "founded the Alexandra Hospital for Children with Hip Disease in London" [481:10].

From an early age, Joan Robinson demonstrated a keen mind and seriousness of purpose. These attributes made her a prime candidate for the well-regarded St. Paul's School for Girls in London. At St. Paul's, Robinson was a conscientious student who still found time to volunteer at a settlement house for the underprivileged, thus beginning a lifelong interest in the problems of the poor. In 1921, Robinson left St. Paul's and went to Girton College at Cambridge University, where she was a Gilchrist Scholar.

Her progression from public school to university was somewhat unusual even for someone of her exceptional intellect, as Marjorie Turner explains:

> In England, before the many changes brought about by World War II, it was difficult for intelligent and ambitious boys, and even more so for girls, to go very far unless they were born into fairly wealthy, upper-class families who sent them to private schools to be educated. Schooling in state schools ended at age fourteen, except for the few outstanding students who qualified to go on to a Grammar School. University educations were almost entirely for the privileged classes. For Joan

> Maurice, as a member of an ancient and distinguished family, opportunity was her birthright. [481:9]

At Girton, the first women's college associated with either Cambridge or Oxford Universities, Robinson read for the Economics Tripos from 1922 through 1925. During this period, on July 13, 1924, to be exact, Alfred Marshall passed away. The death of the undisputed leader of the Cambridge School of economic thought, which at the time enjoyed "an unsurpassed international reputation" [482:15], opened the door for the ascendancy of John Maynard Keynes and his approach to economics.

In 1925, Robinson graduated from Girton with second-class honors in economics, "a great disappointment" [449:663] for she was regarded as one of the brightest economic students at Cambridge, having been "the only person to place Class I in the Intercollegiate Examination in Economics" [481:17] in June 1923. Whatever dismay Robinson experienced as a result of her second-class honors was short-lived, for within the year she married Austin Robinson, the Cambridge economist and teacher, and the two left for India, where Austin served as a tutor to the Maharajah of Gwailor until 1929 [481:18].

During her stay in India, Robinson had "her first glimpse of the economically under-developed world" [481:18]. This firsthand observation of a third-world nation was to have a lasting impression on the young Joan Robinson, as she "would never ... turn her back on the problems of the poor as being beneath her interest as an economist" [481:18].

By the time the Robinsons returned to Cambridge, Joan's basic values were firmly established. Her core philosophy not only guided her life but also shaped her scholarship. Unlike many economists of her era, who claimed to shun "normative" economics in favor of "positive" reasoning, Robinson did not hide her beliefs, nor pretend that she had none. She knew that such a subterfuge was not possible or desirable. As she put it,

> It is true that economic terminology is colored. Bigger is close to better; equal to equitable; goods sound good; disequilibrium sounds uncomfortable; exploitation, wicked; and subnormal profits, rather sad. All the same, taking a particular economic system as given, we can describe the technical features of its operation in an objective way. But it is not possible to describe a system without moral judgments creeping in. For to look at a system from the outside implies that it is not the only possible system; in describing it we compare it (openly or tacitly) with other actual or imagined systems. Differences imply choices, and choices imply judgment. We cannot escape from making judgments and the judgments that we make arise from the ethical preconceptions that have soaked into our view of life and are somehow printed in our

> brains. We cannot escape from our own habits of thought. [158:14]

In assessing the role of moral judgments in the development of Robinson's economics, Hans E. Jensen argues [482:20-33] that values played a pivotal role in shaping her vision of society. Robinson's notion of vision was normative and akin to that of Marshall's--a "hopeful view of the possibilities of human progress" in the future--as opposed to Schumpeter's sense of vision, which is positive and based on the reality of today [482:21]. Robinson's vision of the future reflected a number of specific values, which when taken together, formed the basis of an ideology, a set of processes and goals that describe the formation and function of an ideal society. And what were her habits of thought, the moral judgments and ethical beliefs imprinted in her mind and ultimately revealed in her economics?

Robinson's consummate society is one that provides "a decent and comfortable level of living for all ..." [482:23]. In this world, the worst of poverty is eliminated, and "the cult of self-interest and competition" [241:16-17]--the twin cornerstones of laissez faire--give way to a system of social behavior based on ethical principles that value world harmony, progress, and peace. In concrete terms, this means an economic system that can promote continuous prosperity and full employment without relying on the arms race to stimulate growth or an inflationary bias to keep employment high. Convinced that the maldistribution of income was a prime source of many problems plaguing modern capitalism, Robinson also believed in a more equal distribution of income as a way of improving both economic efficiency and social equity. A self-described "archetypal left-wing Keynesian" [482:23], Robinson brought to the study of economics a set of values inherited from her family, nurtured by the experiences of her youth, tempered by her academic training, and ultimately embodied in what she wrote and how she wrote it. According to Jan Keppler,

> Perhaps the most distinguished personality to combine theoretical achievement and social engagement was Joan Robinson. ... The daughter of a Christian Socialist family, she displayed all her life a passionate advocacy for the disadvantaged, whether as a member of the Capital Supply subcommittee of the New Fabian Research Bureau or as a diligent and gratefully acknowledged proofreader of and collaborator on several books by the Labor politicians John Strachey and Hugh Dalton. Yet her leanings to leftist policy prescriptions and later her professed openness to Marxist economists were countered by the foundation of her analytical apparatus in neoclassical Marshallian economics. [487:35]

> When I was a student ... [t]here seemed ... to be an accepted and well-established body of "economic principles" to learn. But I think mine was the last generation for whom this was true. Very soon all the seeming-solid ground began to quake and change.
>
> Joan Robinson [143:88]

THE QUAKING DISCIPLINE

In 1929, the year Joan Robinson and her husband returned to Cambridge from India, the Western world lapsed into an economic downturn of cataclysmic proportions. The Great Depression lasted a full decade and was deeper and longer than any previous recession the West had experienced. Diehard communists were convinced that the self-destructive nature of capitalism, which Marx had predicted nearly a century before, was finally playing itself out. They pushed for societal change--the more and the faster, the better. Orthodox economists pleaded for patience, maintaining that laissez-faire capitalism would and could right itself if its cybernetic properties were given an opportunity to self-correct.

As the depression wore on, misplaced hope gave way to desperation as societies sought to bring order out of chaos. Stalin's Russia embraced socialism with a vengeance, Hitler's Germany and Mussolini's Italy turned to fascism, and Western democracies threw up tariff barriers as each scrapped the long-cherished faith in free trade and adopted a zero-sum philosophy of well-being. 1929 through 1949 was arguably the most tumultuous period of world history during the twentieth century. It was also an era of unparalleled change in Western economic thought, and as fate would have it, Joan Robinson was at the epicenter of the quake.

Soon after returning to Cambridge University, Robinson "paid her five-pound fee and gained her master's degree" [481:20], which she had earned by virtue of the course work and exams she completed prior to leaving for India. Since she did not earn a Class I degree, she could not break into university teaching on the basis of scholastic achievement; nor was she invited to be a fellow at her old college, another path to the teaching profession [481:20]. Instead, she made herself available for the supervision and tutoring of students, and began to write and publish scholarly works. Her husband's position as a lecturer in economics at Cambridge obviously gave her a chance to capitalize on this opportunity, but it was her good work in the classroom and emerging scholarly agenda that eventually earned her a faculty position as an assistant lecturer in 1931. From then on, Robinson's career was in her own hands.

During the early 1930s, two major themes dominated economics at Cambridge University. The first theme involved the re-examination of Marshallian value theory. After Marshall's death in 1924, Neoclassical value theory came under intense scrutiny as Piero Sraffa and other economists of the time, no longer inhibited by a sense of loyalty to the master, pointed out inconsistencies in Marshall's economics. Most troubling, says Turner, "was that Marshall, in elaborating the economies of scale wherein firms grow larger and larger, had failed to give up the idea of perfect competition."

> A world of perfect competition meant that price would always just cover cost because of that competition. A demand curve where price equals marginal revenue is termed "perfectly elastic." On the traditional diagram, such a horizontal curve indicates that the producer can sell all of his product without affecting the price, a condition associated with "perfect competition." However, if there were increasingly large firms, perfect competition would be impossible. [481:25]

Marshall's theory of value implied that firms produced at maximum efficiency or not at all. Sheer observation during the Great Depression showed that firms could and did operate at suboptimal levels of production and remain in business. Perfect competition requires all firms to be price takers, but the reality of the marketplace, where large, dominant companies in well-defined industries dictate price, suggested that this was not the case. The relevance of Marshall's theory of value was suspect and a paradigm shift was in order.

Inspired by Piero Sraffa's 1926 *Economic Journal* article "The Laws of Return Under Competitive Conditions," Robinson began to rework the theory of the firm and in the process rewrote microeconomics [428:106]. The first substantive output of this effort, and Robinson's first major article in a prominent economics journal [004], was a precursor of what mainstream economists regard as her magnum opus, *The Economics of Imperfect Competition* [005]. More than an instant success that established Robinson's reputation as an economist of note, the book also went on to become a classic. Published in 1933, it was reprinted ten times through 1959 and reissued in a new edition in 1969.

To this day, the treatment of imperfect competition that Robinson expounded at the ripe old age of thirty is still embodied in basic economics texts. Her many contributions--the concept of marginal revenue and the discontinuous or kinked demand curve to cite just two--are fundamental to modern price theory analysis. Robinson's breakthrough work is so integrated into economic theory that she is no longer referenced and has not been for some time. The concept of imperfect competition is part and parcel of orthodox economics thanks largely to this book [428:108].

Just about the time that Robinson was reinventing microeconomics, the American economist Edward H. Chamberlin (1899-1967) was exploring the same territory. His analysis and conclusions, similar to Robinson's, were first developed in a Harvard University dissertation in 1927 and subsequently published in the 1933 book *The Theory of Monopolistic Competition*. While the simultaneous publication of two path-breaking books on the same general topic sparked a controversy over originality, significance, and priority [487 and 481: Chapter 4], they together changed the nature of microeconomics, the first great revolution of which Joan Robinson was a participant. Keppler writes:

> The simultaneous publication of these two classics of economic theory at a certain point in the scientific debate entitled them to define the synthesis of monopolistic competition, and the definition holds even today. The merits of the two books do not lie in any single technical advance but in their overview of achieved results, which brought the problem of monopoly to the center of economic attention. Perhaps the lack of actual technical differences between them led to the debate over monopolistic versus imperfect competition, which seems so superfluous today. [487:82]

It was Joan Robinson's great "good misfortune" to be part of a second and even more important revolution in economic thinking, the one involving John Maynard Keynes and the development of modern macroeconomics [470:4]. For Joan Robinson, the "good" in this association was the personal and professional relationship between her and Keynes, undoubtedly the most famous Western economist of the twentieth century. The "misfortune" in this association was the fact that publication of Keynes's magnum opus, *The General Theory of Employment, Interest, and Money* (1936), so eclipsed Robinson's classic on imperfect competition as a work of theory with policy implications that the brightness of her book never reached its full brilliance.

Robinson's involvement with Keynes and the emerging field of macroeconomics began early in 1931 when several younger-generation economists at Cambridge University, responding to a suggestion from Piero Sraffa, formed a discussion group dubbed the "Circus." Created to help Keynes realize the employment implication of his recently published *Treatise on Money* (1930), the Circus began as informal talks in Richard Kahn's rooms at Cambridge's King's College [470:14]. Initially, participation was by invitation only, but this format eventually gave way to a seminar held at Trinity College and to which students were invited [470:15].

The original participants in the Circus were Sraffa, Kahn, James Meade, Joan Robinson, and her husband, Austin. Keynes did not attend meetings of the group even though his work was usually the principal topic of discussion. Rather, members of the Circus would attend Keynes's lectures and then discuss and debate the contents thereof at their meetings. Afterward, "Kahn would report orally to Keynes the subject matter and lines of argument" [481:51]. Robinson became so engrossed in the new economics emerging from Keynes's work that she came to regard her own work on value theory as a distraction and her need to complete *Imperfect Competition* as a "nightmare" [481:39].

Unlike Chamberlin, who, after developing the concept of monopolistic competition, devoted the rest of his academic career to perfecting, embellishing, and reviving that one idea, Robinson turned her time and energy to macroeconomics after publishing *Imperfect Competition.* This is not to say that she embraced employment theory to the exclusion of microeconomics. Hardly. It is just that employment theory and related topics, especially investment and saving theory and the accumulation of capital, would occupy the center of her scholarship for the rest of her life, while microeconomics topics would be recurring but not dominant themes in her writings from the mid-1930s onward.

In 1937, just one year after Keynes's *General Theory* appeared, Robinson published two major works that helped define the new field of macroeconomics. *Essays in the Theory of Employment* [032] was a collection of essays, some original to the book and some reprinted from other sources, in which Robinson applied the principles of Keynesian analysis to a variety of problems including disguised unemployment, the nature of unemployment, and beggar-my-neighbor remedies for economic depressions. *Introduction to the Theory of Employment* [033] was Robinson's attempt to explain Keynesian economics in down-to-earth terms. Judging by the popularity of the book--eight printings between its initial publication and the final printing in 1956--Robinson had a considerable degree of success. Together, both books helped establish Robinson as one of the preeminent new economists in the Keynesian movement.

Her published articles also enhanced her reputation as a Keynesian. Beginning in 1933 with her essay "A Parable on Saving and Investment" [006], through the publication of "The Concept of Hoarding" [038], which appeared in 1938, Robinson published six major articles on topics originating with the Keynesian movement. These articles, together with her books, gave Robinson international stature as an economist and earned her worldwide respect as "the only woman ever to have achieved outstanding eminence in economic theory (which, no doubt, tells us more about economic theory than about women)" [471:207].

> Modern developments in academic theory, forced by modern developments in economic life--the analysis of monopoly and the analysis of unemployment--have shattered the structure of orthodox doctrine and destroyed the complacency with which economists were wont to view the workings of laissez-faire capitalism. Their attitude to Marx, as the leading critic of capitalism, is therefore much less cocksure than it used to be. In my belief, they have much to learn from him.
>
> Joan Robinson [049:xxii]

ROBINSON AFTER MARX

Of the six decades over which Joan Robinson's career arched, none was as remarkable as the first. In the 1930s, she published three major books, one a recognized classic; she authored several seminal articles for prestigious journals; she established an international reputation as an economic theorist; and, as if that was not enough, she gave birth to two daughters, one in 1934 and another in 1936. Robinson packed more into the years 1930-1939 than just about any other intellectual in the Western world.

If the 1930s were Robinson's most prolific years, the 1940s were her most fallow. She actually had more publications in the 1940s than in the 1930s--42 compared with 40--but the impact of that output was not nearly so dramatic. Instead of spending the 1940s pushing the envelope of macro theory outward, she devoted herself to popularizing Keynesian economics. "In a series of articles and pamphlets written in the early forties, Joan Robinson dealt with the problems of a full employment economy and its political consequences in a broad way" [442:49]. To be sure this was important work, but interpreting Keynes was not the comparative advantage of someone who just a few years earlier had been on the cutting edge of the revolutions in both micro- and macroeconomics. What happened? Why did Robinson go into intellectual hibernation?

One can only speculate as to the cause. Possibly it was a simple case of burnout. She, nor anyone else for that matter, could have maintained the frenzied personal and professional pace she kept in the 1930s. Taking this view, the 1940s can be looked at as a respite during which Robinson renewed her energies in preparation for the 1950s and 1960s, the years students of the Post-Keynesian school would argue were her most productive period. Then again, the intellectual lethargy Robinson experienced could have been a reaction to the growing prospects of world war, which began to unfold in Europe in 1936 with the Spanish Civil War and escalated until September 1939, when Germany invaded Poland, an event that caused Britain and France and several other nations to declare war on Germany. The stress of conflict affected every nation, institution, and individual, and was probably "the cause of Joan Robinson's missing a term of teaching in 1939" [481:66].

Perhaps Robinson's intellectual ennui was a response to the lack of recognition from her peers at Cambridge University. As the threat of world war descended on Europe in 1938, several of the prominent economists at Cambridge became involved in the British war effort, either in the military or in wartime posts with the government. Not Robinson. She instead was granted a full lectureship, a promotion no doubt meant to bolster a sagging cadre of teachers and thus "probably not as satisfying as it might have been in more peaceful times" [481:66]. While John Maynard Keynes was brilliantly negotiating at Bretton Woods, Robinson was assigned trivial tasks, having been appointed in April 1944 to a minor government commission charged with considering "whether any, and if so what, changes are desirable in the Patent and Design Acts" [470:36]. This appointment and a subsequent one in 1948 to a government commission on Monopolies and Restrictive Practices were for politically correct reasons and not to engage the intellectual prowess of the appointee. Indeed, Robinson is quoted as having said that she was asked to join the Commission on Monopolies "because they could get rid in one person of those two tiresome categories, an economist and a woman" [470:36].

Unappreciated at home, Robinson undoubtedly became even more frustrated because of the obvious shift of the locus of economic theory from Cambridge University to Cambridge, Massachusetts. More than just the home of two great institutions of higher learning, Harvard University and Massachusetts Institute of Technology, Cambridge (MA) was also where the brightest star in the American constellation of economists, Paul Samuelson of MIT, taught. Thorstein Veblen and the Institutional movement had taken American economics on a different path than that of its British counterpart. The diversity of approaches coexisting in the American economic tradition created an environment ripe for a new approach to economics, one that could explain the causes of and suggest the cures for the Great Depression, things with which orthodox British theory had difficulty. Paul Samuelson was clearly the most important scholar in this new cohort of economists who sought to fuse the economics of Keynes with the existing Neoclassical school of thought.

Early in his career, Samuelson demonstrated that he would be a potent force in shaping the scope and methods of the new economics. In 1939, he published an article[2] that provided the "first major addition to Keynes's insights" by "exploring the implications for macroeconomics stability of a model that included not only the multiplier but the accelerator."[3] Through the use of simple differential equations, Samuelson had taken Keynesian analysis into the new dimension of dynamics and had done so in just three short pages. This was the

---

[2] "Interaction between the Multiplier Analysis and the Principle of Acceleration," *Review of Economics and Statistics*, May, 1939: 75-78.

[3] M. P. Niemira and P. A. Klein, *Forecasting Financial and Economic Cycles*, New York: Wiley & Sons, 1994: 67.

extension of a methodology developed in his *Foundations of Economic Analysis*, a book written before the war but not published until 1947. This book and other American works, especially Wassily Leontief's *The Structure of American Economy, 1919-1929: An Empirical Application of Equilibrium Analysis* (1941), signaled the "takeover of the mathematical economists from conceptualists" [481:74], and symbolized the shift of power in economics from Cambridge (UK) to Cambridge (MA).

For whatever reasons, the 1940s represented a low point in Robinson's career. The decade, however, was not without its moments. These were the years during which Robinson published a number of major works on Marxian economics. The first and most memorable was her short book *An Essay on Marxian Economics* [049]. "The process of abandoning the Pigouvian side of Marshall's teaching reached a turning point in *An Essay on Marxian Economics* where, impressed by Marx's emphasis on accumulation, technical progress and continuous disequilibrium, Joan Robinson became convinced that the static model gives a grossly unreal picture of the process of accumulation and distribution in a capitalist society" [442:iii].

Robinson's initial interest in Marx was sparked by a review she wrote of Strachey's *The Nature of the Capitalistic Crisis* [025]. Writing the review inspired Robinson to read Marx, and when she did she found that for her, "the main message of Marx was the need to think in terms of history, not equilibrium" [267:x]. Marx helped Robinson to see "the methodological error of confusing a metaphor based on space to explain a process through time" [482:93]. As Robinson would write in one of her most important and influential articles:

> Time is unlike space in two very striking respects. In space, bodies moving from A to B may pass bodies moving from B to A, but in time the strictest possible rule of one-way traffic is always in force. And in space the distance from A to B is of the same order of magnitude ... as the distance from B to A; but in time the distance from to-day to to-morrow is twenty-four hours, while the distance from to-day to yesterday is infinite, as the poets have often remarked. Therefore a space metaphor applied to time is a very tricky knife to handle, and the concept of equilibrium often cuts the arm that wields it. [099:87-88]

In the 1950s, the issue of history versus equilibrium would be at the center of a war that Robinson waged almost single-handed against the economists of Cambridge (MA), whom she dubbed "bastard" Keynesians because they had distorted Keynes's message to fit the prevailing Neoclassical paradigm.

Robinson's interest in Marx changed her spiritually as well as intellectually or, more accurately, put her in touch with the values she had acquired long before she became an economist. No doubt that was part of the attraction of Marx; his core beliefs and hers were similar. Robinson and Marx were, in effect, soulmates. Each believed in the perfectibility of humankind and both railed against the orthodoxy of the day. *An Essay on Marxian Economics* and other Robinson writings that reflected a Marxian perspective changed her image among American economists from that of a brilliant theoretician to that of a left-wing Keynesian [481:78-79]. Her socialist-oriented publications also contributed to a split among economists at Cambridge University, which after Keynes's death in 1946 divided into two camps: the non-Keynesians, led by Dennis Robertson, and the Keynesians headed by Joan Robinson [481:68].

Some believe that the loss of influence among her peers at Cambridge (UK) and her loss of prestige among the economists at Cambridge (MA) had a pronounced affect on Robinson's career. The change in how she was perceived "had an effect on the reception of all of her subsequent work" and ultimately "on her eligibility for a Nobel Prize" [481:79]. The net result was that Robinson became increasingly isolated from all the branches of economics popular in the 1940s. Driven as much by necessity as desire, over the next two decades she set about creating her own school of thought, which eventually evolved into the Post-Keynesian movement.

> My main concern is to get economic analysis off the mud of static equilibrium theory.
>
> Joan Robinson [159:iv]

THE WAR BETWEEN THE CAMBRIDGES

The fondness that Robinson developed for things Marxian in the 1940s flowered into a comprehensive and coherent attack on mainstream economics in the 1950s. Robinson came to accept that Cambridge (UK) was no longer the center of the economics universe and that she was one of many voices in the diverse world of post-WWII economic thought. In this new and changing environment, she assumed for herself a new role or, rather, reprised an old role. Reverting to her days with the Circus, Robinson became in the 1950s a gadfly of orthodox economics and a seeker of new and different experiences and ideas [481:77].

Her interest in Marxian economics manifested in a desire to see how the theory of socialism worked in practice. In April 1952, as a delegate to the Moscow Economic Conference, Robinson visited the then Soviet Union [481:87]. The following year she made the first of six visits to China, a country that over time she came to admire greatly. She journeyed to China as the vice-president of the British Council for the Promotion of International Trade with China. On subsequent visits, she studied Chinese cooperatives, communes, factories, and universities [481:86]. Her trips to socialist countries provided the information and inspiration for a number of articles that Robinson wrote for the *Monthly Review*, "an intellectual magazine treating political and economic issues from a Marxian point of view" [481:85].

Beginning with a sketch of Moscow [095], Robinson published a total of fourteen articles for the *Monthly Review*, essays that, during the McCarthy era, no doubt solidified the American perception of her as a Marxist. The reality of course was different, as Turner points out:

> The record is clear. Robinson never shrank from seeing herself as a bourgeois rather than a Marxian economist; she never flagged in her determination to criticize orthodox theory; she was equally eager to criticize Marxists when she thought them wrong; her contempt for "believers" as distinguished from "scientists" extended in all ideological directions [481:85].

Robinson's critiques drew fire from both the right and the left as each end of the economics spectrum took exception to her characterizations [481:94]. From the right, the American economist Joseph Schumpeter and the English/Canadian economist Harry Johnson crossed swords with Robinson over her faith in socialism, a faith that they thought was totally unjustified given the repressive nature of life in the Soviet Union and China. From the left, Robinson was attacked for her complete lack of understanding of the Marxian system, especially the labor theory of value, a concept that she criticized unmercifully [463:545].

For her part, Robinson dismissed as fundamentalist dribble diatribes from the left, particularly those coming from Marxists who, in her opinion, had a political agenda and really did not appreciate the meaning of Marx. To those individuals, she wrote in a pamphlet she published in 1953 [097], "I understand Marx far and away better than you do ... What I mean is that I have Marx in my bones and you have him in your mouth." In the same essay she also severed her ties with the old Marshallian Classical School and reaffirmed the values of her youth when she wrote: "The more I learn about economics, the more I admire Marshall's intellect and the less I like his character."

While taking aim on both the right and the left, Robinson trained her energies primarily on the former and with good reason. Even in its heydays, Marxian analysis had but a negligible influence on mainstream Western economics. Those on the right, however, had a definite imprint on mainstream thinking, and so orthodox economics and its right-of-center supporters became the object of Robinson's attention. In a conflict which essentially pitted Cambridge (UK) against Cambridge (MA), 1953 was a pivotal year.

In a now classic article [099], Robinson challenged the idea of the aggregate production function and the ancillary theoretical implications that Cambridge (MA) economists had firmly planted in the mainstream of Western economic thought. Ostensibly about the technical shortcomings of the aggregate production function, this article was in fact a broad salvo on the emerging Neoclassical paradigm of the "bastard" Keynesians [165], a term Robinson reserved especially for American Keynesian teaching at Harvard and MIT [481:59]. Robinson objected to much of orthodox theory, reserving her harshest criticisms for three concepts: the notion of equilibrium, the mainstream theory of economic growth, and the uncritical acceptance by Western economists of income distribution based on marginal productivity theory.

Robinson had always regarded the concept of long-run equilibrium as a misplaced metaphor, the product of fertile imaginations and not hard science because it did not square with observed reality. The Neoclassical tenet of equilibrium made for elegant mathematical models but shoddy economics in Robinson's view. Furthermore, the concept of general equilibrium was an intellectual affront to the Keynesian breakthrough. "The key insight of Keynes is that an unregulated economy contains no dynamic process that would tend, if left alone, to get it into a position of general equilibrium" [463:521]. To argue otherwise was, in Robinson's opinion, a bastardization of Keynesian thought.

Having accepted the notion of general equilibrium, the Neoclassical synthesis was, of logical necessity, committed to a theory of growth based on consumer choice without regard to the level of employment or the composition of output. In the self-proclaimed, values-free theory of the Neoclassical school, full employment was an incidental by-product of economic activity, not one of its purposes. Moreover, the composition of output was immaterial as long as it satisfied consumers wants. A Gross Domestic Product built on the arms race was, to Neoclassical economists, just as legitimate as one based on eliminating poverty or renewing the urban infrastructure. For Joan Robinson, this was never the case; to believe otherwise would have been to repudiate Keynes. To Robinson, the central message of Keynes when extended to the long run was that "employment ... depends primarily on the accumulation of capital, and the accumulation of capital depends primarily on the uncertain expectations of profit held by capitalist firm" and not "the intertemporal consumption choices of independent households in a dynamic model of neo-Walrasian general equilibrium.

The assumption of general equilibrium in a world of perfectly competitive markets also forced the Neoclassical school to accept the marginal productivity theory of distribution when observation by even the most uninitiated would suggest that comparative productivity was only one of a number of factors determining who gets what. As a young economist, Robinson had taken exception to marginal productivity theory, first in *The Economics of Imperfect Competition* [005] and again in an article on Euler's Theorem [015]. Marginal productivity theory stressed efficiency over equity, something Robinson would have nothing to do with.

While the war between Cambridge (UK) and Cambridge (MA) was more about values than economic theory, the latter became the focus of the controversy for better or for worse. More specifically, the Neoclassical theory of the production function, which Robinson believed was rooted in the fallacious idea "that it is possible to specify purely technical relations, not involving prices, in a human economy" [108:67], became the lightning rod for what was essentially a philosophical debate. The conflict between the Cambridges was protracted, intense, and often arcane [414]. At its essence, however, was a clash between Joan Robinson and two MIT economists, Paul Samuelson and Robert Solow [481:113], both of whom would go on to win Nobels in economics--Samuelson in 1970 and Solow in 1987.

The friction between Robinson and Solow centered on the theory of the aggregate production function and "whether or not it is possible to measure 'capital' as a factor of production" [449:667]. The particulars of the debate involved: what unit to measure capital by if there is a unit of measure independent of distribution and prices; the validity of equating the marginal product of capital to the rate of profit; and the role of the time versus the concept of equilibrium in aggregate analysis [449:667]. The debates between Robinson and Solow were frequent and sharp [481:113-23].

The Robinson/Solow exchanges were heated and engaged both parties to the fullest. By contrast, the Robinson/Samuelson debate was muted and basically one-way. Robinson had, she believed, found a technical error in Samuelson's theory of capital, a point that she considered significant but that he downplayed.

This was evident in an exchange of letters between the two in which he wrote: "I used to joke with Bob Solow that the distance between me and Joan Robinson is less than the distance between Joan Robinson and me" [481:128].

The controversy that separated Robinson and Samuelson is known as reswitching. To make a point--that "there is no meaning to be given to 'a quantity of capital' apart from the rate of profit, so that the contention that the 'marginal product of capital' determines the rate of profit is meaningless" [245:309]--Robinson created a concept which Robert Solow dubbed [470:41] the "pseudo-production function" [108]. During a discussion with a colleague named Ruth Cohen, Robinson found that the Neoclassical (Samuelson) proposition that the rate of profit is a monotonically decreasing function of the capital/labor ratio is not true. As Robinson observed:

> I found that over certain ranges of the pseudo-production function the technique that becomes eligible at a higher rate of profit (with a correspondingly lower real-wage rate) may be less labor-intensive (that is, may have a higher output per man employed) than that chosen at a higher wage rate, contrary to the rule of a 'well-behaved production function' in which a lower wage rate is always associated with a more labor-intensive technique. [245:309-10]

This meant that a technique of production selected at a lower real-wage rate may be less labor-intensive than one selected at a higher real-wage rate, leading to the possibility of "switching" and "reswitching." Neither phenomenon was a possibility with the Neoclassical production function, which predicts a steady progression from lower to higher capital/labor ratios.

Samuelson would eventually concede the correctness of Robinson's point, but he considered the whole issue irrelevant. For mainstream economists, the "Ruth Cohen case," as the reswitching controversy is sometimes called, is akin to the "Giffen paradox." The Giffen paradox is a special case where the price and the quantity demanded of a good are directly related, in contrast to the accepted "law of demand," which states that price and quantity demanded are inversely related. Despite observed occurrences in the real world, the Giffen paradox has never dissuaded mainstream economists of the general correctness of the "law of demand." Similarly, the "Ruth Cohen case" has not disabused orthodox economics of its faith in the aggregate production function, Robinson's tireless efforts to the contrary notwithstanding.

In the Cambridge controversy, Robinson was often portrayed as someone long on criticism but short on contributions, a charge without substance. She did more than just criticize orthodox economics: Robinson offered an alternative to it. That alternative is today called Post-Keynesian economics, the origins of which can be found in many of Robinson's post-WWII writings, especially her book *The Accumulation of Capital* [111].

In that book, one can clearly detect the work of the four economists who most influenced Robinson. Marshall provided the style for the work--seven individual "books" in a single wordy volume; Keynes contributed the macroeconomics; and Marx gave the concept of history to replace the Neoclassical fetish with equilibrium. The index of the book bears witness to the importance of two of these three predecessors: Marshall is cited ten times, as is Keynes; no one else is even close. Yet, the significance of Michal Kalecki and his notion of fusing the theory of imperfect competition with Keynesian economics is not readily acknowledged in either references or footnotes, despite the enormous influence he had on Robinsonian thought.

A relatively unknown Polish economist, Kalecki first came to Robinson's attention in the mid-1930s when he wrote a letter expressing admiration for her article "Disguised Unemployment" [024]. Visiting England at the time on a Rockefeller Scholarship, Kalecki shared with Robinson his theory of employment, which he had published in Poland in 1933 [481:63]. Robinson observed that Kalecki's theory was remarkably similar to that of Keynes, save that Kalecki came to his conclusion from the Marxian tradition while Keynes's thinking evolved from Marshall. So taken with Kalecki was Robinson that she was instrumental in getting him to come to Cambridge University, where in the late 1930s he interacted with her and other Keynesian economists. Although he never held a permanent position at Cambridge and thus was not in the strictest sense a colleague, Kalecki was to be a significant influence on Robinson's thinking, thinking that would eventually culminate in the development of Post-Keynesian economics.

Robinson found Kalecki's formulation of employment theory superior to Keynes's on several counts. She considered Keynes's "propensity to consume," resting as it does on the psychological principle that individuals are disposed to increase consumption as incomes increase but not by as much, a weak point in Keynesian analysis. Robinson preferred Kalecki's division of the world into workers and capitalists, where the former earn wages and the latter profits, and where the saving of each group is determined by the distribution of income between the two. In the Keynesian model, saving is an undifferentiated aggregate that depends on the level of national income without regard to its distribution [299].

More important, Kaleckian analysis, as Robinson wrote, "brought imperfect competition in touch with the theory of employment" [470:24], a union reminiscent of the Classical tradition in economics and in sharp contrast to the Neoclassical approach, where the two are divorced.

> The importance of Kalecki's line of argument was in integrating the analysis of prices with the analysis of effective demand. Before Keynes, they were kept in two separate boxes; in America now the division between micro and macro theory is more complete than ever; but no progress can be

> made with either until they are united in a truly general theory. [299:12]

Kalecki's approach to the business cycle and the theory of employment, as revealed in his published works and his many heated discussions with Robinson [481:63], joined micro- and macroeconomics into a single theory of prices, employment, and accumulation [477]. His work also provided Robinson a theory of distribution that she found more appealing than that of either the Neoclassical or Marxian schools. As Maria Cristina Marcuzzo explains,

> Kalecki's analysis of pricing policies by firms based on the degree of monopoly, together with his employment theory, provided not only a short period theory of distribution, according to which the share of wages in the value of output is determined by the degree of monopoly, but also laid the basis for a long run theory of distribution. According to the latter, the distributive shares are determined by the rate of investment and the propensity to consume of each class. [470:24]

In *The Accumulation of Capital*, Robinson's thinking--as shaped by Marshall, Keynes, Marx, and Kalecki--came together to form a new school of economic thought. Prior to the publication of *The Accumulation of Capital*, Post-Keynesian thinking had been (and some believe still is [482:168]) so many fragmented pieces, individually coherent but lacking an integrated framework. Robinson's book gave cohesion to a movement that had lacked a center, and economists who take exception to orthodox analysis have been grateful ever since.

Mainstream economists perceived the value of *The Accumulation of Capital* quite differently. For them, the book is seen as inaccessible on two counts. First there is the matter of style. If, as Marshall McLuhan once said, "the medium is the message," then *The Accumulation of Capital* is the wrong medium. Modern economic methodology, begun in the 1930s and well-advanced when *Accumulation* was published in 1956, is nowhere evident in the book. Extremely wordy and tightly reasoned, the book is often considered incomprehensible. Even a valiant attempt to reduce the book's lengthy message to a few well-chosen equations and functions [383] could not rescue the substance of *Accumulation* from its style.

The second reason orthodox economists question the worth of *Accumulation* is the book's author. By the time the book appeared, Robinson had a well-developed reputation as a gadfly/curmudgeon, and thus mainstream economists tended to prejudge the book without giving it a fair reading, or any reading for that matter. While Post-Keynesians consider *The Accumulation of Capital* Joan Robinson's most significant work, orthodox economists have designated it a classic, i.e., a book most have heard of but few have read.

> The economist has to proceed by interpreting the events which happen to be thrown in the course of history, and there is no generally accepted code of rules for interpreting history.
>
> Joan Robinson [144:xv]

AFFLICTING THE COMFORTABLE

The battle between the Cambridges that began in the 1950s continued into the 1960s, and even though the frequency of clashes diminished, the intensity did not. G. C. Harcourt writes:

> The controversies still rage and judging from one of the more recent exchanges ... , the contestants are as cross with one another as ever and as far away from agreement, even to the extent that one side argues that the other does not know what is being discussed. [414:369]

A stalemate usually saps the vitality of all combatants, but that was not true in this conflict. In the 1960s, both Cambridges thrived.

In the United States, the presidential administrations of John F. Kennedy and Lyndon B. Johnson embraced Keynesian economics in theory and in practice, and in so doing elevated the "bastard" Keynesians to the status of high priests of the social sciences. The then unprecedented economic expansion of the mid-1960s was attributed in large measure to the successful implementation of Keynesian thinking, rightly or wrongly, and this "cause and effect" convinced the world that economists really know what they are doing. The perception was reinforced with the creation in 1969 of the Nobel Prize in economics, an award reserved primarily for mainstream economists.

If the 1960s were the heyday of Cambridge (MA) economics, it was also a time of considerable popularity for the other Cambridge as well. The global distaste for America's war in Vietnam and the unfulfilled expectations of people of color in the United States and South Africa spawned a radical movement in economics that has since been marginalized but was quite prominent in the 1960s. This radical economics was especially strong in the United States, where many economists challenged the prevailing orthodoxy and in the process adopted as one of their champions Joan Robinson, that long-time foe of mainstream thinking.

Robinson's popularity in the 1960s was furthered by a shift in the nature of her research. Concerned less with revolutionizing economics and more with spreading the word among the emerging band of scholars who would listen to her, Robinson began writing for a wider audience than just the close-knit cadre of academics wrapped up in the Cambridge controversies. Turner writes:

> As her ancillary work became less technical, it became more interesting to the general reader, including many economists

> who were either unable or unwilling to wade through the articles that made up the capital controversy. [481:145]

In terms of sheer output, the 1960s were an incredibly prolific period for Robinson. She had more than 100 publications in the decade, including: two volumes of her *Collected Economic Papers*; more than a dozen books and articles on socialism in China, Russia, Cuba, and North Korea; four other books ranging from an economics text [144] to a critique of contemporary economic policy in the West [204]; ten articles in major economics journals; and over twenty book reviews. At a time when most people are contemplating retirement--she turned 65 in 1968--Robinson was more productive than ever.

The eclectic nature of Robinson's output in the 1960s makes it hard to characterize her writing for that period of time. Lacking a single theme, she did have, in the words of John Kenneth Galbraith, an intent: "to comfort the afflicted and afflict the comfortable" [481:169]. In 1961, Robinson visited the United States for the first time on one of a number of trips she made to North America during the decade. While on these trips, she often spoke or taught seminars at major universities where, for the most part, economics departments were staffed with "bastard" Keynesians. Everywhere she taught or spoke she took the opportunity to challenge mainstream thinking, whether it was questioning the merits of the aggregate production function or pointing out the obsession with equilibrium of Western economics [481:170-82]. Regardless of the specifics of her topic, Robinson's basic message was always the same: Mainstream economics was of questionable relevance. Her gospel pained the professors but resonated with many of their students, among whom Robinson found a receptive and responsive audience [481:180].

As for comforting the afflicted, Robinson published many papers in the 1960s sympathetic to the economic progress being made in socialist countries, particularly China. This sort of attention from one of the world's foremost economists certainly did nothing to tarnish the image of these emerging socialist nations and probably mollified to some extent the negative portrayals frequently appearing in the Western press. Robinson's infatuation with China was revealed in many of her writings, e.g., [178, 189, and 230]. She also penned works supportive of Cuba [154 and 200] and published a ringing endorsement of North Korea's so-called "economic miracle" [198].

Her unflinching support for socialist causes, coming as it did during the midst of the Cold War, was courageous; Robinson paid a high price for her convictions. Western economists were prone to dismiss the value of her work, believing it was all tinted "red." This made it easy, and indeed respectable, to ignore her even when she had something of substance to say. In the end, Robinson's affection for socialism, which had its roots in her liberal upbringing, was one of the prime factors that rendered her ineligible for a Nobel Prize [481:79].

Of all Robinson's publications in the 1960s, probably none was more fascinating than *Economic Philosophy* [158], a book that afflicted all economists and

Of all Robinson's publications in the 1960s, probably none was more fascinating than *Economic Philosophy* [158], a book that afflicted all economists and comforted none. In *Economic Philosophy*, Robinson argued "that economics should avoid analysis which is loaded down with untestable or 'metaphysical' propositions," and endeavor instead "to formulate theories in a manner which allows them to be disproved" [476:18-19]. She wrote:

> The process of science ... consists in trying to *disprove* theories. The corpus of science at any moment consists of the theories that have not been disproved. The great difficulty in the social sciences (if we may presume to call them so) of applying scientific method, is that we have not yet established an agreed standard for the disproof of an hypothesis. Without the possibility of controlled experiment, we have to rely on interpretation of evidence, and interpretation involves judgment; we can never get a knock-down answer. [158:23]

Reviewing the so-called scientific contents of the major schools of economic thought, especially Neoclassical and Marxian, Robinson concluded that all are as much a product of metaphysical concepts as objective empirical analysis and logical reasoning. The great tragedy in all this, as she sees it, is not that values shape these schools of thinking, but that "the metaphysical contents of these theories are not explicitly recognized for what they are" [476:1]. Robinson chided her colleagues for this lack of candor, a criticism that she realized applied to everyone in the profession, including herself.

> I have spent my life in economic theory and it has come to pieces in my hands.
>
> Joan Robinson [470:53]

QUESTIONS WITHOUT ANSWERS

Unlike American universities where several faculty members in the same department often hold the rank of full professor simultaneously, British universities usually reserve that distinguished title for one professor at a time. In 1965, Robinson achieved the status of professor, the pinnacle among teaching faculty at British institutions of higher learning. In 1971, she retired from her formal teaching duties, but remained as active as ever through the twilight of her career, which ended with her death in 1983.

Ironically, Robinson's professional popularity exceeded that of nearly all other living economists in the 1970s. She was showered with honors and recognition at a time when the impact of her work on emerging scholars was diminishing. "With the profession, as her honors arrived, her influence had waned, a not uncommon experience" [481:156]. Undoubtedly, the greatest of these honors came when she delivered the Richard T. Ely Lecture at the 1971 Annual Meeting of the American Economics Association held in New Orleans.

Robinson did not have many colleagues among the economists at Harvard University, but she did have one true friend, John Kenneth Galbraith. In a relationship that began in the late 1930s when Galbraith spent a year at Cambridge as a Social Science Research Fellow [481:162-63], Galbraith and Robinson had been intellectual comrades and personal friends for nearly all of their professional lives. When, in 1971, Galbraith became President of the American Economics Association, he used the authority of his position to invite Joan Robinson to give the Richard T. Ely Lecture.

Her presentation has been described as "a personal triumph" which played to an overflow audience that gave Robinson a standing ovation at the end of her address [449:668]. In what some consider the most exciting and electric session ever presented at the Association's annual meeting, Robinson explored a topic--"The Second Crisis of Economic Theory" [262]--that consumed her interests from that point to the end of her life.

For Robinson, the first great crisis of economic theory, the great slump of the 1930s, was resolved when Keynes settled the question of how extensive and prolonged unemployment can persist in an equilibrium-seeking economy. The response to the first crisis led to the development of policies designed to maintain employment at or near full, thereby reducing, if not eliminating outright, the likelihood of economic collapse. Left unresolved was the Keynesian trade-off, an economy with an inflationary bias.

Having solved the employment problem, modern economic theory had to confront, as Robinson saw it, the second crisis: What is employment for? In her words:

> The present situation raises new questions. The long boom of twenty-five years after 1945, interrupted only by shallow and local recessions, blew up into a violent inflation in 1973 and collapsed into a world-wide slump. The economists had sunk into complacency and now do not know what to say. Relatively high employment and continuous growth in the indicators of production and accumulation had been taken to show that an age of permanent prosperity had set in. It was natural scientists, not economists, who first pointed out that exponential growth in perpetuity is an impossibility for any physical entity. On the plane of doctrine, Keynes had been smothered in the neo-classical synthesis, and a new "dynamic" version of Say's Law had come into operation.
>
> Now that the Juggernaut car has come more or less to a halt, we must take stock of the problems that its passage leaves behind. The consumption of resources, including air to breathe, has evidently impoverished the world; the long struggle over relative shares has implanted a chronic tendency to inflation in the industrial countries, which no resort to monetary stringency can master. The uneven development of trading nations has set insupportable strains on the international financial system. Growth of wealth has not after all removed poverty at home, and "aid" has not reduced it abroad. Now unemployment exacerbates social problems and embitters politics.
>
> In this situation, the cry is to get growth started again. The European countries in a weak competitive position plead with West Germany to spend money on something or other to improve the market for the rest so that they can permit employment to increase. Any up turn in the indicators in the United States is greeted as a sign that we shall once more be pulled up out of the slough.
>
> Here we come upon the greatest of all economic questions, but one that in fact is never asked: what is growth for?...
>
> The obvious answer is that there is apparently no way to reduce unemployment except by increasing industrial investment. There is no question of choosing between alternative uses for given resources. Past development has dug deep grooves by physical investment, creation of financial property, and specialization of the labor force; existing resources cannot

be redeployed; our only hope is to pour more resources down the old grooves.

... What is the object of production in a modern industrial nation, and if we could have more ... ,what should we use it for?

For the classical economists, such a question did not arise. The wealth of a nation was its investable surplus; real wages were part of the cost of production, like fodder for cattle, and luxury consumption was deprecated; the neoclassicists conceived the object of production to be provision for consumption. But consumption by whom, of what?

The question was suppose to be settled by appeal to the individual's freedom of choice, but there are three very large objections to such a solution.

The first arises from the inequality of the distribution of purchasing power between individuals. The nature of accumulation under private enterprise necessarily generates inequality and is therefore condemned to meeting the trivial wants of a few before the urgent needs of the many.

Do we want renewed growth in order to maintain and enhance disparities in consumption? Have we not become disillusioned with the doctrine that "disease, squalor and ignorance" will soon be cleared away by the "trickle down" from ever-growing conspicuous consumption?

Secondly, many kinds of consumption that are chosen by some individuals generate disutility for others. The leading case is the spread of private motor cars--the higher the level of consumption, the more uncomfortable life becomes; this fact is painfully obvious, but the orthodox doctrine has not been able to accommodate it.

Thirdly, to keep the show going, it is necessary continually to introduce new commodities and create new wants. In a competitive society, a growth of consumption does not guarantee a growth of satisfaction.

Here is the problem. The task of deciding how resources should be allocated is not fulfilled by the market but by the great corporations who are in charge of the finance of development.

These questions involve the whole political and social system of the capitalist world; they cannot be decided by economic

> theory, but it would be decent, at least, if the economists admitted that they do not have an answer to them. [306:1137-39]

Robinson did not have the answers, but she did spend the balance of her career raising the questions and searching for a process that would yield the solutions. Her probing inquiries are evident in the more than 100 publications she produced during the 1970s and 1980s. In the articles, books, essays, and reviews she published during this period, economic theory, the staple of her life well into her sixties, gave way to an insatiable interest in ancillary topics such as an economic interpretation of history [241], the case against the European Economic Community [256], and the inflationary bias inherent in Keynesian economic policy [280]. It would be a mistake, however, to conclude that she abandoned theory in the twilight of her career. On the contrary, she continued to write solid, albeit academic, economics, as when she declared the capital controversy over [257] or penned a highly technical note comparing Samuelson and Marx [275]. Still, the body of her work from 1970 onward dealt less with the formal logic of economic theory and more with the softer, broader issues of the arms race [345], the state of economics [342], and the moral conflicts inherent in capitalism [311].

Toward the end of her life, Robinson became "the challenging critic, asking profound questions, but often providing no more than hints to answers" [475:50]. She did not develop a comprehensive and coherent theory to explain the many questions she asked, nor did she propose a policy agenda to reduce or at least ameliorate the myriad of social problems she felt economics had left unresolved or avoided altogether. She did, however, stimulate the creation of a new school of thought that she hoped would offer a different approach to the perception of these problems than that likely to flow from the orthodox tradition.

Arguably, Post-Keynesian economics owes its origin to Joan Robinson. While Kalecki's macro-theory no doubt influenced Robinson's thinking and thus indirectly the development of the Post-Keynesian school, she is the one whose lifetime of work wove together the individual threads that have become the principal tenets of this movement. Of course, it is an open question as to whether Post-Keynesianism is sufficiently coherent to justify the designation "school" [482:168]. At one time or another, the terms Anglo-Italian, neo-Ricardian, neo-Keynesian, and neo-Marxian have been used to describe the various strands of economic thinking that today are part of the fabric that is Post-Keynesian economics. Even the spelling of the name is a matter of debate as post Keynesian, Post Keynesian, and Post-Keynesian are used inter-changeably by those who identify with this school of thought. Still, there are some core beliefs to which nearly all Post-Keynesians subscribe, and these precepts have their intellectual roots in the writings of Joan Robinson.

Fundamental to Post-Keynesian thought is the rejection of the Neoclassical school, which is viewed as an aberration in the line of reasoning that connects the Classical tradition and Keynesian analysis. Second, Post-Keynesians see the micro/macro dichotomy as false and unproductive, believing instead that macroeconomics events have their origins in microeconomics conditions, which in turn are affected by aggregate economic activity. Third, the concept of equilibrium is seen as irrelevant in a Post-Keynesian world where risk, uncertainty, and unrealized expectations abound. Finally, Post-Keynesians think that positive economics is neither desirable nor possible, and favor instead a normative approach reminiscent of early political economy, the source of all modern Western economic thought.

If the emergence of Post-Keynesianism gave Robinson hope that at least some economists would address the pressing issues of the day from a perspective she believed in, the events of the world at large seemed to confirm her worst suspicions as she neared the end of her life. In the mid-1970s, the oil crisis disrupted the economies of the West as few shocks had since the Great Depression. The near hyper-inflation of the late 1970s and early 1980s, the severe economic downturn of 1980-1982, and the crushing financial burden these occurrences placed on third- world nations were all events that Robinson had predicted in one form or another. The ascendancy of Ronald Reagan in the United States and Margaret Thatcher in England, and Britain's Falkland war and America's "star wars" only confirmed Robinson's lament that fifty years of trying to clarify economic thinking had been for naught. When she died on August 5, 1983, less than three months shy of her eightieth birthday, the world seemed headed for the second crisis Robinson's life work was meant to avoid.

> Controversies in economics persist, not because economists are necessarily less intelligent or more bad tempered than the rest of mankind, but because the issues involved arouse strong feelings.
>
> Joan Robinson [033]

ASSESSING A LIFE

Robinson's fascinating life can be examined on so many different levels, it is hard to know where to begin. The length and productivity of her professional career is difficult to capture and assess in a few short paragraphs. Still, we need to identify some salient benchmarks if we are to make sense of a life so rich and full. Three pegs, more illustrative than exhaustive, can help us triangulate Robinson's life: the power and influence of her intellect; the controversies associated with her work; and the complexity of her personality.

That Joan Robinson was one of the foremost Western economists of the twentieth century there is no doubt. She displayed her intellectual brilliance early and often, beginning in the 1920s with her success as an economics student at Cambridge University and ending more than fifty years later with the publication of hundreds of books, articles, essays, and reviews, many considered classics in the field. "The most widely known of Joan Robinson's works is still the first, *The Economics of Imperfect Competition*" [477:214]. The seminal ideas and techniques that Robinson introduced in that book have stood the test of time, making the work one of the masterpieces of modern economic thought.

As an economic theoretician, Robinson was more than just a one-stage rocket flashing across the sky for a few fleeting moments and then disappearing forever. "For Joan Robinson, the *Economics of Imperfect Competition* was only the first step on a very long way to a series of works in quite different and varied fields of economic theory" [477:214]. The culmination of that journey was the creation of a new school of economic thinking, Post-Keynesian economics. Others contributed, in some cases significantly, to the development of this novel approach to economic reasoning, but none can claim the proprietorship of Joan Robinson.

This is evident in the dedication of the provisional edition of Alfred S. Eichner's *The Macrodynamics of Advanced Market Economies*:[4]

> To Joan Robinson who, by first putting together into a coherent whole the alternative post-Keynesian paradigm, showed us the path out of the Valley of Darkness that is the neoclassical theory.

Eichner's book, a work in progress, was to be a summative volume on Post-

---

[4] Armonk, NY: M. E. Sharpe, 1987: v.

Keynesian economics in which he hoped "to present, within a single text, a comprehensive treatment of the post-Keynesian (and institutionalist, post-Marxian and behavioralist) alternative to the conventional (neoclassical) theory."[5] Having completed twelve of an intended fifteen chapters, Eichner published the provisional text seeking feedback from interested colleagues. In February, 1988, before he could revise the manuscript, at the age of 51, Eichner suffered a fatal heart attack. The project remains unfinished, and although the definitive work on Post-Keynesian economics has yet to be written, this school of thought owes its life to Joan Robinson, and its very existence remains a vital part of her legacy to the discipline.

The grandeur of Robinson's intellectual achievements is all the more remarkable considering the hostile environment in which she had to labor.

> On a strictly academic level, Joan Robinson slowly ascended the academic ladder: Junior Assistant Lecturer in 1931, Full Lecturer in 1937, Reader in 1949. It was suggested in Cambridge that the fact that her husband was in the same faculty kept her back at all stages of her academic career. She became full professor only on Austin Robinson's retirement in 1965. [477:212]

> The male chauvinism Robinson encountered was not restricted to her colleagues at Cambridge but also seemed to be a general attitude of the profession at large, especially early in her career. An inordinate number of critiques of her work contain her name in the title, e.g., [354, 356, 368, 383, and 384]. Rather than a mark of respect or courtesy, such references appear condescending, and seem to imply that the work under review is the product of a scholar inherently different from the usual practitioner. Eventually, Robinson was accepted as an intellectual with few equals, but only after establishing herself as a world-renowned economist.

Whatever problems the profession had in accepting Robinson, she was for years the best-known economist at Cambridge University and ultimately became one of only a handful of theoreticians whose fame transcends the academy. Her accomplishments warranted inclusion in "Engagement Calendar 1985: Great Economists,"[6] a publication featuring the portraits of fifty-four economists of distinction. She also earned an intellectual profile in *Applied Economics*, one of only fourteen economists so recognized in a textbook designed for American

---

[5] Personal letter of October 28, 1987.

[6] Compiled by G. J. Stigler and C. Friedland: Chicago, IL: University of Chicago Press, 1984.

high school students.[7] And of course, she was featured in *Business Week* in 1975, the year most economics pundits thought she would win the Nobel Prize in economics.

Curiously, the very aspects of Robinson's work that captured popular attention--the elegance of her prose, her affinity for socialism, and the seemingly endless battle with American Keynesians--were the source of much of the controversy in her professional life. Mark Blaug writes:

> A glance at Joan Robinson's five volumes of *Collected Papers* ... shows that she is one of the best counter-examples of the generalization that all economists write badly: her style, marked by the frequent use of colloquialisms, rhetorical barbs, and a peculiar but intoxicating type of verbal algebra is a sheer delight to read. On the other hand, her admiration of Mao's China and Kim-Sung's North Korea was a continual embarrassment to her friends and foes alike. [484:x]

Especially damaging to her professional image was her long and sometimes nasty dispute with the American economists Samuelson and Solow. Robinson's critique of their work began as a professional rebuke but eventually gave way to a personal crusade in which she exhibited at times a degree of righteousness she often criticized in others. "Few economists of this century have been as personal as Joan Robinson in her attacks on individuals" [481:112].

What made her assault on the two economists from MIT particularly vexing was its reflection of a deeper resentment that Robinson seemed to harbor for nearly all Americans, with the notable exception of John Kenneth Galbraith. For Samuelson and Solow, and economists of their ilk, she had coined the term "bastard Keynesians," hardly a flattering moniker. For those Americans she deemed less well endowed intellectually, Robinson had another term: "hippopotami" [481:172], which in her private lexicon had a distinctly pejorative meaning.

Her disdain for things American is evident in the references in her research to American scholars, or rather the lack thereof. Just as the exception proves the rule, this anti-Americanism is obvious in the one time she went out of her way to cite the scholarship of an American not directly involved in the capital controversy. This happened in 1971 when Robinson discussed with praise the work of Franklin Fisher, research that she concluded shows aggregate production function do not exist [254 and 257]. Although Fisher subsequently claimed that Robinson completely misinterpreted his results [254], she argued nonetheless that Fisher's work proves that "marginal productivity of capital in industry as a whole ... (is) a meaningless expression" [257], and with that pronouncement, she declared the capital controversy over.

---

[7] Colorado Springs, CO: Junior Achievement, 1990: 89.

Since Robinson rarely cited empirical research, this incident suggests one of two possibilities, neither of which enhances her reputation as a scholar: Either she was largely unaware of the growing body of empirical scholarship that developed after WWII, especially in the United States, or she chose to ignore it. Either way, Robinson's aversion to American scholars not only diminished her image in the eyes of her contemporaries, it also denied her access to research that could have supported her own.

Consider, for example, what Robinson could have accomplished had she incorporated Herbert Simon's path-breaking studies on satisficing behavior into her work on the micro-economics foundations of Post-Keynesian macroeconomics. There is, however, no evidence by implicit reference or explicit citation that Robinson knew of Simon's work on the psychological dimensions of decision making and its impact on economic behavior. There exist other missed opportunities of a comparable nature, all of which magnified the controversies surrounding her scholarship.

A propensity to stereotype is only one of the personal idiosyncrasies that made Robinson a complex individual, difficult to understand and nearly impossible to characterize. She was, for instance, capable of profound tenderness and yet was openly rude to even her closest allies. A single anecdote demonstrates the latter point.

In the preface of her marvelous biography [482:xiii], Marjorie Turner describes an exchange of letters with Joan Robinson concerning the book Turner was writing about Robinson's life. Turner sought Robinson's assistance in the development of the work, and, even though Robinson considered herself an unsuitable subject for a biography, she agreed to help: "I think the best plan would be for you to send to me your drafts or any queries you want to raise and I will reply to them as they come." When Turner tried to followup on Robinson's offer, she (Turner) got a one-line reply: "It is your business to do this research, not mine" [482:xiii].

Though her charm was not always evident to her peers, Robinson was kind almost to a fault with her students. According to Harcourt,

> Her concern for students and what they are taught has been expressed in a number of areas. Generations of Cambridge undergraduates and research students have paid tribute to her as a demanding but devoted supervisor. She has lectured to students across the world, often at their request. [449:670]

The affection students had for her is quite understandable, for compared with most professors she was colorful, almost dashing. Peter Allen writes:

> She was extremely popular with the students--a clear, brilliant, stimulating teacher. She was a person who inspired strong feelings--of love and hate. Her opponents were frightened by

> her, and her friends really admired, almost worshipped her. Her nonconformism in everyday life and even in her clothing (most of which she bought in India) was renowned. [447:213]

Above all, she had the capacity not to take herself or her subject matter too seriously. Examples of her sharp wit are legendary, such as the time she was told that Milton Friedman had won the Nobel Prize in economics, Robinson is alleged to have replied: "I'm spinning in my grave."

Where then does all this leave us? Surely, no one-line summary of Robinson, her life or her work can capture the essence of one of the preeminent, controversial, and most influential intellects in the history of Western economics. Indeed, we are probably better off just to absorb Robinson rather than categorize her. But this still leaves unresolved the issue of the Nobel Prize.

Did Robinson deserve the award, and if so, why was it denied her? The answer to the first part of the question is an unequivocal yes. *The Economics of Imperfect Competition* alone entitled her to the prize, and while that book may be four or five times better than anything else she subsequently wrote, the overall scope, originality, and volume of her scholarship is on a par with just about every recipient to date of the Nobel in economics. The sad truth is that had she stopped writing after publishing *Imperfect Competition*, she probably would have gone on to win the prize, for it was the controversies surrounding her subsequent scholarship that ultimately cost her the Nobel.

Unfortunately, the members of the Swedish panel who select the winner in economics could not find in their hearts the charity that Martin Bronfenbrenner showed when he wrote:

> Speaking as a "bastard" Keynesian purveyor of "rubbish" and "stinking fish," ... I do not agree with most of what Joan Robinson has been saying these past forty years, but hope she wins a Nobel Prize for saying it. [452:446]

Instead, the panel's missed opportunity has left open a debate that will be renewed every October when the Nobel Prize in economics is announced. One suspects that Joan Robinson would have wanted it that way.

Chapter 2
Works by Joan Robinson

A USER'S GUIDE

The purpose of this bibliography is to provide those interested in the scholarship of Joan Robinson an annotated listing of works by and about her. The bibliography is, we believe, user friendly in that it enables the curious scholar--novice or professional--to ascertain what Joan Robinson thought and what others thought about her and her works. The annotations try to capture the essence of each publication, often indicating the level as well as the contents of the material under review. The citations are as complete as necessary to locate each item, either by searching a library's holdings directly or through interlibrary loan.

The bibliography of works by Joan Robinson is based on the unannotated listings of Maria Cristina Marcuzzo [470], which establish the order of Robinson's publications but do not take into account all the anthologies in which her writings can be found. Robinson's works are grouped by years starting in 1930 and numbered sequentially from [001] through [347]. The progressive numeration corresponds to the chronological order of publication. If there is more than one publication in a given year, books and pamphlets are listed first, followed by other works listed chronologically by seasons, months, and/or dates.

If a publication is reprinted elsewhere, the citation is followed by a bracketed number referring to the location of the other printing. For example, in 1933 Robinson published "The Theory of Money and the Analysis of Output." The work is listed as:

[011] "The Theory of Money and the Analysis of Output," *Review of Economic Studies*, 1(1), October: 22-26. Reprinted in [086] and [308].

Thus, this work is the eleventh publication annotated in this bibliography. It appeared in Volume 1, Number 1 of the *Review of Economic Studies* in October 1933, on pages 22-26. The article is reprinted in [086], Volume 1 of Robinson's *Collected Economic Papers*, and in [308], *Contributions to Modern Economics*.

Joan Robinson published numerous books in her life, some original volumes, others collections of previously printed essays, and still others a mixture of reprinted and original materials. If an essay in a book is original to that book, it is identified with a bracketed number/letter combination to the left of the title. If, however, the essay is reprinted in the book, the title of the essay is followed by a bracketed number showing the original printing.

So, for example, in 1937 Robinson published *Essays in the Theory of Employment* [032]. "Full Employment" is an original essay in that book and assigned the number [032a], followed by a brief annotation. Also appearing in that book is the reprinted essay "Disguised Unemployment" [024]. There is no annotation following this entry as the bracketed number to the right of the title indicates that this is item [024], a work already cited and annotated. Referring to [024], the reader can determine the original citation for the work and review its annotation. The reader would also discover that the work is reprinted in [032], a cross-reference, and [263], another cross-reference.

Sometimes reprinted works and the original differ. When this occurs, such changes are noted. For instance, in [032], the essay "The Long-Period Theory of Employment" is reprinted with section five of the original omitted. The citation so indicates. In addition to variations in completeness, other modifications such as changes in titles or language of translation are noted where appropriate.

The bibliography of works about Joan Robinson--the third portion of this book--is a selective, annotated listing of books, articles and reviews about her work and life. Listed in chronological order, these writings are numbered sequentially from [348] through [488] and grouped by decades beginning with the 1930s. A brief user's guide precedes the annotated bibliography of works about Joan Robinson.

1930

[001] A review of H. Clay, *The Problem of Industrial Relations*, in *Political Quarterly*, (1), April: 293-96.

It seems entirely appropriate that Robinson's first published work should be a book review. She published well over 100 book reviews during her career, and in many ways these reviews reveal more about Joan Robinson, the person and the economist, than the sum total of her other publications.

In this review, Robinson takes exception to Clay's definition of a "fair wage," noting that Clay accepts the orthodox theory of the distribution of wealth, something against which she argued throughout her life.

1932

[002] *Economics Is a Serious Subject. The Apologia of an Economist to the Mathematician, the Scientist and the Plain Man*, Cambridge: Heffer and Sons.

In this, the first of a dozen or so pamphlets she would publish in her career, Robinson makes the case that economics is a serious subject despite at times being "utterly heartless." She concedes that the techniques of economics are "imperfect, primitive, incomplete, only capable of giving unreal answers to unreal questions." Nevertheless, Robinson cites the astonishing accomplishments of Pigou and Keynes regarding the theory of value and the analysis of total output, respectively, as genuine progress for a discipline still in its infancy.

For Robinson, the study of economics is torn between two competing but equally valid approaches. On the one side are "the optimistic, analytical, English" economists who develop models that are manageable but unrealistic. Their optimism stems from the belief that manageable models provide insights, however, incomplete, into economic phenomena, the realistic details of which can be developed later, when more precise information is available.

The other approach to economics is that of the "pessimistic, methodological, Continental" economists who build realistic, though unmanageable, models. Their pessimism comes from the notion that realism is essential even if it means not being able to come to definitive conclusions.

For Robinson, each school has much to recommend and neither is inherently superior to the other. Indeed, each approach serves as a check and balance on the other, ensuring real progress in the serious study that is economics.

[003] A review of L. S. S. O'Malley, *Indian Caste Customs*, in *Cambridge Review*, (54), November 25: 138.

This one-paragraph critique is full of praise for O'Malley's book, which Robinson describes as "a clear and concise account of the ... workings of the caste system."

[004] "Imperfect Competition and Falling Supply Price," *Economic Journal*, 42(168), December: 544-54.

Following the intellectual protocol of the Neoclassical school, of which in 1932 she was an integral part, Robinson uses orthodox reasoning to show that "when average cost for the firm is falling, it by no means follows that supply price for the commodity is falling." Her first major article in a prominent journal, this work is clearly a precursor of Robinson's classic book *The Economics of Imperfect Competition* [005].

1933

[005] *The Economics of Imperfect Competition*, London: Macmillan, (Second edition, 1969).

For Post-Keynesian economists, *The Accumulation of Capital* [111] is Robinson's magnum opus, but for mainstream economists, *Imperfect Competition* holds that distinction. The popularity of the book is self-evident; it was reprinted ten times through 1959 and reissued in a new edition in 1969.

To this day, the treatment of imperfect competition that Robinson expounded in 1933 at the age of 30 is still embodied in basic economics texts. Her contributions--marginal revenue and the discontinuous demand curve to name just two--fill much of modern price theory analysis. Robinson's material is so integrated into microeconomic theory that she is no longer referenced and hasn't been for some time. The concept of imperfect competition is part and parcel of mainstream economics, thanks largely to this book.

In the foreword of the first edition, Robinson acknowledges a debt of gratitude to R. F. Kahn, Alfred Marshall, and A. C. Pigou, claiming that the latter two laid the foundation on which the thesis of this work is built.

[005a] Preface to the Second Edition: "Imperfect Competition, Then and Now."

Robinson compares price theory analysis circa 1969 with that in vogue in 1933 and concludes, much to her dismay, that the unrealistic, if not irrelevant, economics of perfect competition "still reign supreme" despite the existence of this book and the body of work that it stimulated.

[006] "A Parable on Saving and Investment," *Economica* (old series), (13), February: 75-84.

In the early 1930s, Keynes and Hayek became involved in a controversy over saving and investment. Hayek claimed that voluntary savings always equals investment, while Keynes, in his *Treatise on*

Money, said that no automatic mechanism exists in the economy to equate the two.

In an attempt to resolve the controversy in favor of her friend Keynes, Robinson develops an elaborate parable that is supposed to simplify the problem so that the solution becomes self-evident. The result is mixed at best. For the reader lacking technical expertise, the parable muddles rather than clarifies, and it could easily have caused Keynes to exclaim, "With friends like these, who needs enemies?"

[007] "The Imperfection of the Market: A Further Comment," *Economic Journal*, 43(169), March 124-25.

Responding to G. F. Shove's critique of her article on "Imperfect Competition and Falling Supply Price" [004], Robinson takes exception to some of the critical comments. Shove's essay immediately precedes Robinson's short comment, and both pieces are incorporated under the single title of this article.

[008] "Shakespeare and Mr. Looney," *Cambridge Review*, (54), May 12: 389-90.

Most of Robinson's publications deal with economic theory; many of her writings focus on economic policy; some of her works discuss tangential issues such as world peace or preserving the environment; then there is this essay.

In this short piece, Robinson takes up the cause of a schoolmaster named Looney who published in 1920 a book claiming that "Shakespeare" was really Edward de Vere, the Seventeenth Earl of Oxford and a prominent sixteenth-century British poet. Robinson thinks Mr. Looney's hypothesis has merit and explains why.

[009] A review of P. H. Wicksteed, *The Coordination of the Laws of Distribution*, in *Economic Journal*, 43(170), June: 301-4.

Finding much to admire in the reissue of this Wicksteed classic, Robinson notes the proposition that rewarding each factor of production according to its marginal contribution exhausts output holds only if (a) competition is perfect and (b) returns to scale are constant. She would spend a great deal of her career challenging these two assumptions and, thus, the Neoclassical theory of distribution.

[010] "Decreasing Costs: A Reply to Mr. Harrod," *Economic Journal*, 43(171), September: 531-32.

Responding to another essay critical of her article on "Imperfect Competition and Falling Supply Price" [004], Robinson gets involved in what is essentially a squabble over definitions.

[011] "The Theory of Money and the Analysis of Output," *Review of Economic Studies*, 1(1), October:22-26. Reprinted in [086] and [308].

Robinson argues that because Keynes was a captive of the Classical Quantity Theory of Money, he failed to appreciate the revolutionary analysis of national output he developed in his 1930 book *The Treatise on Money*. This essay reflects the discussions Robinson and Keynes were having in the early 1930s. Those discussions helped Keynes sharpen his thinking on saving, investment and the equilibrium of national income at less than full employment, ideas that made his next book, *The General Theory of Employment, Interest and Money* (1936), a classic in economic literature.

[012] A review of A. da Empoli, *Theory of Equilibrium*, in *Economic Journal*, 43(172), December: 666-69.

Robinson believes that "the development of the pure theory of value is in a curious state of confusion" and that da Empoli's book only adds to the chaos. While generally critical of the book, Robinson does commend the author for his "interesting and important" analysis on aspects of imperfect competition such as duopoly.

1934

[013] "Mr. Fraser on Taxation and Returns," *Review of Economic Studies*, 1(2), February: 137-40.

With this comment, Robinson gets involved in the Neoclassical debate concerning the efficacy of increasing social welfare by taxing increasing cost industries while subsidizing decreasing cost industries. The argument is couched in orthodox microeconomicese.

[014] A review of J. E. Meade, *The Rate of Interest in a Progressive State*, in *Economic Journal*, 44(174), June: 282-85.

While critical of Meade's fascination with "monetary mysticism," Robinson is nonetheless full of praise for this book, which she describes as "a considerable feat of bold and independent thinking." She is particularly impressed with Meade's analysis of the conditions of dynamic equilibrium and his notion of the supply curve of capital goods.

[015] "Euler's Theorem and the Problem of Distribution," *Economic Journal*, 44(175), September: 398-414. Reprinted in [086].

Robinson discusses Wicksteed's realization that under conditions of imperfect competition, the Marshallian notion that factors of production are paid according to their marginal product does not appear to hold, an apparent contradiction with Euler's Theorem.

[016] A review of G. T. Jones, *Increasing Returns*, in *Journal of Political Economy*, (42), October: 694-96.

The purpose of Jones's book is to discover whether any causality exists "between the expansion of an industry and an increase in its efficiency." In other words, are increasing returns real? Because of a number of complicating factors such as economies associated with technological breakthroughs that occur independently of industrial expansion, Robinson believes Jones's conclusion is destined to be inconclusive. Nevertheless, she thinks the book has merit because Jones makes many interesting discoveries on the way to his bland conclusion.

[017] "What Is Perfect Competition?" *Quarterly Journal of Economics*, 49(4), November: 104-20. Reprinted in [086].

After defining perfect competition--"a state of affairs in which the demand for the output of an individual seller is perfectly elastic"--Robinson goes on to compare and contrast her definition with those of Chamberlain (who distinguishes between "pure competition" and "perfect competition") and Harrod.

1935

[018] "A Fundamental Objection to Laissez-Faire," *Economic Journal*, 45(179), September: 580-82. Reprinted in [086] as "An Inherent Defect in Laissez-Faire."

Robinson claims that marginal cost pricing answers the question of how much to produce of existing commodities but does not address the larger, normative issue of what ought to be produced. Laissez faire leads to efficient production of present commodities, given the prevailing distribution of income. Robinson believes, however, that total social welfare could be increased with the production of nonexistent commodities that would be introduced under a different--indeed, ideal--distribution of social resources.

[019] A review of H. S. Ellis, *German Monetary Theory* in *Economic Journal*, 45(180), December: 729-31.

Robinson thinks that Ellis's book is competent but uninspiring because the author refuses to take on German and Austrian monetarists such as Mises and Hahn even when they are clearly wrong.

1936

[020] "Dr. Machlup's Commonsense of the Elasticity of Substitution," *Review of Economic Studies*, (3), February: 148-50.

Robinson believes that Machlup's "commonsense" interpretation of the elasticity of substitution will cause the ordinary reader more difficulties than will her interpretation or that of John Hicks.

[021] "The Long-Period Theory of Employment," *Zeitschrift fur Nationalokonomie*, March: 74-93. Reprinted in [032] with section 5 omitted.

In this essay, Robinson extends Keynesian employment theory to the long run with pretty much the same results as short-run analysis, notably the ineffectiveness of monetary policy in restoring full employment.

[022] A review of P. Einzig, *Bankers, Statesmen and Economists*, in *Economic Journal*, 46(181), March: 122-23.

During the Great Depression, books on monetary topics were immensely popular. Robinson felt that most of those books were written by "self-appointed monetary expert[s]" who presented themselves as necromancers to gaping audiences. "Mr. Einzig is not a writer of this class." Robinson finds his "style ... limpid, his ideas commonsensical, his conclusions definite and clear."

[023] "Banking Policy and the Exchanges," *Review of Economic Studies*, (3), June: 226-29.

Written in a narrative style common in economics tracts of Marshall's time, this technical essay purports to show "that the tendency for exchange rates to fluctuate in response to altered conditions is far less powerful than it is nowadays usual to suppose."

[024] "Disguised Unemployment," *Economic Journal*, 46(182), June: 225-37. Reprinted in [032] and [263].

Robinson's notion of disguised unemployment--"the adoption of inferior occupations by disgusted workers"--is referred to today as underemployment. In this essay, Robinson analyzes the causes and the consequences of disguised unemployment, especially as it impacts on and is affected by various unemployment compensation systems.

[025] A review of J. Strachey, *The Nature of the Capitalistic Crisis*, in *Economic Journal*, 46(182), June: 298-302. Part of this review is reprinted in [032] as "Some Reflections of Marxist Economics."

Although not an academic economist, Strachey is, in Robinson's view, an intelligent amateur who has written a book "all professional economists should read and remember." Robinson is taken by Strachey's keen observation that orthodox theory cannot possibly explain massive unemployment as the theory itself is "erected upon the assumption that unemployment cannot exist."

[026] A review of N. Angell, *The Money Mystery*, in *International Affairs*, 15(4), July-August: 598-99.

"In writing popular economics," Robinson observes, "it is a matter of utmost difficulty to strike exactly the right balance--to be lucid without condescension and simple without inaccuracy." As Robinson sees it, Angell's book is condescending without being accurate.

[027] A review of R. F. Harrod, *The Trade Cycle*, in *Economic Journal*, 46(184), December: 691-93. Reprinted in [086] as "The Trade Cycle."

Robinson has general praise for Harrod's essay "as the first advance into the territories opened up by *The General Theory of Employment, Interest and Money*." She is particularly taken by Harrod's analysis of the multiplier-accelerator interaction that shows that a decrease in the rate of increase of consumption is enough to cause a decline in investment, thereby turning an economic expansion into a contradiction.

[028] A review of *Britain Without Capitalists* by a Group of Economists, Scientists and Technicians, in *Economic Journal*, 46(184), December: 704-6.

Robinson is full of praise for this book. She believes its Marxian perspective immunizes the authors "against the sophistication's of laissez-faire economics" and enables them "to review their problems in the light of common sense." Whatever flaws the book has, Robinson considers them minor compared to the overall message of identifying what's wrong with British capitalism.

[029] A review of A. Radford, *Patterns of Economic Activity*, in *Economic Journal*, 46(184), December: 706-7.

Robinson finds Radford's intention--to write a new textbook for post-WWI economic theory--admirable, but the results disappointing.

[030] "Disguised Unemployment: A Rejoinder," *Economic Journal*, 46(184), December: 759-60.

Responding to a comment on her paper "Disguised Unemployment" [024], Robinson contends that, save for two minor points, the comment "is concerned with a subject largely different from that of my article." Additionally, she is convinced that her approach to reducing unemployment is not so risky as that suggested by the author of the comment.

[031] "Mr. Keynes and Socialism," *Left Review*, (2), December: 853.

In her review of A. L. Rowse's pamphlet *Mr. Keynes and the Labor Movement*, Robinson notes that Keynes's *General Theory*, far from providing a way to save capitalism, offers instead "the clearest case for a Socialist policy." This is essentially Rowse's message, with which Robinson wholeheartedly agrees.

1937

[032] *Essays In the Theory of Employment*, London: Macmillan. (Second edition, London: Basil Blackwell, 1947).

In this collection of essays, some original to this book and some reprinted from other sources, Robinson applies the principles of Keynesian macroeconomics to a variety of problems, including disguised unemployment, the concept of zero savings, foreign exchange rates, and beggar-my-neighbour remedies for unemployment. The 1947 edition is nearly a photocopy of the 1937 edition, save for a few minor corrections Robinson describes in the foreword to the later edition.

[032a] "Full Employment" (Reprinted in [263])

Robinson discusses in fairly standard Keynesian terms full employment and unemployment, and the interplay of money and real wages in determining both. The impact of countercyclical fiscal and monetary policies is also evaluated.

[032b] "Mobility of Labour"

Robinson discusses what we now call cyclical, structural, and frictional unemployment, and the difficulty of measuring each precisely.

[032c] "Certain Proposed Remedies for Unemployment"

Robinson reviews the merits and shortcomings of four methods for increasing employment, each of which had some popular support in the 1930s. The four methods discussed are a compulsory reduction in the length of the work day, an increase in compulsory education, emigration, and a wage subsidy. Robinson concludes that all four proposals deal more with the consequences of unemployment than with the root causes.

"Disguised Unemployment" [024]

"The Long-Period Theory of Employment" [021]

[032d] "The Concept of Zero Savings"

In this essay, Robinson contrasts the ease of generating long-run equilibrium with zero savings in a Classical world where the interest rate can vary, with the difficulty of achieving equilibrium in the face of the Keynesian liquidity trap (the rate of interest is given and the level of employment must vary to have equilibrium).

[032e] "Disinvestment"

In this short piece, Robinson compares the impact of a declining population in an economy where most of the capital stock is maintained by "repair" with the impact in an economy where most of the capital stock is maintained by "renewal."

[032f] "Diagrammatic Illustrations"

For those familiar with the narrative style of Robinson's later works, this essay is an anachronism, laced as it is with fifteen diagrams. The diagrams are used "as an alternative method of expressing some" basic Keynesian propositions such as the short- and long- period supply and demand curves of labor.

[032g] "The Foreign Exchanges" (Reprinted in [263])

Robinson reviews the determination of foreign exchange rates from the Keynesian perspective as revealed in the *Treatise on Money* and the *General Theory*. She concludes "that there is no one rate of exchange which is the equilibrium rate corresponding to a given state of world demands and techniques." Rather, there is an equilibrium exchange rate for each combination of interest rate and level of national income, and any rate of exchange can be brought into equilibrium by changing the rate of interest appropriately.

[032h] "Beggar-My-Neighbour Remedies for Unemployment" (Reprinted in [263] and [308])

From a Keynesian perspective, Robinson examines the effects of beggar-my-neighbour policies--programs aimed at the reduction of imports and stimulation of exports to promote domestic employment--in times of worldwide recession.

[032i] "Indeterminacy"

Robinson is critical of the economist's fixation with determinacy, believing that this obsession leads to superficial analysis of complex issues, issues that often require recourse to noneconomic explanations to understand.

[032j] "An Economist's Sermon" (Reprinted in [263])

In this brief "sermon," Robinson maintains that one effect of orthodox economics is to provide the privileged class with a conscience-saving, integrity-preserving rationale for ignoring the plight of the less fortunate.

"Some Reflections on Marxist Economics" [025]

[033] *Introduction to the Theory of Employment*, London: Macmillan. (Second edition, 1969).

This book is Robinson's attempt to explain in lay terms the meaning of Keynes's *General Theory.* Judging by the popularity of the book--eight reprintings between its initial appearance and the final publication of the first edition in 1956--Robinson had a certain degree of success. By comparison, however, Robinson's book had nowhere near the impact of Alvin Hansen's *A Guide to Keynes* (1953) in disseminating the meaning of the *General Theory* to the economics profession and the public at large.

[034] "The Economic System in a Socialist State," *Cambridge Review*, (58), February 26: 289-90.

According to Robinson, some socialists, captivated by the beauty and benefits of the theoretical market economy, are convinced that "if private enterprise were abolished and all production controlled by a central plan, it would be possible to reproduce by artificial means the workings of the ideal competitive system, and to achieve the results which the actual system has failed to bring about."

In this review of R. L. Hall's *The Economic System in a Socialist State*, Robinson writes that Hall is of this ilk. While she respects his point of view, she thinks that it is too narrow. Robinson contends that there are many social issues, such as the composition of output, that ideal capitalism does not address, and neither would "market socialism." For Robinson, a true socialism would be involved in many aspects of human activity, not just the economic.

[035] A review of A. W. Knight, *Abolish Slumps: A Diagnosis of the Trade Cycle,* in *Economic Journal*, 47(186), June: 339-40.

Robinson believes that the main contribution of this book is an "ingenious method for estimating the value of the multiplier," a method that provides a useful cross-check for other estimations.

[036] A review of S. E. Harris, *Exchange Depreciation*, in *Economic Journal*, 47(188), December: 699-701.

Robinson considers Harris's book on exchange depreciation in the United States and Great Britain since 1930 "a very useful analytical and statistical study" but believes that, viewed in total, the work "is somewhat diffuse and repetitive."

1938

[037] "The Classification of Inventions," *Review of Economic Studies*, (5), February: 139-42.

This is a technical discussion in which Robinson compares and contrasts her definitions of neutral, labor-saving, or capital-saving inventions with the definitions of Hicks and Harrod.

[038] "The Concept of Hoarding," *Economic Journal*, 48(190), June: 231-36. Reprinted in [086] and [308].

Robinson identifies several definitions of hoarding, then describes the implication of each for consumption, saving, investment, and the level of national economic activity.

[039] A review of C. Bresciani-Turroni, *The Economics of Inflation*, in *Economic Journal*, 48(191), September: 507-13. Reprinted in [086] as "The Economics of Hyper-Inflation."

Robinson rejects Bresciani-Turroni's claim that the sole cause of the hyperinflation in post-WWI Germany was a dramatic increase in the quantity of money in circulation. She favors a more complicated chain of events involving an increase in the supply of money, a growing national debt, and rising money wages.

1939

[040] A review of Gunnar Myrdal, *Monetary Equilibrium*, in *Economic Journal*, 49(195), September: 493-95. Reprinted in [086] as "Monetary Equilibrium."

Robinson claims that the eminent Swedish economist Gunnar Myrdal has in this book--the original version of which appeared in 1931--many ideas that predate those of Keynes in the *General Theory*. She finds of special interest Myrdal's distinction between ex ante and ex post saving and investment, and the role expectations play in affecting the level of aggregate economic activity.

1940

[041] A review of R. A. Lester, *Monetary Experiments*, in *Economic Journal*, 50(198-99), June-September: 280-82.

Robinson is favorably impressed with Lester's narratives of monetary experiments in colonial America and in Scandinavia during the 1930s, despite his tendency to interpret history "in light of a strictly orthodox Quantity Theory."

[042] A review of G. Crowther, *Ways and Means of War*, and J. K. Horsefield, *The Real Cost of the War*, in *Economic Journal*, 50(200), December: 505-7.

Robinson commends the authors for trying to explain war economics to the "plain man." At the same time, however, she takes exception to unnecessary technical analyses in both books, especially the "treatment of inflation in terms of the supply of money and credit." Robinson believes such monetary theory does more to confuse than to educate.

[043] "War Savings Campaign," *The Times* (London), December 3: 5.

In what is essentially a letter to the editor, Robinson supports Keynes's position that voluntary savings, when combined with tax yields and foreign reserves, will be insufficient to cover the cost of WWII for Britain. Like Keynes, Robinson believes some forms of involuntary saving will be necessary to finance the war.

1941

[044] "The Financial Problem of 1941," *The Banker*, (57), January: 8-13.

Estimating that the war effort will cause a twenty-five percent reduction in the availability of consumer goods while simultaneously increasing purchasing power by twenty percent, Robinson reasons that wartime inflation is inevitable. She reviews three proposals for controlling this inflation: Kalecki's rationing plan, increased taxation, and Keynes's scheme of deferred pay. While concluding that all three approaches may be necessary, Robinson shows a clear preference for Keynes's.

[045] "Rising Supply Price," *Economica* (new series), 8(29), February: 1-8. Reprinted in [086].

An arcane analysis of the conditions that accelerate the tendency to rising supply price. Robinson readily admits in the opening paragraph that "what follows has no relevance to any problem of importance in the real world."

[046] A review of R. F. Bretherton, F. A. Burchardt, and R. S. G. Rutherford, *Public Investment and the Trade Cycle in Great Britain*, in *Economic Journal*, 51(201), April: 127-29.

Robinson is generally impressed with the book, which is basically a historical description of public investment in Great Britain in the interwar years. She does note, however, that the authors use Kahn's multiplier concept incorrectly as they appear to be confused by its technical aspects.

[047] "Marx on Unemployment," *Economic Journal*, 51(202-3), June-September: 234-48. The first two paragraphs are in [076], which originally appeared in Italian but is reprinted in English in [086].

Robinson's stated purpose in writing this article "is to examine what I take to be Marx's analysis of unemployment in language intelligible to academic economists." Though ostensibly targeted at all mainstream economists, this article seems to have been written to educate just one of them, J. M. Keynes, at that time the editor of the *Economic Journal.* Keynes had confessed on a number of occasions not to understand Marx, and Robinson was hoping that this article would give Keynes insights into Marx and Kalecki. It did not work.

[048] A review of M. Dobb, *Soviet Economy and the War*, in *Economic Journal*, 51(204), December: 489.

Of all the books Robinson reviewed in her career, this is the only one she "recommended without qualification."

1942

[049] *An Essay on Marxian Economics*, London: Macmillan. (Second edition, 1966).

As a freshly minted college professor, I assigned the students in my very first class the task of writing a review on the economics book of their choice. One enterprising student selected the slimmest economics volume in the library, believing that such a work would require a minimal effort to read and review. He learned the hard way that Joan Robinson's *An Essay on Marxian Economics* is a thin book with a vast amount of complex information that requires a solid understanding of economics to grasp.

Besides presenting a concise yet thorough review of Marxian economics, Robinson connects Marxian thought to Keynes's General Theory, Kalecki's *Essays in the Theory of Economic Fluctuations*, and Robinson's own work on imperfect competition. This book cements Robinson's appreciation of the role of history in economic growth and development, a recurring theme in her works published after this date.

[050] *Private Enterprise or Public Control*, London: Association for Education in Citizenship, Handbooks for Discussion Groups, no. 11.

In the preface to this pamphlet, the Association for Education in Citizenship states, "The object of this series of pamphlets is to encourage discussion of the social, economic and political problems ... arising out of the war." In striving for a balanced approach to issues, the Association claims that the writer of each pamphlet "has been asked to remember that his function is not to provide propaganda for any particular plan ..., but to place before his reader the principal facts and points of view that must be taken into account if any agreed solution is to be found."

Apparently, Robinson missed the point because her biases against capitalism and for socialism are abundantly evident throughout the twenty pages of this pamphlet.

[051] A review of J. H. G. Pierson, *Full Employment*, in *Economic Journal*, 52(206-7), June-September: 240-41.

Robinson believes that Pierson's approach to maintaining full employment--by having the federal government underwrite consumer spending without regard to the distribution of the benefits--will not find popular support once the general public understands how the system operates.

[052] A review of S. E. Harris, *Economics of Social Security*, in *Economic Journal*, 52(206-7), June-September: 241-43.

Although Robinson believes the book has a number of defects, she thinks that Harris's encyclopedic work is an interesting, descriptive, and analytical study "of a fascinating subject."

[053] A review of N. H. Borden, *The Economic Effects of Advertising*, in *Economica* (New Series), 9(53), August: 394-96. Reprinted in [086] as "The Economic Effects of Advertising."

This generally favorable review is innocuous save for one revealing thought. Characterizing Borden's discussion of the ethics of advertising as superficial, Robinson concludes her review by observing, "The question [the ethics of advertising] is bound up with the question of the ethics of the profit system, which his [Borden's] terms of reference forbid him to discuss." The latter question was one of prime importance throughout Robinson's life.

[054] "Industry and the State," *Political Quarterly*, (13), October: 400-6.

Midway through WWII, the Federation of British Industries published a report outlining its vision of postwar reconstruction. In this article and elsewhere [056], Robinson takes exception to the report's recommendations. She believes that the report represents the self-interest of industry at the expense of social welfare. Robinson finds particularly objectionable the recommendation that each industry "possess a Trade Association with clearly defined functions to suit its needs."

[055] A review of T. Wilson, *Fluctuations in Income and Employment*, in *Economic Journal*, 52(208), December: 352-54.

While favorably impressed with the book as a whole, Robinson has special praise for the historical chapters in which Wilson applies the prevailing trade-cycle theories to U.S. economic activity from 1919 to 1937.

1943

[056] *The Future of Industry*, London: Commonwealth.

Continuing her indictment of a report by the Federation of British Industries, Robinson expands on her earlier criticisms [054] in part 1 of this pamphlet, then devotes part 2 to a persuasive essay touting socialism as an alternative to monopolistic capitalism.

[057] *The Problem of Full Employment: An Outline for Study Circles*, London: Workers Educational Association. (Second edition, 1949; third edition, 1953).

After outlining the basis of Keynesian economics in easy-to-understand language, Robinson discusses the "false" and the "true" remedies for unemployment. She concludes this short pamphlet with a discussion on the importance of planning investment, improving the distribution of income, and controlling inflation.

[058] "Creating Money," *Accountancy*, (54), January: 64-65.

In simple, straightforward terms, Robinson describes the process by which central banks "create and destroy" money.

[059] "Planning," *Fabian Quarterly*, (36), January: 4-8.

Maintaining that "socialism involves planning, but planning is not necessarily socialism," Robinson argues that the crux of socialist planning is who does the planning and for what purpose. New Deal planning done in the United States or industrial planning as proposed by the Federation of British Industries will not create a socialist state. True socialism requires government planning done in the best interest of the community, not pseudoplanning done to preserve capitalism or further the interest of monopolistic industries.

[060] "Planning Full Employment," *The Times* (London), January 22: 5; and January 23: 5. Reprinted in [086].

In the first part of this two-part article, Robinson argues that to promote full employment and avoid mass unemployment, it will "be necessary to remove certain substantial spheres of activity from the hands of private enterprise and put them under the control of the government." In the second part of the article, Robinson recognizes that guaranteeing high levels of employment could lead to inflation and declining productivity. To counter these tendencies, she recommends the socialization of capital, arguing that if the means of production become community property, it will be self-evident that the interest of all are furthered by moderation and innovation.

[061] A review of R. T. Norris, *The Theory of Consumers' Demand*, in *Economic Journal*, 53(209), April: 115-17. Reprinted in [086] as "The Theory of Consumers' Demand."

While lauding the attempt to overhaul the Marshall-Hicks view of consumer behavior so at odds "with the teachings of modern psychology," Robinson finds Dr. Norris's treatment still entangled in the obsolete apparatus of utility theory, indifference maps, and marginal utility curves.

[062] "The International Currency Proposals," *Economic Journal*, 53(210-11), June-September: 161-75.

Robinson begins by describing the purpose and shortcomings of the gold standard. She then goes into a lengthy comparative analysis of two international currency systems being proposed as replacements for the gold standard.

The systems she considers are: (1) the *Proposals for an International Clearing Union*, put forth by the British Chancellor of the Exchequer and referred to as the Bancor plan, and (2) the *United States proposal for a United and Associated Nations Stabilization Fund*, called the Unitas plan.

In a careful comparison of the two plans, Robinson exhibits a clear preference for the Bancor plan, which she claims is based on the creation of a real international medium of exchange, unlike the Unitas plan, which operates more or less like an international central bank.

[063] A review of J. Schumpeter, *Capitalism, Socialism and Democracy*, in *Economic Journal*, 53(212), December: 381-83. Reprinted in [334] and in [086] as "Capitalism, Socialism and Democracy."

In 1934, Schumpeter wrote a glowing review [354] of Robinson's *The Economics of Imperfect Competition*, considered by many her most significant book. Nine years later, Robinson returns the favor in this laudatory review of what is arguably Schumpeter's magnum opus. Drawn to Schumpeter's analysis of Marx, Robinson finds the book highly original, fresh, and provocative.

[064] "Economics and Unemployment," *New Statesman and Nation*, 27(667), December 4: 372-73.

Discussions about post-WWII British employment policy were in full swing at this time. In this review of G. D. H. Cole, *The Means to Full Employment*, Robinson divides the competing schools of thought into those "who regard full employment as the best means for saving capitalism and those who regard it as the starting point for a gradual transition to socialism." She considers Cole's book representative of the former.

1944

[065] "Abolishing Unnecessary Poverty," in N. Kaldor, J. Robinson, A. Evans, E. F. Schumacher, and P. L. Yates, *Planning for Abundance*, (Peace Aims Pamphlet No. 21), London: National Peace Council: 3-7.

Based on presentations made at the Peace Aims Conference of the National Peace Council held at Oxford on July 23-26, 1943, this pamphlet addresses the prospects of prosperity after WWII. In her essay, Robinson argues that the real problem confronting England "is not so much unemployment as unnecessary poverty." She makes this point because she believes that "it is important to keep in mind the real nature of the problem." Otherwise, there will be confusion between true remedies to poverty and false ones that merely reduce unemployment by creating make-work jobs.

[066] "Implications of a Full Employment Policy," in D. Tyerman, editor, *Ways and Means of Rebuilding*, London: Faber and Faber: 20-27 and 30-31.

In this address given at the London Conference of Town Planning, Housing, and Full Employment held in July 1943, Robinson argues that putting people to work solely to achieve full employment is short-sighted. To have lasting full employment, a long-term plan is required to put labor to work producing what is needed. In her estimation, this means the coordination of aggregate consumption, the control of national investment, and a redistribution of income toward greater equality.

[067] "The Currency Plan," *Socialist Commentary*, June: 245-50.

In a rare display of praise for things American, Robinson speaks highly of the international currency plan the United States proposed to put in place after WWII. That plan eventually became the International Monetary Fund, and Robinson believes it speaks highly for American insight and "sense of responsibility to the world." This position represents a change of heart for Robinson, who one year earlier expressed a contrary view [062].

[068] "Official Paper" (a review of H. B. Larry and Associates, editors, *The United States in the World Economy*), in *Economic Journal*, 54(215-16), December: 430-37. Reprinted in [086] as "The United States in the World Economy."

Calling the Department of Commerce report of the U.S. balance of payments from 1919 to 1939 "probably the clearest and most penetrating analysis that has yet appeared on the whole history of international trade and capital," Robinson shows how these flows contributed to the worldwide depression of the 1930s.

1945

[069] A review of B. Wootton, *Freedom Under Planning*, in *Girton Review*, 129(Michaelmas Term): 20.

Robinson has much praise for Ms. Wootton's examination of "the points at which national economic planning is liable to conflict with traditional liberties." She is particularly taken by Wootton's discussion of the apparent incompatibility of planning and the individual's choice of employment.

[070] A review of *The Economics of Full Employment* by the Economists of the Oxford Institute of Statistics, in *Economic Journal*, 55(217), April: 77-82. Reprinted in [086] as "The Economics of Full Employment."

Acknowledging individually the six studies in applied economics that make up this book, Robinson centers her remarks on the papers by Kalecki and Balogh. In the Kalecki paper, she finds a thorough review of alternative employment policies, while in the Balogh paper she praises the treatment of the relationship between international trade and domestic employment, "the most intricate part" of the economics of full employment.

[071] A review of League of Nations, *International Currency Experience*, in *Economic Journal*, 55(220), December: 405-7.

Noting that the book is subtitled "Lessons of the Inter-War Period," Robinson observes that the main lesson to be gleaned from this work "is that monetary problems cannot be solved by monetary measures alone."

1946

[072] "Obstacles to Full Employment," *Nationalokonomisk Tidsskrift*, 85(5): 169-78. Reprinted in [086] and [308].

Based on a lecture given to the Nationalokonomisk Forening in Copenhagen on December 6, 1946, this penetrating and insightful essay reviews the obstacles to full employment that confound policy makers to this day.

Robinson considers the use of countercyclical government spending to stabilize economic activity an internal obstacle to full employment. She believes such a policy is impractical--government investment can't be turned on and off like a faucet--and ineffective because it is aimed at controlling the overall level of employment without regard to the composition.

Of greater significance in Robinson's view are the external obstacles to full employment, namely the dual problems of maintaining a high level of employment and a neutral balance of payments. Robinson argues that the impediments to full employment can be eliminated or at least mitigated with "a high degree of central control over the economic system," though she realizes that "the problem of combining the necessary degree of control with the traditional methods of democracy is the dominating political problem of the present time."

[073] "Budget et Inflation," *Institut de Science Économique Appliquée Bulletin*, (1-2), September: 4-11 (in French).

Arguing that post-WWII inflation is real and must be dealt with in real terms, not monetary terms, Robinson suggests that a rationing system, vigorously enforced, will provide some relief from the inflation associated with reconstruction.

1947

[074] "The Pure Theory of International Trade," *Review of Economic Studies*, 14(36): 98-112. Note that the number of this journal is actually dated 1946-47. Reprinted in [086].

Critical of the Classical theory of international trade because it presupposes a natural tendency toward equilibrium, Robinson reviews at length the basic assumptions of the Classical model and its theoretical operations, the principle of comparative advantage, and the rationale for free trade. She then considers what happens to the model when complex international lending arrangements are allowed, concluding that under this condition "the notion of a unique national position of equilibrium is a mirage" and so requires that international trade be managed by conscious policy.

1948

[075] "Wages in Our Present Crises," *Listener*, 39(997), March 4: 363-64.

This is a two-part essay. The first part, "Case for a Double Price Level," is written by Robinson. The second part, "Reducing Internal Demand," is authored by F. W. Paish.

For her part, Robinson suggests that a double price level can deal with the postwar demand-pull inflation while not necessarily exacerbating cost-push inflation. Her idea is to control prices of basic utilities and put a purchase tax on everything else. Such a plan, she believes, would preserve the purchasing power of the wages of the middle-class, making workers less inclined to seek inflationary wage increases.

Another approach to control inflation, represented by Paish, would curb domestic demand and promote exports.

[076] "Marx e Keynes," *Critica Economica*, (2), November: 33-45 (in Italian). Reprinted in English in [086]. The first two paragraphs of this version are taken from [047].

For many years, Marxist and mainstream economists did not communicate because of the fundamental differences between Marx's theory and Classical economic thought. In Robinson's view, this estrangement changed with the development of Keynes's *General Theory*. Despite some obvious differences, the theories of Marx and Keynes are more complementary than contradictory. Indeed, Robinson believes that the ascendancy of Keynesian analysis relative to Classical thinking has taken mainstream thought on a path that resembles Marx's system, a proposition Neoclassical economists would readily challenge.

[077] "Neo-Keynes" (a review of E. V. Morgan, *The Conquest of Unemployment*), *New Statesman and Nation*, 35(895), May 1: 359.

Categorizing Morgan as belonging "to the group of economists who use Keynes's methods of analysis to shore up the breach which Keynes made in the ramparts of traditional doctrine," Robinson nonetheless commends him for writing a book that lay persons interested in Keynesian economics can easily understand.

[078] A review of A. P. Lerner and F. D. Graham (editors), *Planning and Paying for Full Employment*, and T. Morgan, *Income and Employment*, in *Economic Journal*, 58(230), June: 248-50.

Robinson finds nothing new or terribly interesting in the Lerner-Graham book and recommends Morgan's work, "written from a purely American point of view," for teaching purposes because it is "an excellent introduction to the theory of employment."

[079] "La Théorie Générale de l'Emploi," *Économie Appliquée*, (1), September: 185-86 (in French).

Claiming that the *General Theory* is not really "general," Robinson examines the Keynesian position that full employment depends primarily on interest rates and the wage level. Robinson believes Keynes placed too much emphasis on the importance of interest rates and not enough on other factors such as real and money wages, the level of aggregate demand, and the rate of investment.

1949

[080] "Mr. Harrod's Dynamics," *Economic Journal*, 59(233), March: 68-85. Reprinted in [086].

More than a review of Harrod's *Towards a Dynamic Economics*, this essay is a thorough summary of Harrod's economic classic, which Robinson considers highly abstract and hard to follow because of his idiosyncratic exposition. She explains in depth Harrod's concepts of the actual, natural, and warranted rates of economic growth. Robinson also goes to great lengths to show how Harrod comes to the conclusion that there is no guarantee that thriftiness (with a constant rate of interest) will adapt itself to the rate of capital accumulation required to sustain steady economic expansion.

Characterizing Harrod's analysis as the missing link between Keynes and Hobson, Robinson finds much to admire in this systematic body of long-run dynamics, which she likens to the work of Marx. For all its merits, the book has, Robinson believes, a significant shortcoming: Harrod's reluctance "to discuss either the distribution of income or measures to increase useful investment" because of his desire to avoid bringing politics into the economic argument.

[081] A review of M. Dobb, *Soviet Economic Development Since 1917*, in *Soviet Studies*, (1), October: 60-64. Reprinted in [086] as "The Theory of Planning."

Robinson finds this a valuable book because Dobb has illuminated (1) the history of Soviet development by analyzing it through the lens of economic theory, and (2) the theory of planning by showing how economic theory actually worked in the Soviet experience. While questioning the validity of the historical part of the book because it relies so heavily on official evidence, she believes, nonetheless, that Dobb "has made an invaluable contribution to the understanding of a passage of history of which it is impossible to exaggerate the importance."

As to the book's theoretical content, Robinson is taken with Dobb's description of the process by which Soviet planners answer the dual questions of what to produce and how much to produce.

[082] A review of D. Lynch, *The Concentration of Economic Power*, in *Economic Journal*, 59(236), December: 580-81.

Robinson calls Lynch's book "a shrewd and lively commentary" on the voluminous documents of the temporary National Economic Committee, a committee that studied the extent and consequences of the concentration of economic power in the U. S. Economy.

1950

[083] "The Soviet Family," *Soviet Studies*, (1), January: 234-37.

In this review of R. Schlesinger's *Changing Attitudes in Soviet Russia: The Family*, Robinson thanks the author for providing so much "fascinating material" on the topic.

[084] "Exchange Equilibrium," *Economica Internazionale*, (3), May: 396-406. Reprinted in [086].

Robinson takes exception to the policy articulated at Bretton Woods which says "A member shall not propose a change in the par value of its currency except to correct a fundamental disequilibrium." She dislikes the statement because she knows of no definition of disequilibrium which can hold water. Robinson reasons that the term "disequilibrium" implies a state of equilibrium, which in fact may not exist. She explains how disequilibrium can occur in international economics and how it can become a "permanent" state, not an aberration.

[085] "The Labour Theory of Value," (a review of E. von Bohm-Bawerk, *Karl Marx and the Close of his System*; R. Hilferding, *Bohm-Bawerk's Criticism of Marx*; and L. von Bortkiewecz, *On the Correction of Marx's Fundamental Theoretical Construction in the Third Volume of Capital*), in *Economic Journal*, 60(238), June: 358-63. Reprinted in [086].

Robinson argues that Marx's critics and supporters alike miss the point by focusing on Marx's admittedly flawed labor theory of value instead of the broader questions with which he was concerned--variations in aggregate production, the development of economy-wide productivity, and the distribution of output between labor and capital.

1951

[086] *Collected Economic Papers*, Volume 1, London: Basil Blackwell. Republished by the MIT Press (Cambridge) in 1980.

A potpourri of essays featuring two sections of particular interest. Part 2 of the book is a collection of essays and reviews that reflect Robinson's interpretation and defense of Keynes's General Theory, and part 3 contains materials that reveal Robinson's views of Marx and Marxian economics.

[086a] "Introduction"

Robinson acknowledges how the influence of Sraffa caused her to question Marshall's *Principles*, which students at Cambridge University in the 1920s accepted as gospel.

"Euler's Theorem and the Problem of Distribution" [015]

"What is Perfect Competition?" [017]

"Rising Supply Price" [045]

"The Theory of Consumers' Demand" [061]

"The Economic Effects of Advertising" [053]

"An Inherent Defect in Laissez-Faire" [018]

"The Theory of Money and the Analysis of Output" [011]

"The Trade Cycle" [027]

"The Concept of Hoarding" [038]

"The Economics of Hyper-Inflation" [039]

"Monetary Equilibrium" [040]

"Planning Full Employment" [060]

[086b] "War-Time Inflation"

In this, the basis of a lecture delivered in Paris in January 1945, Robinson distinguished three stages of inflation: (1) a sharp rise in prices relative to cost or demand-pull inflation, (2) the wage-price spiral or cost-push inflation, and (3) hyperinflation. She then discusses the various tactics--price controls, taxation, voluntary savings--Great Britain used during WWII to prevent the first stage of inflation from developing into the second or the third.

"The Economics of Full Employment" [070]

"Obstacles to Full Employment" [072]

[086c] "Economic Consequences of a Decline in the Population of Great Britain"

Written during WWII, this paper reflects Robinson's thinking on how an expected decline in the population of Great Britain would affect the country's level of employment, investment, consumption, standard of living, and balance of trade. The fall in population did not materialize, thereby diminishing the significance of this essay.

"Marx and Keynes" [076]

"The Labour Theory of Value" [085]

"Capitalism, Socialism and Democracy" [063]

"Mr. Harrod's Dynamics" [080]

"The Theory of Planning" [081]

"The Pure Theory of International Trade" [074]

"The United States in the World Economy" [068]

"Exchange Equilibrium" [084]

[086d] "Beauty and the Beast" Reprinted in [308].

Written in collaboration with Dorothea Morison while both were undergraduates at Griton, this parody of Marshall's writing style uses Classical economic reasoning to describe the trials and triumphs of a merchant from Urbania who returns from the Orient bearing gifts for his three daughters.

[087] "Introduction" to Rosa Luxemburg, *The Accumulation of Capital* (English edition), London: Routledge and Kegan. Reprinted in [143] as "Rosa Luxemburg's *Accumulation of Capital*."

One of Robinson's missions in life was to serve as a "translator" of economics classics, putting into ordinary language the difficult and sometimes exasperating proses of some of the world's foremost economic thinkers. She did this for Keynes's *General Theory* [033] and Harrod's economic dynamics [080]. In this introduction, Robinson does the same for Luxemburg.

One gets the distinct impression that Robinson does not believe that the Luxemburg book is in the same class as the works of Keynes or Marx, for despite the book's considerable bulk, Robinson reduces Luxemburg's central thesis to one crisp phrase, "that it is the invasion of primitive economies by capitalism which keeps the system [capitalism] alive."

[088] "The Rate of Interest," *Econometrica*, (19), April: 92-111. Reprinted in [089], [143], [308] and [320], with the last section omitted in [143] and [308].

While claiming that the most important determinants of interest rates are social, legal, and institutional, Robinson ignores these factors and focuses instead on how interest rates in a closed, laissez-faire economy are influenced by the structure of the market, expectations, the quantity of money, the rate of investment, and thriftiness.

1952

[089] *The Rate of Interest and Other Essays*, London: Macmillan. Republished in 1979 as *Generalization of the General Theory and Other Essays* [320].

This short book consists of four essays, two of which--"Notes on the Economics of Technical Progress" and "The Generalization of the General Theory"--contain much of what would eventually become the foundations of the Post-Keynesian movement.

[089a] "Introduction"

Robinson sets out the theme of the book: the analysis of a dynamic economic system.

"The Rate of Interest" [088]

[089b] "Notes on the Economics of Technical Progress"

Taking exception to conventional analysis of technical progress which relies on the production function and related concepts of marginal productivity and the elasticity of factor substitution, Robinson develops a theory of technical progress that embellishes and extends Schumpeter's work. She examines the impact of innovations on real wages, the relative shares of labor and capital, investment opportunities, and the capital-labor ratio.

[089c] "The Generalization of the General Theory"

Robinson claims that Keynes's *General Theory* is an application of Marshall's short-period analysis of an industry to output as a whole. In this essay, Robinson seeks to extend Keynes's analysis to the long run, examining along the way the rate of interest as a regulator of economic conditions, and the role of finance in economic growth. She discusses in detail a model of accumulation in a dynamic economy, with particular reference to the vicissitudes of development, especially technical progress, which is the mainspring of an expanding economy as well as its most important source of disturbance.

[089d] "Acknowledgments and Disclaimers." Parts 1 and 2 reprinted in [143] as "Notes on Marx and Marshall." The full essay is in [320].

Robinson examines the well-developed dynamics of Marx's system, notably the interactions of the rate of exploitation, the rate of profit on capital, and the organic composition of capital. She then proceeds to articulate the "dynamics" of Marshallian economics, imputing to Marshall's statics a latent dynamism that some economists might view as more imaginary than real. She concludes the essay by acknowledging her intellectual debts to Rosa Luxemburg, Michal Kalecki, and Roy Harrod.

[090] *Conference Sketch Book: Moscow, April 1952*, Cambridge: Heffer. Reprinted in [095] as "Moscow 1952."

In April 1952, the government of the then Soviet Union organized a conference on Soviet life for delegations from 48 countries. In this 28-page pamphlet, Robinson has put together, in no particular order, 27 word sketches on "Meeting Russians," "Nylons," "Spy Mania?" and other aspects and institutions of life in Moscow. No economics here; not even the word. Just impressions, most favorable, like this one: "Russians, Chinese, and English understand each other's style--reserve, understatement, common sense. Amongst some other nations (irrespective of race, clime and social system) these qualities are not so marked."

[091] "The Model of an Expanding Economy," *Economic Journal*, 62(245), March: 42-53. Reprinted in [143].

In a discussion about models of an expanding capitalist economy, Robinson examines the contributions and shortcomings of the models developed by Karl Marx, Gustav Cassell, R. F. Harrod, and E. D. Domar.

[092] "A Comment," *Economic Journal*, 62(246), June: 325.

Referring to E. H. Chamberlin's article on "Full Cost and Monopolistic Competition" that immediately preceded her comment, Robinson argues that the standard assumption about entrepreneurs maximizing profit is too simplistic, and economists need to discover "what in reality are the motives governing decisions."

[093] "Theory and Practice of Planning," *Soviet Studies*, (4), July: 53-58.

In this review of the second edition of C. Bettelheim's *Problèmes Théoriques et Pratiques de la Planification*, Robinson notes a sharp separation in the book between the theory and practice of planning, "without much cross illumination from one to the other." She concludes that in the Soviet Union "common sense and administrative rule of thumb play a larger part in running a planned economy than principles derived from the theory of value."

[094] "Monetary Policy Again," *Bulletin of the Oxford University Institute of Statistic*, (14), August: 281-84. Reprinted in [143] as "A Note on Bank Rate."

Robinson argues that the contemporary (early 1950s) eagerness to return to pre-WWI orthodox monetary policy is based on the unfounded notion that the cybernetics of financial markets solved balance of trade problems without causing undue side effects. Robinson claims that in its heyday the gold standard was relatively successful because it had little to do. In the post-WWII era, correcting balance of payments problems often meant a worsening of domestic unemployment problems, and this trade-off diminishes the attractiveness of orthodox monetary policy in favor of an interventionist one.

[095] "Moscow 1952," *Monthly Review*, (4), September: 157-72. For annotation, see [090].

[096] A review of J. K. Galbraith, *American Capitalism: The Concept of Countervailing Power*, in *Economic Journal*, 62(248), December: 925-28.

Robinson finds much to appreciate in this American classic, calling Galbraith's book "shrewd, witty and forceful." She doubts that it would be successful in fulfilling its purpose, that of debunking the prevailing belief in the efficacy of laissez faire.

1953

[097] *On Re-Reading Marx*, Cambridge (UK): Students' Bookshop. Reprinted in [263] as "Essays 1953." The "A Lecture ..." essay is reprinted in [308] and the "An Open Letter ..." essay in [334].

This short pamphlet is one of the most difficult of Robinson's works to find. Luckily, it is reproduced as part 3 in volume 4 of the *Collected Economic Papers* [263].

The three essays contained in the pamphlet--"Would You Believe It?"; "A Lecture Delivered at Oxford by a Cambridge Economist"; and "An Open Letter from a Keynesian to a Marxist"--focus on the shortcomings of Classical, Keynesian, and Marxian theories. Robinson contends all three schools trace their roots to Ricardo, a declaration that probably does not sit well with any of the schools. Still, the essays do have their moments, as when she writes in her open letter to Marxists, "I understand Marx far and away better than you do." With remarks like this, it is easy to see why this pamphlet is among the least cited of Robinson's works, save for one famous sentence: "The more I learn about economics the more I admire Marshall's intellect and the less I like his character."

[098] "'Imperfect Competition' Revisited," *Economic Journal*, 63(251), September: 579-93. Reprinted with a postscript in [143] and [308].

Twenty years after the original publication of her classic *The Economics of Imperfect Competition* [005], Robinson is generally satisfied that the relevance of the book has withstood the test of time. She has, however, one reservation: "In my opinion, the greatest weakness of *The Economics of Imperfect Competition* is one which it shares with the class of economic theory to which it belongs--the failure to deal with time."

[099] "The Production Function and the Theory of Capital," *Review of Economic Studies*, 21(2), No. 55: 81-106. The number of this journal is actually dated 1953-54. A shortened version is reprinted in [143] and [308].

Robinson argues that the Neoclassical production function has limited relevance to actual problems and is particularly ill suited for analyzing the process of capital accumulation because it presupposes the existence of equilibrium. This article generated much controversy when it appeared, and triggered a vociferous response from mainstream economists.

[100] "Letters from a Visitor to China, July 1953, Part I," *Monthly Review*, (5), November: 302-10. For annotation, see [104].

[101] "Letters from a Visitor to China, July 1953, Part II," *Monthly Review*, (5), December: 397-410. For annotation, see [104].

1954

[102] "Letters from a Visitor to China, July 1953, Part III," *Monthly Review*, (5), January: 477-80. For annotation, see [104].

[103] "Letters from a Visitor to China, July 1953, Part IV," *Monthly Review*, (5), February: 536-43. For annotation, see [104].

[104] *Letters from a Visitor to China*, Cambridge (UK): Students' Bookshop. Reprinted in [295] and as a series of articles in the *Monthly Review*. See [100], [101], [102], and [103].

In 1953, Robinson spent over three weeks in China, her first visit to that country. She went to China with seventeen British business practitioners on a trip organized by the British Council for the Promotion of International Trade. She was not there to promote trade but to observe, and this pamphlet is a record of what she saw.

Robinson is clearly impressed with the New China and its state of mind, which she describes as "something new and powerful." She finds China clean, honest and upbeat. Minorities are treated with respect, criminals with compassion; land reform is in progress, and the arts flourish. Robinson's rapture is obvious and complete; nothing or almost nothing is wrong with the New China.

[105] "The Labor Theory of Value: A Discussion," *Science and Society*, (18), Spring: 141-51. Reprinted in [143] as "The Labor Theory of Value."

In the process of discussing such concepts as relative value, absolute value, value without capital, and money values, Robinson writes, "By giving up an untenable claim to complete exactness, the labor theory can establish the right to be considered broadly true and highly important." For Robinson, value is social. It cannot be measured exactly by prices or any other mechanism. To her, the labor theory of value and the Neoclassical supply-and-demand theory of price are complements, not contraries.

[106] "The Impossibility of Competition," in E. H. Chamberlin, editor, *Monopoly and Competition and Their Regulation*, London: Macmillan: 245-54.

Not only does Robinson believe that "the assumption of perfect competition is highly unrealistic and that competition in practice is very imperfect," but she also argues that there are "logical contradictions in the basic conception of competition as an equilibrium state of affairs." Robinson credits three tendencies of competition for making this so. The three tendencies are product differentiation, the search for economies of scale, and collusion.

1955

[107] "Marx, Marshall and Keynes," *Delhi School of Economics*, Occasional Paper No. 9, University of Delhi. Reprinted in [143] and [308].

In these lectures, Robinson associates the three economists named in the title with three different attitudes toward capitalism. "Marx represents revolutionary socialism" as he seeks to understand the capitalist system "in order to hasten its overthrow." Marshall represents "the complacent defense of capitalism" as he seeks to make the system "acceptable by showing it in an agreeable light." Keynes stands for the "disillusioned defense of capitalism" as he seeks out the inherent defects of the system in order to devise corrective policies that will save capitalism from destroying itself. Robinson elaborates on the strengths and weaknesses of each of these attitudes, noting that all have something to contribute to economics if one is willing to study them with an open mind.

[108] "The Production Function," *Economic Journal*, 65(257), March: 67-71.

Robinson challenges the validity of the production function, claiming that it is rooted in the fallacious idea "that it is possible to specify purely technical relations, not involving prices, in a human economy." In Robinson's world, when prices, uncertainty, and history are taken into account, the production function becomes an intellectual curiosity that has no practical significance or meaning. In this article, she describes the paradox of switching, an issue which became the focal point of an esoteric debate between her and the prominent Neoclassical economists of this era.

[109] "A Theory of Long-Run Development," *Economic Review* (Tokyo), 6(4), October: 382-85. Printed in English and Japanese.

In what is essentially a generalization of Harrod's growth model, Robinson describes a system in which a scarcity of labor develops if accumulation occurs at a faster rate than population growth, while labor becomes redundant if population grows at a faster rate than accumulation. She extends the model by considering the role of technical progress in development, and what happens when accumulation takes place with given knowledge and in an environment marked by technical progress.

[110] "The Production Function and the Theory of Capital: A Reply," *Review of Economic Studies*, 23(3): 247. The number of this journal is actually dated 1955-56.

In this short note, Robinson takes Solow to task for using index numbers as a way of dealing with the problem of measuring capital in the production function. See [376] for Solow's article.

1956

[111] *The Accumulation of Capital*, London: Macmillan. (Second edition 1965; third edition, 1969).

For Post-Keynesians, this is Robinson's magnum opus. Written in the style of the classic nineteenth-century tracts, this book is the nexus of Keynes, Marx, Kalecki, and Harrod as seen through Robinsonian lenses. Indeed, much of what Robinson published from 1956 to the end of her life in 1983 has its origins in this book. For those sympathetic to Robinson's view of economics, this book is must reading.

Mainstream economists have a different opinion. For them, this book is a throwback. Even its style is archaic. Seven individual "books" in a single wordy volume, the book looks more like an economic treatise from the nineteenth century instead of the twentieth. Devoid of data, the book virtually ignores the work of post-WWII economists, especially Americans, referencing other works infrequently and then mostly the classics. Marshall is footnoted ten times, as is Keynes; no one else is even close.

The models offered are built on heroic assumptions, as was done in the nineteenth century when reliable quantitative data were nonexistent. For twentieth-century analysis, especially that appearing after WWII, the failure to quantify is inexcusable, and so the book is seen more as an anachronism than a real contribution.

Although verbose for the most part, the book does contain a section--"Notes on Various Topics"--of pithy essays on a variety of themes that Robinson would turn to repeatedly in the next quarter century. (1956-81).

[112] "Mr. Wiles' Rationality: A Comment," *Soviet Studies*, (7), January: 269-73.

Characterizing Mr. Wiles as a bourgeois economist who has "gone clean off the rails," Robinson thinks that his "rationality"--the function of price is to ration output given resources--is quite irrational and naively simplistic. To her, price is as much cultural as it is economic.

[113] "Employment and the Plan," *The Economic Weekly* (India), (8), March 24: 355-56.

Robinson is critical of India's latest five-year plan, believing it lacks boldness and imagination.

[114] "The Industry and the Market," *Economic Journal*, 66(262), June: 360-61.

In this short comment, Robinson reiterates an old theme: "There is no advantage (and much error) in making definitions of words more precise than the subject matter that they refer to." In this instance, the subject matter in question is the distinctions (and definitions) of a commodity and an industry.

[115] A review of K. Marx, *The Poverty of Philosophy*, in *Economic Journal*, 66(262), June: 334-35.

While Robinson considers the book "a dead horse," she finds particular passages of Marx's work extremely valuable, especially for those interested in What Marx Really Meant.

[116] "British-Soviet Trade Prospects," *British-Soviet Friendship*, October: 2,5.

In this journalistic piece appearing in what is essentially a newsletter, Robinson argues that cold-war politics, not economics, is restricting trade between Britain and the Soviet Union. Noting that the Soviet Union is eager to expand trade with Britain, Robinson writes, "We should seize the opportunity with both hands."

[117] A review of J. Strachey, *Contemporary Capitalism*, in *Economic Journal,* 66(264), December: 697-98.

Robinson finds much to like in this book and praises its author, an active politician, for showing that "the concentrations of modern industry into oligopolies and monopolies" has rendered obsolete the Classical theory of economics. She is also taken by Mr. Strachey's discussion of Marxism, a theory she believes has "hardened into dogma" and, like Classical theory, has been "left high and dry while history has changed its course."

[118] "India, 1955: Unemployment and Planning," *Capital* (Calcutta), Annual Supplement, December: 7-9. Reprinted in [195].

A critical review of India's second five-year plan of the post-WWII era, this essay points out the problems of sustaining economic growth in a country with a booming population such as India's in the 1950s.

1957

[119] "What Remains of Marxism?," in *A Contribution to a Symposium*. Reprinted in [195]. The original publication data are unknown.

Robinson begins this essay by reviewing several Marxian ideas that have failed the test of time, notably the Marxian stages of history and the concept that capitalism would self-destruct. Marxian contributions that have long-term value according to Robinson include the economic interpretation of history, the interplay of class interests and technology on economic development, the notion of ideology ("an orthodoxy prevalent in a particular society not because of its truth but because of its convenience for the dominant authorities"), and Marxian analysis of capital accumulation and the trade cycle.

[120] "Notes on the Theory of Economic Development," *Annals de la Faculte de Droit de Liège* (in French). Reprinted in English in [143].

Robinson specifies the demanding conditions necessary for a capitalist economy to experience continuous growth. Since "the price of prosperity is eternal vigilance," Robinson believes that a socialist economy is better suited than a capitalist society to maintain the delicate environment required for steady expansion.

[121] "Une lettre de Joan Robinson," *Cahiers Internationaux: Revue Internationale du Monde du Travail*, (82), January: 27-28, (in French).

This short letter is another of Robinson's many attacks on dogmatic Marxism.

[122] "The Control of Monopoly in British Industry," *Listener*, 57(1460), March 21: 459-60, 475.

In the mid-1950s, the British Oxygen Company (BOC) had developed a virtual monopoly in the production and distribution of certain industrial gases. The monopoly was largely the result of successful competitive practices, which nonetheless put BOC in a position to exploit the situation. Robinson goes through the litany of orthodox ways to control monopoly for the public good and finds all of them wanting for one reason or another. She concludes that "the most thoroughgoing remedy for monopoly is nationalization" and then proceeds to explain her solution.

[123] "Full Employment and After," *Universities and Left Review*, (1), Spring: 66-68. This journal merged with *New Reasoner* to form *New Left Review.*

Robinson notes the success of Britain's post-WWII full-employment policy: "For the last ten years recorded unemployment has only once (in 1947) exceeded 2%." Having solved the problem of unemployment, Britain must deal with inflation and its related ills: diminishing investment, an unfavorable balance of trade, and the wage-price spiral. Robinson is deft at pinpointing the problems but short on specific solutions, recognizing that policies to control inflation almost always result in increasing unemployment.

[124] "Economic Growth and Capital Accumulation: A Comment," *Economic Record,* (33), April: 103-8.

A year earlier, Professor Swan had published in the same journal an article [378] critical of Robinson's book *The Accumulation of Capital* [111]. In her reply, Robinson claims not to understand what he finds in the book that is so "indigestible." Furthermore, Robinson finds Swan's alternative model of economic growth to be unsatisfactory because, in her estimation, he has violated two basic methodological rules of theoretical analysis: (1) "to draw a clear distinction between a comparison of positions which differ in some specified respect and an analysis of a change taking place in a given position" and (2) "not to express a quantity without stating the units which it is a quantity of."

[125] A review of E. E. Nemmers, *Hobson and Under Consumption*, in *Economic Journal*, 67(267), September: 511-12.

Although Robinson believes Hobson deserves to be praised for his willingness to challenge the orthodoxy of his time, she thinks that this book "is not worthy of its theme, either as theory or as biography."

[126] "La Théorie de la Réparation," *Économie Appliquée*, (10), October: 523-38, (in French). Reprinted in English in an amended version in [143] as "The Theory of Distribution."

Drawing on the works of Nicholas Kaldor and Michal Kalecki, Robinson develops a theory of distribution that integrates factor supplies, elasticity of substitution, the degree of monopoly, the rate of investment, the propensity to consume, and the state of technology into models that explain the relative shares of labor and capital in the short- and the long-run.

1958

[127] *China: An Economic Perspective*, (with S. Adler), Fabian Tract No. 314, London: The Fabian Society.

In the introduction to this twenty-page pamphlet, Harold Wilson, at the time a member of Parliament, writes that this tract "is not written to present a slanted view ..., or to tailor facts to fit ideological theories." Nevertheless, one would hardly expect Robinson to be critical of China, especially since she had by 1958 published so many favorable pieces about that country.

One's expectations are confirmed in the pamphlet, which is essentially a reiteration of official Chinese statistics (supplemented by casual observations) about agriculture, industrialization, national income, and population growth in China.

[128] "Birth Control in China," *New Statesman* (The Week-end Review), 55(1401), January 18: 66-67.

Robinson discusses why, after having long ignored the problem of population growth, China has come to recognizing the importance of birth control. Of the factors responsible for this change in attitude, she cites (1) the drive to raise the per capita standard of living, (2) a dramatic drop in the infant mortality rate, and (3) the desire of women to work outside the home.

[129] "Plein Emploi et Inflation," *Bulletin de Conjoncture Régionale* (Rennes), (3), January-March: 26-30, (in French). Reprinted in English in [143] as "Full Employment and Inflation."

Based on a lecture given at the University of Rennes in March 1958, this essay offers Robinson's thoughts on two of the major economic problems confronting the Western world in the post-WWII era: the inflation/unemployment trade-off and the wage-price spiral. Robinson readily admits that the West has been relatively ineffective in dealing with these problems, and she attributes this lack of success to the high level of defense spending (unproductive employment) in the postwar period. "It seems to me," she writes, "that the question of whether it is possible to have full employment without a falling value of money cannot be answered until we know whether it is possible to have full employment without the cold war."

[130] "Some Reflections on the Philosophy of Prices," *Manchester School of Economics and Social Studies*, (26), May: 116-35. An altered version is in [143] and [308] as "The Philosophy of Prices."

True to its title, this is a philosophical essay about the nature of prices. As Robinson sees it, there are two types of prices--those set in a Walrasian or exchange economy and those set in a Marshallian or wage economy. The essential difference between the two types of prices is in the basis of specialization: natural conditions as found in a commodities-based, exchange economy; and economies of scale as occur in an industrial-based, wage economy.

Having established this dichotomy, Robinson examines its implications in an exchange economy, a wage economy, and under conditions of laissez faire and socialism. She concludes that a simple general theory of prices that fits all cases does not exist. "Prices are a social phenomenon and the pricing system in any economy is geared to its social and political system."

[131] "The Real Wicksell Effect," *Economic Journal*, 68(271), September: 600-5. Reprinted in [143].

Using an arcane methodology reminiscent of nineteenth-century economics, Robinson argues that there is a difference between the "financial pseudo-Wicksell effect," in which a change in prices has only a bookkeeping effect on the value of an item of capital equipment, and the "real Wicksell effect," in which a change in productive capacity leads to variations in output, consumption, and the distribution of income.

[132] "Il Milo Della Concorrenza," *Il Mercurio* (Italy), (9), December: 15-20, (in Italian). Reprinted in English in [143] as "'Imperfect Competition' Today."

The Great Depression shattered forever the simplistic notion that laissez-faire capitalism naturally tends to produce the maximum social benefit possible. General discontent among professional economists with this "economics of naivete" produced (1) a new microeconomics (*The Economics of Imperfect Competition*), (2) a new aggregate economics (*The General Theory*), and (3) a new school of economics (Post-Keynesianism) based on the works of Michal Kalecki, whose theory shows that "the determination of gross profit margins is the key to the distribution of the product of industry between wages and profits, and is therefore highly relevant to the problem of effective demand and the level of employment."

[133] "Populación Y Desarollo," *Investigación Económica* (Mexico), 18: 275-81 (in Spanish). Reprinted in English in [143] and [146] as "Population and Development."

In this paper based on a seminar given at Moscow University in July 1956, Robinson notes that no general conclusion can be drawn from history concerning the relationship between population growth and economic prosperity. Believing that analysis and not observation can reveal the association between population and growth, Robinson discusses how variations in population affect and are affected by economic development.

1959

[134] "Economic Possibilities of Ceylon," in *Papers by Visiting Economists*, Colombo: Planning Secretariat (National Planning Council of Ceylon): 35-71.

In 1957, the government of Ceylon (now Sri Lanka) invited several noted economists from abroad to visit the country and advise the National Planning Council on the broad issues of economic growth and development. The visits lasted four to six weeks, after which each visiting scholar prepared a paper outlining his or her suggestions.

In her proposal, Robinson stresses the need for population control if development (rising per capita income), as well as growth (rising aggregate income), is to be experienced. With population control as a backdrop, she elaborates an intricate plan to increase investment and regulate consumption in hopes of increasing foreign earnings.

Robinson was one of a truly distinguished group of economists asked to come to Ceylon. The others to pen essays were J. R. Hicks, N. Kaldor, O. Lange, J. K. Galbraith, U. K. Hicks, and G. Myrdal.

[135] "The Falling Rate of Profit: A Comment," *Science and Society*, 23(2): 104-6.

Commenting on Dr. Gillman's *The Falling Rate of Profit*, Robinson takes exception to the claim that the profit rate in capitalist economies is falling because of increasing advertising costs and a rising tax burden. She believes more "Marxian causes" are at the root of the problem.

[136] "A Comment," *Oxford Economic Papers*, (11), January: 141-42.

Responding to G. D N. Worswick's paper, "Mrs. Robinson on Simple Accumulation: A Comment with Algebra" [383], which immediately precedes her paper, Robinson makes two points regarding Worswick's attempt to translate into algebra her model of accumulation developed in *The Accumulation of Capital* [111]. She believes that (1) he makes too much of the absence of machines in the investment sector, and (2) his assumption that the wage rate is fixed complicates instead of simplifies.

[137] "Some Problems of Definition and Measurement of Capital." *Oxford Economic Papers*, (11), June: 157-66. Reprinted in [143] and [139], the latter in French.

While arguing that "formidable difficulties surrounding the concept of capital ... make it impossible to give an unambiguous simple meaning to the phrase 'the value of a stock of capital good,'" Robinson identifies a set of operationally descriptive questions, which if answered would help clarify the concept of capital and explain the decision-making process of individual entrepreneurs that leads to capital accumulation. If this synopsis seems confusing, you should read the article.

[138] A review of K. K. Kurihara, *The Keynesian Theory of Economic Development*, in *Economic Journal*, 69(274), June: 352-53.

Though commending the author for this "forthright and shrewd" criticism of United Nations development policy, Robinson believes

Kurihara has many blind spots, not the least of which is the contemporary inclination to reduce Keynesian analysis "to the same idle pattern of definitions (written out to look like equations) as the Quantity Theory which it superseded."

[139] "Quelques Problèmes de la Définition et de la Measure du Capital," *Colloques Économiques Franco-Britanniques*, 85(3), Juillet, (Numero special): 5-20; 48-49. (NB: Libraries may classify this publication as a book instead of a journal.) French version of [137]. Reprinted In English in [143] as "Some Problems of Definition and Measurement of Capital."

Written in English, then translated and printed in French, this essay repeats a familiar Robinson theme: Capital is too difficult to define and/or measure for empirical work, especially work in which "capital" is treated as an aggregate for the entire economy. The theme of this issue of the journal is "L'Accumulation du Capital."

[140] "Letter to the Editor," *Econometrica*, (27), July: 490.

In his favorable review [382] of Robinson's *The Accumulation of Capital*, L. R. Klein raised a question which Robinson addresses in this letter. As phrased by Robinson, the question is "Can the level of wages and profits and the rate of profit on capital be deduced from a production function?"

Robinson's answer is no and yes. No because of the ambiguity in the meaning of "capital," but yes if some unrealistic assumptions about the nature of the economy are made, assumptions that are so unreal that the value of the resulting analysis is questionable and incomplete.

[141] "Accumulation and the Production Function," *Economic Journal*, 69(275), September: 433-42. Reprinted in [143].

Robinson takes to task Robert Solow, I. M. D. Little, T. W. Swan, and other economists of the mid-1950s who were trying to explain economic accumulation using the production function. Much of the material presented is a rehash of the ideas that appear in [099].

[142] "Depreciation," *Revista di Politica Economica*, (49), November: 1703-17. Published in English with an Italian translation. Reprinted in English in [143].

Using an uncharacteristically heavy does of mathematical analysis, Robinson concludes that "the value of capital as measured by profit much underestimates its value to society," a recurring theme in her published works of the 1940s and 1950s.

1960

[143] *Collected Economic Papers*, Volume 2, London: Blackwell. Reprinted in 1975. Republished by the MIT Press (Cambridge) in 1980.

Save for two essays in which Robinson reflects on the state of imperfect competition, the bulk of the papers in this volume belong to the field of Post-Keynesian economics. Many of the essays associated with the Cambridge UK/Cambridge USA debate are included in part 2 of this book.

[143a] "Preface" (1959)

A one-page synopsis of the contents of this volume.

[143b] "Introduction" (1974). Amended version reprinted in [334] as "Survey: 1950s."

Robinson reviews the development of a dynamic economics, interpreting the academic milieu of the 1950s from the intellectual perspective of the 1970s.

"Marx, Marshall, and Keynes" [107]

"Notes on Marx and Marshall" [089d]

[143c] "The Philosophy of Prices"

In this reworking of some of the material covered in [130], Robinson compares and contrasts the philosophy of prices under capitalism with that of a planned economy. Robinson argues that under capitalism prices are used as a self-regulating mechanism for allocating scarce resources among competing alternatives. Prices are efficient but not very equitable, because the distribution of income in the capitalist systems depends more on the value of output than on the value of inputs even though the latter may be of comparable worth, especially when the input is labor. As a result, income distribution in a capitalist society depends as much on luck as on ability, and this capriciousness "does not appeal to normal human notions of what is just and reasonable." Under socialism, equity comes first, efficiency second. The distribution of income is more important than the allocation of resources. To minimize inefficiencies in a planned economy, Robinson suggests several policies, including a land tax that operates like Ricardian rent to produce the "right" distribution of income among agricultural and other sectors of the economy.

"The Labor Theory of Value" [105]

"Rosa Luxemburg's *Accumulation of Capital*" [087]

"The Model of an Expanding Economy" [091]

"Notes of the Theory of Economic Development" [120]

"Population and Development" [133]

"The Production Function and the Theory of Capital" [099]

"Accumulation and the Production Function" [141]

"The Theory of Distribution" [126]

[143d] "Capital, Technique and Relative Shares"

During the mid-1950s, Robinson got into an intellectual feud with econometricians who used historical data to derive ex post production functions to explain capital accumulation, the distribution of income, and economic growth. In this previously unpublished paper, Robinson shows the technical choices that might be made under different economic conditions and factor prices. Her point in this exercise is to illustrate that "progress in this field is bound to be difficult; it is certainly not made easier by the meaningless formulae and self-contradictory terminology in which much of the current argument goes on."

"The Real Wicksell Effect" [131]

[143e] "Saving without Investment"

In this previously unpublished paper, Robinson offers an alternative to Paul Samuelson's model as expressed in his paper "Exact Consumption-Loan Model of Interest" (*Journal of Political Economy*, December 1958). In that paper, Samuelson develops what he claims is "a complete general equilibrium solution to the determination of the time-shape of interest rates." Robinson tackles the same basic problem in a narrative, nonmathematical way.

"Some Problems of Definition and Measurement of Capital" [137]

"Depreciation" [142]

"'Imperfect Competition' Revisited" [098]

"'Imperfect Competition' Today" [132]

"The Rate of Interest" [088]

"A Note on Bank Rate" [094]

"Full Employment and Inflation" [129]

[144] *Exercises in Economic Analysis*, London: Macmillan.

This is a Post-Keynesian economics text and thus quite unlike its orthodox competition of the era. Robinson's stated purpose in writing this book is to show students "how propositions in economic theory are arrived at" so that they can carry on where the book leaves off, i.e., think for themselves and not merely master ideology as in the orthodox approach.

In pursuit of this goal, Robinson uses three basic methodological rules: (1) Time is taken seriously; (2) a quantity is meaningless unless specified in measurable units; (3) technical relations between humans and nature must be distinguished from social relations between humans. Robinson's presentation is analytical but not in a conventional way. Instead of drawing diagrams to make a point, she describes in words the relationships in question, leaving as an exercise for the reader the task of drawing the relevant picture.

When reading this book, it becomes clear why Joan Robinson was such a favorite among students. Her writing is clear, the thinking provocative. She tells a story but doesn't preach. Above all, she genuinely cares for the student as is abundantly evident in the way this book is crafted.

[145] "Teaching Economics," *Economics Weekly*, (Bombay), (12), January: 173-75. Reprinted in [195].

Robinson argues that British (orthodox) economics as taught in India is largely irrelevant for that country because such economic thinking focuses too much on price determination and how the relative prices of commodities allocate scarce resources, and too little on the fundamental issues of production, accumulation, and the distribution of income.

[146] "Population and Development," *Pakistan Economic Journal*, (10), March: 1-7. Reprinted in [143]. For annotation, see [133].

[147] A review of T. J. Hughes and D. E. T. Luard, *The Economic Development of Communist China, 1949-1958*, in *Economic Journal*, 70(278), June: 409-10.

Robinson considers this a "valuable book" because it is a reasoned, "cool, objective, documented account of the story" it tells.

[148] A review of B. S. Keirstead, *Capital, Interest and Profits*, in *Canadian Journal of Economics and Political Science* (now *Canadian Journal of Economics*), 26(3), August: 488-90.

While applauding Keirstead's rejection of the "traditional doctrines on the subject of interest and profits," Robinson finds his alternative explanations wanting. Robinson offers a different view of the subject, a view that she claims avoids the stock-and-flow confusion that mars Keirstead's work.

[149] "General Liquidity," *The Banker* (London), (110), December: 790-95. Reprinted in [195].

In this essay, Robinson is critical of the Radcliffe Report, which reexamined monetary policy in the post-WWII era and appears to reject Keynes's *General Theory* in favor of a Neoclassical emphasis that substitutes "general liquidity" for the old "quantity of money."

[150] "The Choice of Models," *Journal of the Royal Statistical Society*, (123), 274-78.

As one of a group of economists discussing the topic "The Present Position of Econometrics," Robinson begins her contribution by quoting from T. Haavelmo's address on the occasion of the publication of the 25th number of *Econometrica* (1958). The essence of that quote is captured in the following sentence:

> The concrete results of our efforts at quantitative measurements often seem to get worse the more refinement of tools and logical stringency we call into play!

For Robinson, the main source of this measurement problem is the dependence of economic theory on the concept of equilibrium. She cites two examples--the theory of induced investment and the production function--where neglecting the nature of time has led both theorists and econometricians astray.

1961

[151] "Prelude to a Critique of Economic Theory," *Oxford Economic Papers*, 13(C1), February: 53-58. Reprinted in [195]; also reprinted in [334] as "Piero Sraffa: *Production of Commodities by Means of Commodities*."

The title of this paper is the subtitle of Piero Sraffa's book *Production of Commodities by Means of Commodities*, of which this essay is a review. Robinson begins her review with an extensive description of the book and then concludes her analysis with an examination of the three main propositions of Sraffa's work, which taken in total are a critique of orthodox economics.

[152] "Equilibrium Growth Models," *American Economic Review*, 51(3), June: 360-69. Reprinted in [195].

Robinson provides a crisp and reasonably objective synopsis of several equilibrium growth models, including those of Meade, Harrod, Kahn, and Duesenberry. She gives a particularly faithful summary of Nobel Laureate J. E. Meade's model as developed in his book *A Neo-Classical Theory of Economic Growth* (1961). Her sensitivity to Meade's model is extraordinary given her belief that the concept of equilibrium is irrelevant in a world where economies blunder from one situation to another, "following no simple predictable path."

[153] "Beyond Full Employment," *Annals of Collective Economy* (Liege), (33), April-June: 159-67. Reprinted in [195]. (The journal has been retitled *Annals of Public and Cooperative Economy.*)

Noting that "full employment is not a firmly established article of conservative orthodoxy," Robinson predicts that the two major economic difficulties that will beset governments pledged to full employment within a capitalist environment are (1) the balance of payments problem and (2) inflation. The experience of the 1960s and 1970s proved her correct, painfully so.

[154] "From the United States to Cuba," *Listener*, 66(1691), August 24: 265-67, 280.

After briefly visiting both Cuba and the United States in 1961, Robinson concludes that the view of the former country held by the people in the latter one is myopic and wrong. Rather than seeing Fidel Castro as a ruthless dictator, Americans should, according to Robinson, take the Cuban perspective which sees Castro as a progressive leader and savior of the country. Robinson is convinced that America's unfounded dread of "communism" causes it to misperceive the significance and benefits of Castro and his revolution.

[155] "Own Rates of Interest," *Economic Journal*, 71(283), September: 596-600. Reprinted in [195].

In trying to clarify "the mysterious chapter in the *General Theory* entitled 'The Essential Properties of Interest and Money,'" Robinson succeeds in obfuscating Keynes's concept of liquidity preference, particularly Keynes's reasoning as to why owners of wealth become more (or less) willing to supply capital as an economy grows.

[156] A review of S. Tsuru, *Has Capitalism Changed?* in *Monthly Review*, (13), October: 265-71. Reprinted in [195] and [308] as "Has Capitalism Changed?"

The title of this essay is taken from a symposium of the same title in which a number of prominent economists, many of them socialists, argue that after the next Great Depression most capitalist countries will experience a peaceful transition to socialism. Robinson believes that this scenario smacks of wishful thinking, and goes on to explain why she thinks capitalism has a long future.

[157] A review of S. Tsuru, *Has Capitalism Changed?*, in *Journal of Political Economy*, 69(5), October: 504-5.

This is a condensed version of the review that appeared in the *Monthly Review* [156].

1962

[158] *Economic Philosophy*, London: Watts and Company. Reprinted by Pelican Books in 1964.

In this thought-provoking book, Robinson examines the philosophical underpinnings of Classical, Neoclassical, and Keynesian economics, as well as the policy implications of each school, particularly as they relate to the questions of economic growth and development.

[159] *Essays in the Theory of Economic Growth*, London: Macmillan. (Second edition, 1963).

[159a] "Preface"

Robinson explains that the purpose of the book is to clarify and simplify the analysis in *The Accumulation of Capital* [111], her attempt to develop a dynamic, long-term Keynesian model.

"Normal Prices" [161]

[159b] "A Model of Accumulation"

In this 65-page essay, Robinson captures the essence of her 400-page book *The Accumulation of Capital* and does so with such economy and clarity that the reader can understand the argument even if he or she does not accept it. Those who wish to comprehend Robinson's economic perspective are urged to start with this essay.

"A Model of Technical Progress" [162]

"A Neo-Neoclassical Theorem" [160]

[160] "A Neoclassical Theorem," *Review of Economic Studies*, 29(1), January: 219-26. Reprinted in [159] as "A Neo-Neoclassical Theorem."

This essay describes the history and derivation of a theorem stating that if (1) the rate of profit is determined by the rate of accumulation of capital and thriftiness conditions, and (2) technical progress allows for the simultaneous possibility of many techniques, then (3) the "highest rate of output of consumption goods is achieved when the rate of profit on capital is equal to the rate of accumulation."

[161] "The Basic Theory of Normal Prices," *Quarterly Journal of Economics*, 76(1), February: 1-29. Reprinted in [159] as "Normal Prices."

Robinson's goal in this essay is to disentangle the microeconomic notions of the Walrasian system of demand-and-supply prices from those derived from the Marshall/Marx idea of normal profits.

[162] "A Model of Technical Progress," *Rivista di Politica Economica*, (52), February: 147-75. Reprinted in [159].

Robinson attempts to develop a model of technical progress that is theoretically sound and relatively realistic. The result is a complex model offered as an alternative to the orthodox Cobb/Douglas production function.

[163] "Draft of a Multilateral Trade Clearing Agency," (with R. Frisch), *Memorandum from the Institute of Economics*, University of Oslo, (a typed manuscript dated July 20).

Summarizing a speech R. Frisch had given a day earlier and included in the *Memorandum,* Robinson writes that a number of independent countries, each confronting balance of payments difficulties, can solve their problems with cooperative efforts and not with unilateral cuts in imports and other cutthroat tactics that lower rather than raise global economic activity.

[164] "Latter-Day Capitalism," *New Left Review* (London), (2), July-August: 37-46. Reprinted in [195] and [308].

Wondering "whether capitalism, even when prosperous, can provide us with what we really want," Robinson argues that capitalism is healthy despite signs to the contrary. She claims that the postwar expansion, a by-product of the cold war, has masked certain fundamental problems such as the political trade cycle (first defined by Kalecki) and stagflation, which she discusses in detail without calling it such.

[165] A review of H. G. Johnson, *Money, Trade and Economic Growth*, in *Economic Journal* 72(287), September: 690-92. Reprinted in [195] as "The General Theory After Twenty-Five Years."

While generally at intellectual loggerheads with Neoclassical economists, Robinson did have a genuine like for some (Joseph Schumpeter) and a personal animosity toward others (Harry Johnson). The latter attitude is evident in this review, in which Robinson characterizes Johnson's version of macroeconomics as silly and illogical.

[166] A review of E. S. Kirby (editor), *Contemporary China*, in *Economic Journal*, 72(287), September: 734.

For Robinson, this book is "of considerable service to specialist students" despite the editor's obvious lack of sympathy for what was then referred to as Mainland China.

[167] "Marxism: Religion and Science," *Monthly Review*, (14), December: 423-35. Reprinted in [195] and [334].

Arguing that Marx was as much prophet as scientist and that Marxism is as much religion as science, Robinson takes exception with modern Marxists who portray Marxism as a scientific ideology. She argues that the "religious" aspects of Marxism are as important as its science and a necessary element for broad-based acceptance.

[168] "Comment on the Production Function Symposium," *Review of Economic Studies*, 29(1): 258-66.

In this lengthy comment, Robinson reviews the growth models and/or production functions hypothesized by Solow, Samuelson, Arrow, and Kaldor. While finding deficiencies with all the models, she aims her harshest criticisms at Solow and Samuelson, whose models she believes are built on unrealistic assumptions and confuse short-and long-run analysis. For her follow-up criticism of Arrow, see [175].

[169] A review of R. Frisch, *Planning for India*, in *Journal of the Royal Statistical Society*, 125(3): 504-6.

Claiming that mathematical methods are an adjunct to common sense, not a substitute for it, Robinson questions the relevance of this highly analytical approach for India. She finds particularly objectionable the input-output tables which seem to condemn "practitioners to accepting the existing technical coefficients and pattern of production." Paraphrasing Marx, Robinson suggests that the job for Indian planners "is not to calculate the coefficients, but to change them."

1963

[170] A review of P. Moussa, *The Underprivileged Nations*, in *International Affairs*, 39(1), January: 93-94.

Robinson considers this discussion of underdeveloped nations to be "very right-minded" but nonetheless "superficial."

[171] A review of A. K. Cairncross, *Factors in Economic Development*, in *International Affairs*, 39(1), January: 97.

In reviewing this collection of papers, Robinson believes that Cairncross's approach to economic development is too skeptical to leave anything but a "blank impression."

[172] "Public and Private Enterprise," *Applied Economic Papers*, (3), March: 1-12.

Only near the end of this essay does Robinson discuss the topic implied in the title: the specific pros and cons of public and private enterprises. The bulk of the work concerns the larger issue of the costs and benefits of capitalism versus socialism. For Robinson, there are real trade-offs associated with both systems: "Capitalist economies have many features which are nauseating; the socialist economies have many features which are terrifying." She concludes that choosing between the two depends on what people want and how best to get it.

[173] A review of J. M. Montias, *Central Planning in Poland*, in *Economic Journal*, 73(289), March: 124-26.

Robinson remarks that Poland, being an open society, "is the best country in which to study socialist planning," and that Montias has made optimal use of all available sources of information in this book.

[174] A review of G. Maynard, *Economic Development and the Price Level*, in *Economic Journal*, 73(290), June: 299-300.

Robinson has high praise for this book, which she considers "an interesting example of how economic analysis can be combined with 'institutionalist' conceptions to throw light on history."

[175] "Learning by Doing: A Further Note," *Review of Economic Studies*,

30(4), October: 167-68.

In this follow-up comment to the one she published in this journal a year earlier [168], Robinson continues to respond to a Kenneth Arrow article. She points out an error in her reformulation of Arrow's model and then goes on to criticize Arrow for accepting the Neoclassical notion that investment is independent of the distribution of income between wages and profits. That investment is influenced by the distribution of income is a basic Post-Keynesian tenet.

[176] "Findlay's Robinsonian Model of Accumulation: A Comment," *Economica*, 30(119), November: 408-11. Reprinted in [195] as "Robinson on Findlay on Robinson."

While praising Findlay's succinct, formal (mathematical) representation of her model, Robinson takes exception to his treatment of her theory as stated in her *The Accumulation of Capital* [111]. Her main criticism is the lack of causality in Findlay's interpretation of her work. She believes Findlay sees her model as a mere one-dimensional extension of Marxian analysis, while she herself believes the model's ancestry is more complex than that, with its lineage traceable to Marx, Keynes, Wicksell, and Kalecki.

[177] "Are We Exerting Ourselves Enough?" *Yojana* (India), 7(1): 7-8.

In this interview, Robinson discusses ways that India can prepare itself to deal with the military and economic threats coming from China. As she has done on other occasions, Robinson notes that the Chinese have made considerably more economic progress in the post-WWII era than have the Indians.

The sentiments expressed in the interview are basically a rehash of positions Robinson has staked out elsewhere in her writings. There is, however, one distinctive aspect to this piece, that being a photo of Joan Robinson smiling.

1964

[178] *Notes from China*, New York: Monthly Review Press. Also published by Basil Blackwell (Oxford).

[178a] "Foreward"

As a firsthand observer--Robinson had visited China in 1953, 1957, and 1963, for six or eight weeks each time--she offers this slim volume as a way to counterbalance much of the "malicious representation of China in the Western Press."

"The Chinese Point of View" [182]

"The People's Communes" [183]

[179] "Communes in China," *Listener*, 71(1818), January 30: 177-79.

Contrary to propaganda coming from Russia, as well as from the West, Robinson reports that the commune system in China is alive and well. After a two-month stay in that country, Robinson's firsthand observations have convinced her that the communes have survived and prospered despite the Great Leap Forward of 1958 and the three years of natural disasters--drought, floods, typhoons--that followed.

[180] "Notes from China," *Economic Weekly*, (Bombay), (16), February: 195-203. Partially reprinted in [295] as part of "Economic Recovery."

Robinson returned to China in 1963 and writes that the 1958 "great leap forward" and the "bitter years" of shortages and natural disasters that followed did not have a pronounced negative impact on China, as many in the West were led to believe.

[181] A review of L. Zeitlin, *Life's Value in Cash*, in *Economic Journal*, 74(293), March: 219-20.

Robinson is ambivalent toward this work by "an economist now eighty-six years old." She clearly finds fault with the author's reasoning but cannot bring herself to criticize him in a manner she reserves for lesser works or better-known economists.

[182] "The Chinese Point of View," *International Affairs*, 40(2), April: 232-44. Reprinted with minor alterations in [178] and [295].

In this essay, Robinson seeks to explain the Chinese point of view on a number of matters, including the USA, Krushchev's Soviet Union, Tibet, India, and Western Europe. The essay is particularly interesting because it begins with a criticism of China, something rarely found in Robinson's writings on that country.

[183] "A British Economist on a Chinese Commune," *Eastern Horizon*, (3), May: 6-11. Reprinted in [178] as "The People's Communes," and in [295] as part of "Economic Recovery."

In contrast to Western characterizations of the Chinese agricultural communes as wicked places aimed at destroying family life and reducing peasants to virtual serfs, Robinson finds much to admire in the communes and their organization.

[184] "Factor Prices Not Equalized," *Quarterly Review of Economics*, 78(2), May: 202-7. Reprinted in [195].

Essentially a review, and not a very flattering one, of B. S. Minhas's *An International Comparison of Factor Costs and Factor Use* (1963). To Robinson, this book exemplifies all that is wrong with orthodox, Neoclassical economics. She laments in no uncertain terms the enormous waste of talent and effort the book represents. In her words: "It is a sad comment on the state of education that a talented young man should be fetched from India to be bamboozled like this." Don't hold back, Joan; speak your mind.

[185] "Statement Submitted by Miss R. Cohen, Mr. R. F. Kahn, Mr. W. B. Reddaway, and Mrs. J. Robinson to the Committee on Resale Maintenance," *Oxford Bulletin of Economics and Statistics*, (26), May: 113-21.

Resale maintenance occurs when manufacturers try to influence or even dictate the price retailers can charge for their products. In good Neoclassical fashion, the writers find the practice objectionable because it inhibits price competition and promotes increased advertising and other forms of nonprice competition.

The statement printed here was originally submitted to the Lloyd Jacob Committee on Resale Price Maintenance in 1947 and reported in 1949. Robinson and her co-authors believe that the argument still has merit even though the economic conditions which prompted the statement had changed considerably.

[186] "Chinese Agricultural Communes," *Co-Existence*, May: 1-7. Reprinted in C. K. Wilber, editor, *The Political Economy of Development and Underdevelopment*, New York: Random House: 1973: 209-15.

This is a straightforward description of the organizational structure of a Chinese agricultural commune and its component parts: the household, the team, and the brigade. Robinson considers the Chinese commune system "ingenious" for reconciling the efficiency requirements of large-scale operations with the social advantages of small-scale enterprises.

[187] "Solow on the Rate of Return," *Economic Journal*, 74(294), June: 410-17. Reprinted in [195].

Robinson takes exception to the production and distribution ideas of Nobel Laureate Robert Solow as expressed in his *Capital Theory and the Rate of Return* (1963), a book based on three lectures he delivered in 1963 for the F. de Vries Foundation at the Netherlands School of Economics.

[188] A review of H. G. Shaffery, editor, *The Soviet Economy: A Collection of Western and Soviet Views*, in *Cambridge Review*, (85), June 6: 491-93.

"This was a good idea," writes Robinson, praising a book of essays by Western (mainly American) and Soviet writers comparing and contrasting their respective economic systems. The execution, however, she finds flawed. The American writers are "spiteful", the Russians, "self-righteous." Still, Robinson believes that "there is much to be learned from this compilation."

[189] "China, 1963: The Communes," *The Political Quarterly*, (London), (35), July: 285-97. Reprinted in [195].

Based on her travels in China, Robinson provides an upbeat description of how communes operate. There are minimal references to the disastrous aftermath of the Great Leap Forward of the late 1950s and absolutely no inkling of the Cultural Revolution that would begin less than two years after the publication of this article. The lack of criticism or critical analysis suggests that Robinson did not know what was happening or did not want to know.

[190] A review of C. Cheng, *Communist China Economy, 1949-1962*, in *International Affairs*, 40(3), July: 560.

Robinson finds little of value in a book whose main purpose "is to give pleasure to American readers by drawing a gloomy picture of the situation in China."

[191] "The Final End of Laissez-Faire," *New Left Review* (London), (26), Summer: 3-9. Reprinted in [194].

Robinson describes in broad terms the fall of laissez faire and the rise of its successor--growth-oriented, government-assisted capitalism dominated by large-scale, self-perpetuating enterprises.

[192] A review of S. H. Chou, *The Chinese Inflation, 1937-1949*, in *Economic Journal*, 74(295), September: 680-81.

Robinson finds considerable value in this book, principally because the author "lived through the history that he describes as an official of the Central Bank of China."

[193] "Pre-Keynesian Theory After Keynes," *Australian Economic Papers*, (3), December: 25-35. Reprinted in [195] and [308].

This is probably the single best synopsis of Robinson's anti-Neoclassical writings published in the 1960s. Among the topics she lines up in her cross hairs are the production function, Walrasian accumulation, technical progress, and marginal product distribution.

[194] "India, Wake Up!" *Economic Weekly*, (16), December 5: 1917-20.

Robinson recites the successes of fifteen years of socialism in China and contrasts this progress with the stagnation India has experienced in the same period, 1949-64.

1965

[195] *Collected Economic Papers*, Volume 3, Oxford: Blackwell. Reprinted in 1975. Republished by MIT Press (Cambridge) in 1980.

This volume of Robinson's papers consists of three groups of essays: ten articles dealing with basic economic analysis; eleven papers focusing on topics that are considered the roots of the Post-Keynesian movement; and three papers--one each on India, China, and North Korea--containing observations of her travels in Asia.

[195a] "Preface" (1965)

A short, narrative description of the book's contents.

[195b] "Introduction" (1974). Reprinted in [334] as "Survey: 1960s."

Robinson reviews her nearly "endless dispute" with the neo-Neoclassicalists, especially as it pertains to capital theory and the inherent shortcomings of laissez faire, two topics that receive extensive attention in this collection of papers.

"Teaching Economics" [145]

"Prelude to a Critique of Economic Theory" [151]

"Equilibrium Growth Models" [152]

"Factor Prices Not Equalized" [184]

"Solow on the Rate of Return" [187]

"Robinson on Findlay on Robinson" [176]

[195c] "Harrod's Knife-Edge"

Robinson discusses the conditions under which Harrod's knife-edge is operational. The knife-edge hypothesis is the notion that there is one and only one stable growth path for a capitalist economy. This essay is original to this volume and not previously published elsewhere.

"Pre-Keynesian Theory After Keynes" [193]

"Consumer Sovereignty in a Planned Economy" [196]

"The Political Economy of Communism" [205]

"Kalecki and Keynes" [203]

"The General Theory After Twenty-Five Years" [165]

"Beyond Full Employment" [153]

"Latter-Day Capitalism" [164]

"General Liquidity" [149]

"Own Rates of Interest" [155]

"The Final End of Laissez Faire" [191]

"Marxism: Religion and Science" [167]

"What Remains of Marxism?" [119]

"Has Capitalism Changed?" [156]

"A Reconsideration of the Theory of Value" [197]

"India, 1955: Unemployment and Planning" [118]

"China, 1963: The Communes" [189]

"Korea, 1964: Economic Miracle" [198]

[196] "Consumer Sovereignty in a Planned Economy," in *On Political Economy and Econometrics: Essays in the Honor of Oskar Lange*, Oxford: Pergamon Press. Reprinted in [195].

The alleged beauty of the market system is that competition guarantees consumer sovereignty; that is, scarce means are allocated among alternative ends for the benefit of society as determined by consumers and not producers, government, or any other vested interest group. In reality, Robinson argues, market imperfections prevent this from happening.

Enter theorists such as Oskar Lange who argue, in Robinson's words, that "the true sphere of operation of the rational price system is in the planned economies." The major flaws of the market system evaporate "where there is no income from property and everyone's earnings are what is right that he should have." Thus, in a planned economy the market system can "be made to behave as though ideal competition prevailed." The idea sounds good, argues Robinson, but is not good and sound. She goes on to explain why even in a socialist environment the price system does not ensure consumer sovereignty.

[197] "Piero Sraffa and the Rate of Exploitation," *New Left Review* (London), (5), June: 28-34. Reprinted in [195] as "A Reconsideration of the Theory of Value."

Noting that "the function of pure logic is to liberate us from nonsense, not to tell us what we ought to believe," Robinson tries to reason through the Ricardian puzzle of "the transformation of value into price." Her goal is to replace Marxian ideology concerning the theory of value and the related concept of exploitation with a reasoned argument that reaches the same conclusions. She concludes that there is justification to Marx's thinking, but her "proof" is no more convincing than the ideology she seeks to displace.

[198] "Korea, 1964: Economic Miracle," *Monthly Review*, (16): January: 541-49. Reprinted in [195].

Based on observations made during a short visit to North Korea in October 1964, this essay is full of praise for the economic miracle of North Korea. Indeed, Robinson boasts, "all the economic miracles of the post-war world are put in the shade by these achievements." Only tangential mention is made of the closed, cult-dominated society of North Korea: "Prime Minister Kim Il Sung seems to function as a messiah rather than a dictator." Robinson predicts that "as the North continues to develop and the South [Korea] to degenerate, sooner or later the curtain of lies must surely begin to tear."

[199] "What's New in China?" *Eastern Horizon*, (4), January: 11-15. Reprinted in [295].

Not much, from Robinson's perspective. In the mid-1960s, Robinson could write about a younger generation completely in sync with its elders, especially when celebrating October 1, China's Fourth of July: "In the evening, under fireworks, the drizzle now turning to cold rain, the huge square [Tien An Man] was filled with laughing, singing, dancing students, the wetter the merrier." The events of June 3-4, 1989, are a stark contrast to this earlier, idyllic time.

[200] "Cuba 1965," *Economic Weekly*, (17), July 28: 1341-45.

Noting that the romantic phase of the revolution is over, Robinson argues that it is time for a Cuban form of socialism to emerge, a socialism based on the uniqueness of a third-world island nation and not the irrelevancy of the Soviet model.

[201] A review of T. C. Liu and K. C. Yeh, *The Economy of the Chinese Mainland: National Income and Economic Development, 1933-1959*, in *Economic Journal*, 75(299), September: 604.

Despite believing that "much of the information in the book is very valuable," Robinson is extremely critical of the work because of its derogatory description of Chinese economic development during the period in question.

[202] "Economic Principles in China," *The Broadsheet*, 2(10), October: 1+.

In what is essentially a review of *La Construction du Socialisme en Chine* by C. Bettelheim, J. Charriere, and H. Marchisto, Robinson summarizes the basic economic principles guiding Chinese socialism. She singles out for special attention the ethical foundations of Chinese economics, the Chinese rejection of monetary incentives, and the Chinese policy of pricing.

1966

[203] "Kalecki and Keynes," in *Problems of Economic Dynamics and Planning: Essays in Honor of Michal Kalecki*, Oxford: Pergamon Press. The first edition of this book, published in 1964 by Polish Scientific Publishers of Warsaw, did not include Robinson's essay, which is reprinted in [195] and [308].

In this tribute to Kalecki, the intellectual source of Post-Keynesian economics, Robinson shows how Kalecki anticipated a number of concepts associated with Keynes. Robinson believes that in many respects Kalecki's formulation of modrn employment theory is more complete than Keynes's, and she clearly implies that if Kalecki had come from the orthodox tradition instead of the Marxian, he would probably be recognized today as the discoverer of modern macro-economics.

[204] *Economics: An Awkward Corner*, London: Allen and Unwin. (Second edition, 1968; American edition published by Pantheon Books (New York) in 1967).

The awkward corner to which Robinson refers is the inability of Britain and other Western powers to control inflation without exacerbating unemployment. This leads to policy paralysis that muddles through the problems rather than dealing with either or both issues decisively.

Ironically, the flattering introduction to the American edition of this book is written by Robert Lekachman, one of those "bastard Keynesians," whose own work Robinson trashed [215].

[205] A review of P. J. D. Wiles, *Political Economy of Communism*, in *Indian Economic Review*, 1(1), (New Series): 145-52. Reprinted in [195] as "The Political Economy of Communism."

Joan Robinson was never a favorite among orthodox economists; neither was she the darling of Marxian economists. In a 1964 essay honoring Oskar Lange [196], she criticized his notion that the price system would operate to Neoclassical perfection if it were to function in a socialist environment. One year later, in this essay Robinson takes aim at another "Neoclassical" socialist, P. J. D. Wiles.

In this critical review of his prosocialism book *The Political Economy of Communism*(1962), she contends that Wiles doesn't really understand the difference between socialism and capitalism. As Robinson sees it, Wiles goes awry when he adopts the Walrasian (Neoclassical) tradition of the time, thereby collapsing the long and short run into one. Robinson is also displeased by Wiles's use of Soviet economic success as validation of his claim of the viability of socialism.

In the course of dismissing Wiles, Robinson recites the litany of shortcomings that afflict capitalism as well as the brand of socialism Wiles is pitching. In so many words, she is saying that orthodox economists are wrong, Marxists are wrong, and thus, by the process of elimination, she is the only one who is right. With essays like this, which alienated virtually every major school in the political economy spectrum, it is easy to understand why Robinson was never an odds-on favorite to win a Nobel prize in economics.

[206] "Introduction" to M. Kalecki, *Studies in the Theory of Business Cycles 1933-39*, Warsaw: Polish Scientific Publishers: vii-xii. Also published by Basil Blackwell (Oxford).

Always a devoted fan of Kalecki, Robinson claims in this introduction that he was able to anticipate the Keynesian revolution because his vision of the business cycle, especially of the Great Depression, was not fogged by prevailing orthodox thinking. Robinson also credits Kalecki for bringing together Keynesian theory and the analysis of imperfect competition. The marriage of the two is fundamental to Post-Keynesian economics.

[207] "The New Mercantilism," *An Inaugural Lecture*, Cambridge: Cambridge University Press. Reprinted in [263] and [308].

This essay was delivered as a lecture at the University of Cambridge on October 15, 1965. It focuses on what Robinson calls the "new mercantilism," the desire of every nation to have a surplus in its income account (balance of payments) with the rest of the world. As she has done frequently in her writing, Robinson casts aspersions on the alleged mutual benefits of free trade, noting that the doctrine of free trade is generally professed by nations that gain an advantage from it. As Robinson sees it, modern mercantilism is more sophisticated than its historical predecessor but no less effective when successful.

[208] A review of K. R. Walker, *Planning in Chinese Agriculture*, in *International Affairs*, 42(1), January: 159-60.

While Robinson finds this contribution "useful," she faults the author for relying too much on official reports and generalized articles, and thus overlooking "the importance of the interaction between economic incentive and quasi-property" as worked out on a commune-by-commune basis.

[209] "The Communes and the Great Leap Forward," *New Left Review*, (6), May-June: 69-72.

In what is essentially a review of I. Crook and D. Crook, *First Years of Yangyi Commune*, Robinson says that the authors, by focusing on one commune, have written "the most enlightening study" of the formation and development of the Chinese communal system and the role that that system played in the Great Leap Forward.

[210] "Comment," *Australian Economic Papers*, (5), June: 45-46.

In commenting on D. Bensusan-Butt's *Pre-Keynesian Theory: A Modest Defence*, Robinson sees the work as a derivative of Neoclassical economics, which to her is a school that puts more faith in economic models than observation can support.

[211] A review of A. K. Das-Gupta, *Planning and Economic Growth*, in *Economic Journal*, 76(302), June: 397-98.

Robinson expresses open admiration for this book and its author, who, she claims, is well-grounded in Classical, Neoclassical, and Keynesian economics but not "stuck" in any of them.

[212] A review of C. Chi-Yi, *La Réforme Agraire en Chine Populaire*, and Y. L. Wu, *The Steel Industry in Communist China*, in *International Affairs*, 42(3), July: 546-48.

Robinson finds little to criticize in these two books, save that each has taken so long to appear in print that much of the factual material is out-of-date.

[213] "Comment on Samuelson and Modigliani," *Review of Economic Studies*, 33(4), October: 307-8.

In this highly technical note, Robinson does battle once again with her arch "enemies," American Keynesian or neo-Neoclassical economists. She chastises the Americans for implicit theorizing--a method of argument that consists of deriving a conclusion by using definitions that entail it. In her words, "After putting the rabbit into the hat in full view of the audience it does not seem necessary to make so much fuss about drawing it out again."

1967

[214] "Socialist Affluence," in C. H. Feinstein, editor, *Socialism, Capitalism and Economic Growth: Essays in Honor of Maurice Dobb*, Cambridge: Cambridge University Press. Reprinted in [263] and [308].

In this thoughtful essay, Robinson reviews the problems of capitalism and socialism, with particularly sharp insights into the shortcomings of the latter. It is hard to believe that, as the author of recent essays so unabashedly sympathetic to socialism in China and North Korea, she is so reflective when examining the defects of European socialism. While critical of most socialist systems in Europe, Robinson does have special praise for the former Czechoslovakia, where explosive liberalization was crushed by Russian intervention just one year after this essay appeared.

[215] A review of R. Lekachman, *The Age of Keynes*, in *New York Review of Books*, January 26: 20-22. Reprinted in [317] as "Smoothing out Keynes."

Along with Alvin Hansen, Robert Lekachman was one of the most influential popularizers of Keynes in America. Robinson's review of *The Age of Keynes* might lead one to conclude otherwise. As far as Robinson is concerned, Lekachman's work, despite being subtitled *The*

Life, Times, Thought and Triumph of the Greatest Economist of Our Age, understates Keynes's contributions.

[216] A review of Y. L. Wu, *The Economy of Communist China*; D. H. Perkins, *Market Control and Planning in Communist China*; and J. L. Buck, et al., *Food and Agriculture in Communist China*, in *International Affairs*, 43(1), January: 192-93.

Claiming that there is something pathetic about Chinese expatriates who bash their country and about Western economists who judge China from the Neoclassical framework, Robinson asserts that "to get some nourishment from these books, the reader must ignore the pattern and benefit from the information that they offer."

[217] "Contribution to Sanity," *Economic and Political Weekly*, 2 (Annual Number), February: 111.

An admirer of Sachin Chaudhuri, the recently deceased editor of this influential Indian publication, Robinson penned this letter, one of several memorials printed in this issue.

[218] "Growth and the Theory of Distribution," *Annals of Public and Cooperative Economy*, (38), January-March: 3-7. Reprinted in [317].

From her Post-Keynesian perspective, Robinson traces the theory of distribution from Ricardo to von Neumann, and en route describes the contributions of Marx, Marshall, Bohm-Bawerk, Walras, Kalecki, Sraffa, and others.

[219] "The Soviet Collective Farm as a Producer Cooperative: Comment," *American Economic Review*, 57(1), March: 222-23.

In this brief comment, Robinson chides Evsey Domar for setting up "a very strange model of an ideal cooperative farm." She particularly objects to his assumption that workers of this farm choose to maximize the return per unit of work instead of maximizing some other variable such as income.

In his reply printed immediately below her comment, Domar says he recognized the short-comings of his assumption and devised another model, discussed in the body of his paper, that "embodied the essence of the suggestion" in Robinson's note. Since he believes that he has addressed the issue Robinson raised, Domar confesses to being mystified about the purpose of her comment.

[220] A review of A. N. Young, *China's Wartime Finance and Inflation, 1937-1945*, and C. M. Hou, *Foreign Investment and Economic Devel-*

opment in China, 1840-1937, in *International Affairs*, 43(2), April: 404-6.

Robinson sees many flaws in both books, particularly Young's account of a hyper-inflationary period in China, a description she believes exaggerates the importance of money while downplaying the significance of real factors.

She finds more value in Hou's book, notably an elaborate and complete account of the impact of foreign investment in China during the period in question. Still, she questions his interpretation of events, believing his facts are right but he nonetheless has come to the wrong conclusion.

[221] "Marginal Productivity," *Indian Economic Review*, (2), April: 78-84. Reprinted in [263].

In this essay, Robinson repeats an old theme: Orthodox economic theory has nothing whatsoever to say about the distribution of income. Neoclassical theory looks at how income is distributed among the factors of production but "says nothing about how the factors are distributed amongst the people." Marginal productivity analysis is confronted by three particularly discomforting obstacles: imperfect competition, wage bargaining, and persistent unemployment. Robinson reviews why it is that orthodox theory cannot accommodate these three realities of the modern world.

[222] A review of H. Portisch, *Eyewitness in China*, in *International Affairs*, 43(3), July: 611-12.

Robinson is critical of this book, claiming that its author evidently has had no prior contact with Asia and thus cannot appreciate "the kind of conditions from which China was rescued by the Communists."

[223] A review of R. Pelissier, *The Awakening of China, 1793-1949*, in *International Affairs*, 43(4), October: 797.

Robinson considers this book "an excellent introduction ... to the historical background of modern China," especially the relations of China with the West.

[224] "The Badly Behaved Production Function," (with K. A. Naqvi), *Quarterly Journal of Economics*, 81(4), November: 579-91. Reprinted in [263].

A tightly written, almost arcane discussion of "switching" and "double switching" the unobservable phenomena that Robinson concedes are more a matter of logic than relevance.

[225] "The Economic Reforms," *Monthly Review*, (19), November: 45-50.

The "economic reforms" in the title of this article refers to the Westernization of socialist economies then underway. Robinson applauds these moves to further the democracy of consumers which, for long periods, has been repressed in socialist economies such as that of the old Soviet Union. Her concern is that, as the socialist world becomes affluent, materialism will triumph over morality, turning socialist societies into pale imitations of their capitalist counterparts in the West.

[226] A review of G. Grossman, *Economic Systems*, in *Economic Journal*, 77(308), December: 871-73.

Robinson believes this book is shallow because by comparing capitalism (as represented by the U.S. economy), a command economy (the old Soviet Union), and Yugoslavia's "Soviet market system," the capitalist system is preordained to be determined "best," given the Neoclassical orientation of the author.

[227] A review of M. Wolfson, *A Reappraisal of Marxian Economics*, in *Political Science Quarterly*, 82(4), December: 627-28.

Robinson finds little new in Wolfson's book, which she characterizes as "nothing very much more than Bohm-Bawerk without the witty cracks." Robinson believes that the book will appeal to professors who want to convince their students "that Marx was a silly old duffer whom they need not bother about." For herself and other Post-Keynesian economists, Robinson thinks that the book has missed the real significance of Marx in the history of economic thought.

1968

[228] A review of G. Myrdal, *Report from a Chinese Village*, in *International Affairs*, 44(1), January: 152-53.

Robinson is taken with this book because of its attention to detail in portraying life in China. Robinson considers the book "a social study of a peasant society" and "a fascinating collection of human stories."

[229] A review of W. Leontief, *Essays in Economics: Theories and Theorizing*, in *Econometrica*, 36(2), April: 431-32.

Robinson claims that Leontief's contribution to Western economic thinking--input/output analysis--had not the "slightest effect on his own thinking" as revealed in this hopelessly orthodox collection of essays.

[230] "The Cultural Revolution in China," *International Affairs*, 44(2), April: 214-27.

The purpose of this article is to explain the Cultural Revolution and its many contradictions, e.g., the existence of class warfare in a country where there are no owners of private property to exploit workers. The result is a short, superb description of the Cultural Revolution, how it came about, and what it means to the Chinese.

[231] A review of F. M. Gottheil, *Marx Economic Predictions*; and W. Leontief, *Input-Output Economics*, in *Indian Economic Review*, (3), April: 57-64. Reprinted in [263] as "Economics versus Political Economy."

In this review, Robinson once again comes to the defense of Marx, noting that although specific points in his reasoning may miss the mark, his overall thrust is essentially correct.

[232] "A Defense of Adam Smith's Deer and Beaver Model--A Reply," *Journal of Economic Studies*, (3), July: 33.

In the briefest of comments, Robinson chides Professor Willett for seeking "to find one set of 'laws' that operate in all economies and apply equally to all societies."

[233] A review of G. Myrdal, *Asian Drama: An Inquiry into the Poverty of Nations*, in *Cambridge Quarterly*, (3), Autumn: 381-89. Reprinted in [263] as "The Poverty of Nations."

Robinson uses this review to contrast the lack of economic development in India with the progress she alleges has occurred in China. Myrdal's pessimism about economic development in Asia is not justified in Robinson's view: "Like a positive, China shows the lines of Myrdal's negative in reverse. Development *is* possible, but not in a 'soft state.'"

[234] "Value and Price," *Soviet Studies Information*, (7), December: 632-72. A short version is reprinted in [263].

In an essay that could be subtitled "Marxian Labor Theory of Value Redux," Robinson reviews Marx's theory of value in light of P. Sraffa's classic work *Production of Commodities by Means of Commodities*. Along with other conclusions, Robinson has praise for the pricing system in Czechoslovakia of the mid-1960s, a system she alleges to be superior to the price system of the West and the planned economies of Russia and China.

1969

[235] *The Cultural Revolution in China*, Harmondsworth: Penguin Books. (Second edition, 1970). Reprinted in part in [295] as "The Cultural Revolution."

In a postscript dated October 1, 1968, Robinson writes, "In the course of the year, there were sporadic outbursts of violence an even bloodshed, which the western press fastens upon with gleeful exaggerations ..." If there are any "gleeful exaggerations," this book is surely one of them. Pure propaganda, this is the story of the Cultural Revolution as seen from the perspective of Mao Tse-tung's supporters.

Robinson claims in the preface that "the Centerpiece of this little volume is the report on the Cultural Revolution which I received in Shanghai." In my opinion, Robinson did more than receive that report; she reproduced it. Robinson is credited with publishing over 300 items, including books, professional articles, popular essays, and reviews. It is my unsubstantiated guess that Robinson did not write this book. The vocabulary, sentence structure, and general tone of the book are quite unlike her other publications. My hunch is that she just lent her name to what she firmly believed was a worthy cause--socialism in China.

[236] "A Further Note," *Review of Economic Studies*, 36(2), No. 106, April: 260-62.

This note is directed to J. A. Mirrlees and N. Kaldor, authors of an article on economic growth that appeared in a previous (1962) issue of this journal. In her comment, Robinson argues that the Mirrlees-Kaldor model has a missing link: "The level of employment is not explained." Robinson maintains that this very important and crucially logical gap can be bridged if Kalecki's theory of distribution is brought into play.

[237] "A Model of Accumulation Proposed by J. E. Stiglitz," *Economic Journal*, 79(314), June: 412-13.

Rejecting Stiglitz's proposal for capital accumulation in a socialist economy, Robinson reaffirms her approach, which calls for "a constant division of the labor force between the investment- and consumption-goods sectors of the economy."

[238] "The Theory of Value Reconsidered," *Australian Economic Papers*, (8), June: 13-19. Reprinted in [263] and [308].

Robinson used this essay to trace the evolution of value theory from Adam Smith and David Ricardo, through Marx, Walras, and Marshall, to Neoclassical and neo-Neoclassical economics. Among the points she makes, she repeats her oft-stated belief that the Neoclassical school turned laissez faire from a program into dogma.

[239] "Macroeconomics of Unbalanced Growth: A Belated Comment," *American Economic Review*, 59(4), September: 632.

In a brief technical note, Robinson challenges Baumol's point that the real cost of a wide variety of outputs--urban service, education, the performing arts--is rising because of a decrease in the labor cost of manufacturers.

[240] A review of A. Leijonhufvud, *On Keynesian Economics and the Economics of Keynes*, in *Economic Journal*, 79(315), September: 581-83.

"Keynesian economics" refers to how Keynes is taught, especially by Neoclassical economists; "the Economics of Keynes" is what Keynes really meant. The two are not necessarily the same. Robinson is grateful to Leijonhufvud for separating the two. She is, however, critical of his view of the "British Keynesians" such as herself. She thinks that Leijonhufvud's view of those who worked with Keynes lacks understanding, particularly of the role of Kalecki and the commitment of British Keynesians to political and social policies more radical than those spelled out in the *General Theory*.

1970

[241] *Freedom and Necessity: An Introduction to the Study of Society*, London: Allen and Unwin. Also published by Pantheon Books (New York), a division of Random House.

The title of this short book stems from "the interplay of consciousness and environment, of freedom with necessity, which is the characteristic of human life." Around this theme, Robinson tries to provoke thought about the study of society through an economic interpretation of history seasoned with geography, biology, psychology, social and political relationships, and the history of culture, law, and religion. For the most part, the result is an uninspiring rehash of the ideas and theories of a number of thinkers who have had profound insights into the subject. Robinson doesn't help matters with her unabashed enthusiasm for Chinese socialism, especially in view of the China that has emerged in the generation since the book was published.

While short on revelations about the nature of society, the book provides candid insights into the essence of Robinson's view of life. The last chapters--"False Prophets" and "Science and Morality"--reveal more about the Robinsonian perspective than do nearly any other essays or books she published.

[242] "Chinese Economic Policy," *Studium Generale*, 23(12): 1267-74.

This is another in a long string of essays in which Robinson heaps praise on Chinese economic policy, especially that associated with Mao Tse-tung. As was her practice in these essays, Robinson takes the opportunity to contrast Chinese economic success with Indian stagnation and Soviet brutality, revealing along the way her special admiration for the commune system in China.

[243] "Economics Today" *Basel Wirtschaftswissenschaftliche Vortage*, (2), Zurich: Polygraphischer Verlag. Reprinted in [263].

Based on a lecture delivered at the University of Basel in December 1969, this essay covers familiar material such as the shortcomings of Neoclassical economics, the Keynesian salvation of laissez faire, and the meaning-and-measurement-of-capital debate.

[244] Foreword to E. L. Wheelwright and B. McFarlane, *The Chinese Road to Socialism*, New York: Monthly Review Press: 7-10.

Robinson is sympathetic to this book, which is essentially a firsthand account of China during the Cultural Revolution of the late 1960s.

[245] "Capital Theory Up-to-date," *Canadian Journal of Economics* (Revue canadienne d'Economique), 3(2), May: 309-17. Reprinted in [263] and [308].

In a familiar attack on Neoclassical production theory, Robinson reviews the "reswitching idea," which essentially says that contrary to the implications of a well-behaved production function, the technique of production selected at a lower real-wage rate may be less labor-intensive than one selected at a higher real wage. In Robinson's view, reswitching invalidates Neoclassical production theory, which even if correct would be irrelevant because it makes no allowance for the degree of capital utilizations as determined by the level of imperfect competition, disappointed expectations, and similar real-world phenomena. Robinson charges that Neoclassical production theory is accepted in mainstream economics largely as "a matter of faith."

A response to Robinson's essay was penned by C. E. Ferguson in the May, 1971 issue of the *Canadian Journal of Economics* [422]. Robinson subsequently wrote a reply [255] to this response.

[246] A review of C. E. Ferguson, *The Neoclassical Theory of Production*

and Distribution, in *Economic Journal*, 80(318), June: 336-39.

Ferguson set out to write "a clear, uncompromising statement of the principles of Neoclassical economics." What he did produce, in Robinson's view, is a defense of "pre-Keynesian theory after Keynes," and not a particularly convincing one at that.

Written for the professional well-versed in Neoclassical economic theory and the critiques thereof, this review is in keeping with Robinson's long-held view that modern theoreticians are more interested in preserving economics than in changing it.

[247] "Harrod After Twenty-One Years," *Economic Journal*, 80(319), September: 731-37. Reprinted in [263].

Robinson restates the Harrod growth model which she contends proves "that actual economies cannot be expected to grow at a steady and desirable rate without conscious control and direction." This is what economic policy should be about but isn't, at least not from the Robinsonian perspective.

[248] "Harrod After Twenty-One Years: A Reply," *Economic Journal* 80(319), September: 741.

In a one-paragraph reply to Harrod's comment on her original article [247], Robinson says her intention in writing the article was to examine the relationship between growth and distribution within the limits of Harrod's dynamic analysis, something Harrod chose not to consider.

[249] "Quantity Theories Old and New," *Journal of Money, Credit and Banking*, 2(4), November: 504-12.

Robinson is critical of the "Chicago School" for trying to revive the quantity theory of money. For her and other Post-Keynesians, the general price level is not a monetary phenomenon but depends mainly on money/wage bargaining. For Robinson, the impact of money on prices is more cause than effect, more political than economic.

[250] A review of C. B. Turner, *An Analysis of Soviet Views on John Maynard Keynes*, in *Soviet Studies*, 22(1), July: 134-35.

Calling Turner's work "a useful and thorough compilation," Robinson is nonetheless of the opinion that the book lacks insight into the topic. Among the issues Robinson believes are unresolved is the tacky treatment both Keynesian and Kaleckian analyses received at the hands of Soviet economists.

1971

[251] *Economic Heresies: Some Old-Fashioned Questions in Economic Theory*, New York: Basic Books.

For those with even a casual knowledge of Robinsonian economics, *Economic Heresies* offers little that is new. For the genuine novice, this book may be the best place to start. With the exception of Chapter 6, which is based in large part on "Quantity Theories Old and New" [249], the book is an easy-to-read, nontechnical summary of Robinson's challenge to orthodox economics. The introduction sets the stage for this flowing account of what Robinson finds wrong with mainstream economics and why she believes that the field as we know it today has probably done more harm than good.

[252] "The Relevance of Economic Theory" *Monthly Review*, (23), January: 29-37. Reprinted in [263].

A pretty standard Robinsonian review of what's wrong with Neoclassical economics, especially the misguided meaning and measurement of capital.

[253] "Continuity and the 'Rate of Return,'" *Economic Journal*, 81(321), March: 120-22. Reprinted in [263].

Robinson seeks to clarify a controversy involving the Neoclassicalist Robert Solow and the Post-Keynesian Luigi Pasinetti. The result is almost total obfuscation. As Robinson herself writes, "This is not a point of realism (there is nothing realistic in the whole argument), it is a matter of logic."

[254] "The Existence of Aggregate Production Functions: Comment," *Econometrica*, 39(2), March: 405.

Within a brief two-paragraph comment, Robinson lauds F. M. Fisher for his article that shows aggregate production functions do not exist, but she then chastises him for evading the conclusion "that the marginal productivity theory of distribution is theory rendered meaningless," especially since his analysis suggests just that. (In his reply printed on the same page, Fisher claims that Robinson has completely misinterpreted his article.)

[255] "Capital Theory Up-to-Date: A Reply," *Canadian Journal of Economics* (Révue canadienne d'Économique), 4(2), May: 254-56. Reprinted in [263] with C. E. Ferguson's rebuttal [422] to Robinson's original article [245].

In this brief reply to Ferguson's rebuttal, Robinson claims that the "Great Capital Debate" is tedious and unnecessary. She sees neo-Neoclassical theory as so much sophistry, a smokescreen to divert attention from the real agenda of the neo-Neoclassicalists: restoration of "the pre-Keynesian view of modern capitalism," i.e., a new defense of laissez faire.

[256] "Going to Europe--Again," *Encounter*, 36(6), June: 5-6.

In the summer of 1962, *Encounter* invited a number of prominent British writers to contribute to a symposium on "Going to Europe." A decade later, *Encounter* asked a similar group of writers to return to this theme. In her short contribution, Robinson argues that England should stay out of the European Economic Community, believing that the alleged long-term benefits would not be worth the short-term economic costs.

Among the others contributing to this symposium were Arnold Toynbee, Nicholas Kaldor, C. P. Snow, Harry Johnson, and E. J. Mishan.

[257] "The Measure of Capital: The End of the Controversy," *Economic Journal*, 81(323), September: 597-602. Reprinted in [263].

This essay is a clearly written, balanced summary of the capital controversy. Robinson cites the work of Franklin Fisher as evidence that "marginal productivity of capital in industry as a whole ... [is] a meaningless expression," and concludes that this finding ends the controversy.

[258] "Michal Kalecki," *Cambridge Review*, 93(2204), October 22: 1-4. Reprinted in [263].

An ardent admirer of Kalecki, Robinson offers in this essay a brief review of his *Selected Essays in the Dynamics of a Capitalist Economy* (1971). Among the points Robinson stresses are (1) her view that Kalecki's work on macroeconomics predates Keynes's *General Theory*, (2) her belief that Kalecki does not do justice to Rosa Luxemburg's vision of the decline of investment opportunities as geographical expansion of capitalism ceases, and (3) Kalecki's idea of the political trade cycle caused by governments' vacillation between the fears of unemployment and inflation.

[259] A review of R. Solow, *Growth Theory, An Exposition*, in *Kyklos*, 24(Fasc.1): 189-92. Reprinted in [263] as "Solow Once More."

Robert Solow, an ardent Neoclassical economist and Nobel Prize winner, gave a series of lectures in 1969 and 1970 intended to interpret the process of economic growth in modern industrial countries. In her unflattering review, Robinson writes that "Professor Solow's lectures are so tightly wrapped up in a circular argument that they cannot point anywhere." She is particularly critical of his definition and measurement of capital, and Solow's frequent changes of basic assumptions.

1972

[260] *Economic Management in China*, (Modern China Series No. 4), London: Anglo-Chinese Educational Institute. (Second edition, 1975; third edition, 1976). Replicated in [270].

Robinson visited China six times between 1953 and 1975. This 39-page pamphlet is a record of what she observed during six weeks of travel in the spring of 1972. Largely devoted to a positive description of the Chinese economy, the pamphlet describes how the Chinese economic system is planned and actually operates. There is some analysis of the political structure, but the focus is primarily on the impact the Cultural Revolution of the late 1960s had on the Chinese economic system. The third edition contains a brief postscript written after Robinson's 1975 visit to China.

[261] A review of T. K. Rymes, *On Concepts of Capital and Technical Change*, in *Kyklos*, 25(Fasc. 2): 427-29.

Robinson has considerable praise for this book, which she says shows definitively that her long-standing criticisms of Neoclassical thinking and its belief in empirical estimates of the aggregate production function are well founded.

[262] "The Second Crisis of Economic Theory," *American Economic Review*, 62(2), May: 1-9. Reprinted in [263] and [308]. Also reprinted in R. Fels, editor, *The Second Crisis of Economic Theory* (and other selected papers from the American Economic Association meetings, December 27-29, 1971), Morristown, NJ: General Learning Press, 1972.

A highly readable essay accessible to the nonprofessional, this piece was originally delivered as the Richard T. Ely Lecture at the 1971 American Economic Association meetings held in New Orleans, which some have described as the most exciting and electric economics session ever presented at the Association's annual meetings. What makes this article particularly valuable is that it represents one of the best available short summaries of Robinson's economic philosophy.

As Robinson sees it, the first crisis of economic theory--the great slump of the 1930s--was resolved when Keynesian economics became the new orthodoxy. This settled the question of how prolonged and extensive unemployment can exist in a laissez-faire, equilibrium-seeking economy.

With the problem of maintaining the level of employment solved, economic theory neglected to address the second crisis of theory--"what employment should be for." The composition of employment is an issue that Robinson believes economic theorists have ignored. All jobs are not equal, and economic growth alone cannot eliminate poverty. Indeed, growth only widens the gap between the advanced and the developing nations of the world. These and related problems are at the crux of this second crisis.

1973

[263] *Collected Economic Papers*, Volume 4, Oxford: Basil Blackwell. Republished by MIT Press (Cambridge) in 1980.

This volume of the *Collected Economic Papers* consists of three distinct parts. The first is a collection of essays focusing primarily on the capital-theory debate and written between 1964 and 1972. The second part is basically a reproduction, with minor updates, of several essays on employment theory that originally appeared in Robinson's 1937 book *Essays in the Theory of Employment* [032]. The third section is a reprint of an obscure pamphlet published in 1953 by the Students' Bookshop, Cambridge (UK) [097].

[263a] "Foreword"

A one-page table of contents in narrative form.

"The New Mercantilism" [207]

"The Need for a Reconsideration of the Theory of International Trade" [264]

"Economics versus Political Economy" [231]

"Socialist Affluence" [214]

"Value and Price" [234]

"The Theory of Value Reconsidered" [238]

"Harrod After Twenty-One Years" [247]

"The Badly Behaved Production Function" [224]

"Michal Kalecki" [258]

"The Second Crisis of Economic Theory" [262]

"The Poverty of Nations" [233]

"The Relevance of Economic Theory" [252]

"Economics Today" [243]

"Marginal Productivity" [221]

"Solow Once More" [259]

"Capital Theory Up-to-Date" [245]

"Capital Theory Up-to-Date: A Comment" by C. E. Ferguson and "A Reply" [255] by Joan Robinson.

"Continuity and 'The Rate of Return'" [253]

"The Measure of Capital: The End of the Controversy" [257]

[263b] "Essays 1935: Introduction"

Robinson introduces five essays that originally appeared in *Essays in the Theory of Employment*. [032].

"Full Employment" [032a]

"Disguised Unemployment" [024]

"The Foreign Exchanges" [032g]

"Beggar-My-Neighbour Remedies for Unemployment" [032h]

"An Economist's Sermon" [032j]

[263c] "Essays 1953: Introduction"

Robinson describes a small pamphlet originally published as *On Rereading Marx* [097] and reproduced as part 3 of this volume.

"Would You Believe It?" [097]

"A Lecture Delivered at Oxford by a Cambridge Economist" [097]

"An Open Letter from a Keynesian to a Marxist" [097]

[264] "The Need for a Reconsideration of The Theory of International Trade," in M. B. Connolly and A. K. Swoboda, editors, *International Trade and Money*, London: Allen and Unwin. Reprinted in [263] and [308].

Robinson returns to an old theme: the gap between orthodox economic theory and the realities of international trade. She has a list of shortcomings of Neoclassical trade theory which includes, but is not limited to, the inappropriateness of the underlying assumptions of the orthodox model and the camouflaged ideology of conventional trade theory. Although original to this volume, the essay offers very little that is new.

[265] *An Introduction to Modern Economics* (with John Eatwell), London: McGraw-Hill (Second edition, 1974).

Written from the Post-Keynesian perspective, this one-semester textbook covers three distinct topics: (1) economic doctrine, that is, a survey of economic thinking from Mercantilism through contemporary analysis, (2) economic theory or the Post-Keynesian equivalent of micro- and macroeconomics, and (3) the challenges confronting capitalist, socialist, and third-world economies.

The book definitely reflects Post-Keynesian thinking. Conventional scissor diagrams of demand and supply equilibrium are almost nonexistent and then presented only to illustrate the shortcomings of "would-be elementary textbooks." Kalecki is referenced as frequently as Keynes; Samuelson, the paragon of Neoclassical economists, rates just one footnote. The book is easy to read and narrowly focused.

[266] *After Keynes* (Joan Robinson, editor) Oxford: Basil Blackwell.

The first seven essays in the book, including one by Robinson herself [266a], describe economics "after Keynes" as seen from the Post-Keynesian perspective. Presented to Section F (Economics) at the 1972 Annual Meeting of the British Association for the Advancement of Science, these papers devote more space to criticizing orthodox economics than to describing the development of the discipline in the thirty-seven years since the appearance of the *General Theory* (1936).

The saving virtue of this volume is the inclusion of the proceedings of a joint symposium with Section D (Zoology) on Environmental Quality. These six papers discuss various connections between economics and ecology. The approach is novel, often seminal, in light of what has happened in the field of environmental economics since 1973.

[266a] "What Has Become of the Keynesian Revolution?" Reprinted in [269] and [317].

Robinson takes dead aim at the "bastard," self-styled Keynesians in the United States who she believes subverted the Keynesian revolution by developing the concept of macroeconomic equilibrium, thereby abolishing the role of time in orthodox economic analysis.

[267] "Foreword," to J. A. Kregel, *The Reconstruction of Political Economy: An Introduction to Post-Keynesian Economics*, New York: Wiley and Sons: ix-xiii.

In this pithy essay, Robinson traces her intellectual development as an economist. When she arrived at Cambridge in October 1921, "Marshall *was* economics." By the late 1920s, however, the Neoclassical system was under attack and all but collapsed with the publication of Keynes's *General Theory* in 1936. From her Keynesian phase of the 1930s, Robinson passed on to her Marxian phase in the 1940s. For her, Marx's main message "was the need to think in terms of history, not of equilibrium." When Keynes and Kalecki were combined with Marx, with a dash of Harrod's dynamics thrown in, Robinson moved into her Post-Keynesian phase, where she more or less stayed until the end of her career.

[268] "Ideology and Analysis," *A Contribution to the Festschrift for Edward Marz*, Europ Verlags: AG Wien. Reprinted in [317].

Arguing that orthodox economics has become trivial because its proponents shy away from problems of accumulation and distribution "for fear of being contaminated by Marxism," Robinson contends that Marxists suffer from a similar phobia because their theory would benefit from aspects of mainstream thinking if they, too, were not fearful of "ideological contamination." In particular, Robinson believes that the Marxian analysis of value and prices, effective demand, and the rate of profit would improve from an appreciation of the works of Keynes, Kalecki, and Sraffa.

[269] "What Has Become of the Keynesian Revolution?" *Challenge*, (16), January-February: 6-11. A reprint of [266a].

[270] "Planning and Management in China Today," *Cambridge Review*, 94(2212): March 2: 106-20.

Extracted from Robinson's recently published pamphlet [260], this essay is a condensed but nonetheless extensive replication of the longer study.

[271] A review of W. Brus, *The Market in a Socialist Economy*, in *Economic Journal*, 83(329), March: 358-60.

In critical tones reserved for what she sees as another half-baked Marxian analysis, Robinson finds many faults with "Professor Brus's blueprint for 'a planned economy with a built-in market mechanism.'"

[272] A review of L. G. Reynolds, *The Three Worlds of Economics*, in *Political Science Quarterly*, 88(1), March: 114-15.

Robinson finds the discussion of capitalism, socialism, and less-developed economies so apolitical and ahistorical that she implies the book has little value without coming right out and saying so.

[273] A review of A. Emmanuel, *Unequal Exchange: A Study of the Imperialism of Trade*; and R. G. Wilkinson, *Poverty and Progress*, in *Journal of Contemporary Asia*, (3): 457-61. Reprinted in [317] as "Formalistic Marxism and Ecology without Classes."

Robinson is critical of both books although each is written from a perspective she can presumably relate to. She finds Emmanuel's Marxism too narrow and formal, and Wilkinson's "ecological approach" pointless.

[274] A review of G. Myrdal, *Against the Stream*, in *New York Times Book Review*, September 23: 31-33. Reprinted in [317] and [334] as "Gunnar Myrdal."

In this glowing review of Myrdal's *Against the Stream*--a collection of his essays and addresses--Robinson outlines the contributions of the man she considers one of the most important economists of the twentieth century, though not necessarily, as she admits, one of the most influential.

[275] "Samuelson and Marx," *Journal of Economic Literature*, 11(4), December: 1367.

Robinson uses this highly technical note to chastise modern economists for not taking "as much trouble as Ricardo and Marx to specify the model they are using."

1974

[276] "History versus Equilibrium," *Thames Papers in Political Economy*, London: Thames Polytechnia. Reprinted in [279], [308] and [317].

Robinson contends that the main focus of Classical economics was the "historical process of accumulation" in a capitalist society and its relation to the distribution of output among the various social classes. Neoclassical economists, on the other hand, were preoccupied with the "conditions of equilibrium in a stationary state." Because of this, Post-Keynesian theory (the analysis of micro- and macroeconomic behavior in conditions of uncertainty) is rooted in Ricardo and Marx, bypassing almost completely "the sixty years of dominance of Neoclassical doctrines from 1870 to the great slump." She concludes that the absence of a comprehensive treatment of historical time makes Neoclassical textbook economics with is fixation on equilibrium virtually useless for the analysis of contemporary micro- and macroeconomic problems.

[277] *Reflections on the Theory of International Trade*, Manchester: University of Manchester Press. Reprinted in [317].

This pamphlet is based on a series of lectures given at the university. Robinson reviews the development and shortcomings of orthodox international trade theory from Ricardo through Marshall to the Ohlin/Hechscher/Samuelson model.

[278] "The Abdication of Neoclassical Economics," in A. Mitra, editor, *Economic Theory and Planning: Essays in Honor of A. K. Gupta*, Calcutta: Oxford University Press. Reprinted in [317].

Claiming that the "irrelevance of orthodox economic theory to economic problems" is common knowledge, Robinson sets out to determine why modern theory is so "lame and impotent." What she in fact does is to spend lots of words rehashing the capital theory debate, a topic she has covered in greater depth elsewhere, e.g., [245].

[279] "History versus Equilibrium," *Indian Economic Journal*, (21), March: 202-13. A reprint of [276].

[280] "Inflation West and East," *Frontier* (Calcutta), October 19. Reprinted in [317].

In what is essentially an "I-told-you-so" essay, Robinson argues that as early as the mid-1930s she had warned that maintaining a successful Keynesian policy of full or near-full employment would result in chronic and possibly escalating inflation.

1975

[281] "Value Before Capitalism," *Kyklos*, 28(Fasc.1): 43-48. Reprinted in [317].

Robinson examines the concept of value in a world void of capitalism and concludes that labor is not sufficient to produce value. Capital and/or land is also required, and that in turn means the existence of some form of property rights.

[282] "The Unimportance of Reswitching," *Quarterly Journal of Economics*, 89(1), February: 32-39. Reprinted in [317].

Robinson reviews in straightforward terms the chronology of the reswitching debate.

[283] "Reswitching: Reply," *Quarterly Journal of Economics*, 89(1), February: 53-55. Reprinted in [317].

In this reply to Paul Samuelson's comment on her original article [282], Robinson continues to hammer at Samuelson's analytical methodology, i.e., the neo-Neoclassical logic which Post-Keynesian economists find so offensive.

[284] A review of L. L. Pasinetti, *Growth and Income Distribution: Essays in Economic Theory*, in *Economic Journal*, 85(338), June: 397-99.

Robinson has much praise for Pasinetti, who, along with her, is a principal architect of the Post-Keynesian movement (also referred to as the "Cambridge School of Anglo-Italian" theory). In this review, Robinson clarifies the linkage between Classical and Keynesian economics, and explains why "reswitching" is such a problem to Neoclassical (orthodox) theory.

[285] "National Minorities in Yunnan," *Eastern Horizon*, 14(4): 32-43. Reprinted in [295].

In what is more anthropology than economics, Robinson describes some of the minorities found in Yunnan, an area in southern China near Vietnam.

[286] A review of L. R. Marchant, *The Phoenix Seat: An Introductory Study of Maoism and the Chinese Communist Quest for a Paradise on Earth*, in *History* (London), 60(199), June: 272-73.

Rejecting Marchant's thesis that Mao Tse-tung was a "secular saintly leader" and sole prophet and interpreter of Chinese Communist dogma, Robinson is critical of this book, which she says does not present statistical evidence to support the assertion that the Chinese economy is a failure.

1976

[287] "Introduction," in M. Kalecki, *Essays on Developing Economies*, Atlantic Highlands, NJ: Harvester Press: 7-13.

With great economy, Robinson compares and contrasts Kalecki and Keynes, highlighting the significant contributions of the former. For Robinson, those contributions are the role of political elements in economic development, the integration of imperfect competition into price level determination analysis, and the recognition of "the essential relationship between the principle of effective demand and the distribution of income."

[288] "Introduzione," (in Italian), in R. F. Kahn, *L'occupazione e la Crescita*, Torino: Einaudi: ix-xiii.

Richard Kahn was part of the Cambridge "Circus" of the 1930s, the discussion group which helped sharpen Keynes's thinking as revealed in the *General Theory*. Robinson was also a member of the Circus and is more than happy to introduce this book of essays by her long-time friend.

[289] "Planning Models: Two Views," *Economic and Political Weekly*, (11), February 28: 361-63.

In this essay, Robinson gives A. Rudra's *Indian Plan Models* a mixed review. As a technical description of planning, the book is too full of jargon for Robinson's tastes. The book is useful, however, on another level: "It exposes decisively that the whole concept of mathematical planning in India has been nothing but a day-dream." Robinson observes that Indian planners had to assume linear relationship to use the dynamic Leontief model even when it was apparent that such assumptions were inappropriate. Furthermore, institutional factors were totally neglected, rendering the planning models "useless for any practical purpose."

[290] "Michal Kalecki: A Neglected Prophet," *New York Review of Books*, 23(3), March 4: 28-30.

In very readable terms, Robinson lays out the essence of the Keynesian-Kaleckian point of view, the fundamental defects of the Classical economic system, and the Post-Keynesian notion that "household saving is a consequence rather than a cause of capital accumulation."

In addition to referencing Kalecki's major works, Robinson pays homage to George Feiwel's *The Intellectual Capital of Michal Kalecki* (1975), which she describes as "a gallant attempt to break through the conspiracy of silence that has kept the young generation in the US from learning of Kalecki's work."

For the noneconomist interested in tracing the evolution of twentieth-century economics from the Neoclassical school through the Post-Keynesian movement, this essay is an excellent place to start.

[291] "The Age of Growth," *Challenge*, (19), May-June: 4-9. Reprinted in [317] and [334].

Originally delivered as the Gildersleeve Lecture at Barnard College, Robinson interprets "the age of growth," her name for the period from 1946 through the early 1970s which saw nearly continuous economic expansion in the West. In this discussion, she provides an operational definition of "bastard Keynesian" and describes in detail Kalecki's prediction of the political trade cycle.

[292] "An Eyewitness Account of the Cultural Revolution," *Monthly Review*, (28), October: 50-51.

In this review of J. Collier and E. Collier, *China's Socialist Revolution*, Robinson calls the book "a most valuable contribution to knowledge of a crucial period of modern history." Full of praise for the efforts of this husband-and-wife team, Robinson commends the completeness of their eyewitness accounts and their willingness to describe the good, the bad, and the ugly of China's Cultural Revolution of the late 1960s.

[293] "Class Struggles in Tanzania," *Journal of Contemporary Asia*, (6): 344-45.

In reviewing I. G. Shivji's *Class Struggle in Tanzania*, Robinson notes a similarity between Shivjhi's "bureaucratic bourgeoisie" and Kalecki's "intermediate regime." In both instances, the reference is to a class of individuals that takes over the role of big capitalists and manages the economy in the interest of the petty bourgeoisie. For Tanzania, the development of this class has meant little change in basic economic and political relationships despite the succession of socialism over colonialism.

[294] A review of J. K. Fairbank, E. O. Reischauer, and A. M. Craig, *East Asia: Tradition and Transformation*, in *Journal of the Royal Asiatic Society*, 102(1): 91-92.

Robinson sees this big book--nearly 1,000 pages--as an encyclopedic treatment of the subject: broad coverage but not much depth. Clearly written from an American perspective, the book is intended for general readers in the USA. A specialist like Robinson finds nothing new or fresh between its covers.

1977

[295] *Reports from China: 1953-76*, London: Anglo-Chinese Educational Institute.

[295a] "Foreword"

Robinson uses this foreword to catalog the various trips she made to China and the articles and pamphlets she wrote describing her impressions and insights.

"Letters from a Visitor to China" [104]

[295b] Reminiscences

In 1957, Robinson visited China and wrote a report describing her adventure. She claims that the report cannot be traced, and this brief essay is a recollection of that visit written nearly twenty years later. Among her memories, she writes of meeting for the first time, but not speaking to, Mao Tse-tung.

Economic Recovery [180 and 183]. (The essay in this book is a compilation of two other essays. This version has a postscript describing changes in the commune system through the early 1970s.)

"The Chinese Point of View" [182]

"What's New in China?" [199]

"The Cultural Revolution" [235] (A thirty-five page except from the book)

[295c] "Retrospect"

Written in 1972 and published in this book for the first time, this short essay is a description of the impact the Cultural Revolution had on the life of one factory manager.

"National Minorities in Yunnan" [285]

[296] "Employment and the Choice of Technique," in K. S. Krishnasawy, A. Mitra, I. G. Patel, K. N. Srinivas, editors, *Society and Change*, Oxford: Oxford University Press. Reprinted in [317].

While more or less the standard Robinsonian fare about what is wrong with orthodox economics, this essay is unique in containing a long and detailed discussion--complete with a diagram--on the shortcomings and inappropriateness of the Neoclassical production function, especially when applied to third-world economies.

[297] "The Labour Theory of Value as an Analytical System," *A Contribution to the Conference of the Economic Section of the Academy of Science of Montenegro*. Printed in [317].

Quoting from Joseph Schumpeter's *Capitalism, Socialism and Democracy*, Robinson agrees with him that detractors and supporters of Marx have missed an important point of Marxian analysis, that being the analytical value of the labor theory. Like Schumpeter, Robinson believes Marx was "both a prophet and a scientist," and she explains her position in this paper.

[298] "The Guidelines of Orthodox Economics," *Journal of Contemporary Asia*, 7(1): 1-12. Reprinted in [317].

In her typical, caustic style, Robinson is critical of a UN publication "which purports to advise economic advisers to third-world countries how to set about their task." The source of Robinson's displeasure is her contention that the publication in question--*Guidelines of Project Evaluation*--is an application of orthodox theory to important real-life situations, and thus totally inappropriate for the purpose intended.

[299] "Michal Kalecki on the Economics of Capitalism," *Oxford Bulletin of Economics and Statistics*, (39), February: 7-17. Reprinted in [317] as "Michal Kalecki."

Originally given as the Michal Kalecki Memorial lecture, the article is a contrast and comparison of Keynes's General Theory and Kalecki"s. Robinson considers the less-known Kalecki version superior because it weaves together imperfect competition and effective demand analysis, thereby laying the foundation of Post-Keynesian economic theory.

[300] "What Has Become of Employment Policy?" (with F. Wilkinson), *Cambridge Journal of Economics*, (1) March: 5-14. Reprinted in [308] and [317].

Employment policy refers to the government's pledge to maintain a high and stable level of employment. Such declarations were made in the mid-1940s in England and the United States as a response to the Great Depression.

Robinson and her co-author review the evolution of employment policies from the mid-1940s through the mid-1970s. In the process, the shortcomings of the Neoclassical synthesis are discussed, as are the contributions of Keynes (which Robinson believes have been forgotten) and the contributions of Kalecki (which Robinson knows were summarily ignored). While there is not much new here in comparison with other Robinson publications of the same vintage, the writing is clear, comprehensible, and accessible to the noneconomist.

[301] "Qu'est Ce Que Le Capital?" *Révue d'Économie Politique*, (87), March: 165-79 (in French). Reprinted in English in [308] and [317] as "The Meaning of Capital."

Section 1 of this essay is probably one of the best short summaries of Keynesian economics Robinson ever wrote. Section 4 is a review of the "reswitching" debate as Robinson sees it. The remaining three sections of the article deal with standard Robinsonian views on the ills of mainstream teachings on capital theory, the significance of Sraffa's *Production of Commodities*, and the ties between the Post-Keynesian movement and Classical economic thought.

[302] "Education," *Social Scientist*, (5), June: 131-37.

The education Robinson writes of is that which has occurred in China since the advent of socialism. She describes in some detail education in China from the Great Leap Forward of 1958 through the early 1970s. Her main purpose is to explain why, in pursuit of a uniquely Chinese educational system, both Confucian and Russian approaches to education were rejected.

[303] "Economics in Dismay," *New York Times*, August 12: A21.

In this op-ed piece, Robinson claims that the economic slump of the mid-1970s "exposed the bankruptcy of academic economic teaching." She sees orthodox teaching as primarily a screen to prevent students from considering Marx and other alternative economic thinkers. Among the shortcomings of modern economics, she laments the removal of history from the study of economics, the corralling of Keynes into "macroeconomics," and the ascendancy of Monetarism.

[304] "Socialist Korea," *Monthly Review*, (29), October: 60-62.

According to Robinson, "History does not provide controlled experiments to enable social scientists to observe how the same forces of production develop in different relations of production." The division of Korea into socialist North and capitalist South is the "nearest thing that there has ever been to such an experiment." Robinson welcomes the study of this remarkable situation as presented in E. Brun and J. Hersh, *Socialist Korea: A Case Study in the Strategy of Economic Development*, which she reviews in this essay.

[305] A review of R. L. Meek, *Studies in the Theory of Value* (Second edition), in *Monthly Review*,(29), December: 50-59. Reprinted in [317] and [334] as "The Labour Theory of Value."

Ostensibly a book review, this essay begins with a lengthy description of Marx's labor theory of value; only toward the end of the essay does Robinson get down to the task at hand. When she does, her review is less than flattering. Specifically, she considers Meek a dogmatic Marxist prone "to repeat undigested phrases" in lieu of thinking and writing clearly.

[306] "What Are the Questions?", *Journal of Economic Literature*, 15(4), December: 1318-39. Reprinted in [317] and [334].

Robinson examines once again the shortcomings of orthodox economics when dealing with the questions of equilibrium, the theory of the firm, price determination, growth, and international trade. The truly original material in this article is contained in the last section, "What Now?" In this brief but interesting passage, Robinson addresses "the greatest of all economic questions ... : what is growth for?"

[307] "Michal Kalecki," *Challenge*, (20), November/December: 67-69.

Robinson lays out the basics of Kalecki's "general theory" in this easy-to-read essay. She considers Kalecki's work superior to Keynes's. Robinson readily admits that Keynes's analysis had certain strengths--the multiplier effect and a persuasive exposition. Kalecki's version, though tightly reasoned and terse, has more insights, especially the political trade cycle, which Robinson considers Kalecki's most famous (and correct) prediction.

1978

[308] *Contributions to Modern Economics*, Oxford: Basil Blackwell. Reprinted by the Academic Press (New York) in 1978.

[308a] "Preface"

Robinson notes that the papers in this book are drawn from fifty years of work, and she refers to the five general rubrics under which the papers are grouped.

[308b] "Reminiscences"

In just a few short pages, Robinson provides an insightful review of her intellectual development. Starting with the topic that drew her to economics in 1921--"to understand poverty and how it could be cured"--she describes the path that took her from Marshall, through Pigou, then Keynes, and ultimately to her showdowns with Samuelson. Along the way she pauses to remember in fond details the thrill of the "Circus" and the influence of Kalecki.

"The Second Crisis of Economic Theory" [262]

"The Theory of Money and the Analysis of Output" [011]

"Obstacles to Full Employment" [072]

"The Concept of Hoarding" [038]

"The Rate of Interest" [088]

"Kalecki and Keynes" [203]

"Marx, Marshall, and Keynes" [107]

"The Production Function and the Theory of Capital" [099]

"Pre-Keynesian Theory After Keynes" [193]

"Capital Theory Up-to-Date" [245]

"The Meaning of Capital" [301]

"History versus Equilibrium" [276]

"A Lecture Delivered at Oxford by a Cambridge Economist" [097]

"The Philosophy of Prices" [130]

"Imperfect Competition Revisited" [098]

"The Theory of Value Reconsidered" [238]

"Beggar-My-Neighbour Remedies for Unemployment" [032h]

"The New Mercantilism" [207]

"The Need for a Reconsideration of the Theory of International Trade" [264]

"Has Capitalism Changed?" [156]

"Latter-Day Capitalism" [164]

"Socialist Affluence" [214]

"What Has Become of Employment Policy?" [300]

"Beauty and the Beast" [086d]

[309] "The Organic Composition of Capital," *Kyklos*, 31(Fasc.1): 5-20. Reprinted in [317] and [334].

In an uncharacteristically analytical article (six diagrams), Robinson reviews Marx's concept of the organic composition of capital through Sraffian lenses provided in the *Production of Commodities by Means of Commodities*.

[310] "Foreword" to A. S. Eichner, editor, *A Guide to Post-Keynesian Economics*, White Plains, NY: M. E. Sharpe: xi-xxi. Also published by Macmillan (London) in 1979.

Robinson reviews the basic difference between Post-Keynesian and Neoclassical economics, but does so in a manner that is not nearly so clear and succinct as elsewhere in her writings. She spends considerable effort knocking Neoclassical economists, particularly Paul Samuelson, while simultaneously praising the Post-Keynesian contributions of Piero Sraffa. The end result, however, is that the reader gets a sense of what's wrong with orthodox theory without the benefit of an equally convincing presentation about what's right with Post-Keynesian economics.

[311] "Morality and Economics," *Challenge*, (22), March-April: 62-64. Reprinted in [317].

Originally given as the Commencement Address at the University of Maine in May 1975, this short essay reflects Robinson's view that the pursuit of self-interest does not lead to societal benefit as orthodox economists contend. Instead, the result is often personal gain at the expense of the social good.

[312] "Keynes and Ricardo," *Journal of Post Keynesian Economics*, 1(1), Fall: 12-18. Reprinted in [317] and [334].

Seemingly about Keynes and Ricardo, this essay is really about Post-Keynesian economics and its main task, "to bring the insights of Marx, Keynes, and Kalecki into a coherent form and apply them to the contemporary scene."

[313] "China 1978: Joan Robinson Comments on Bettelheim," *China Now*, September/October: 4-7.

In what is essentially a review of Charles Bettelheim's *Questions sur la chine aprés la mort de Mao Tse-tung*, Robinson chastises the author for forming an opinion of China based on official policies, pronouncements, and publications instead of firsthand observations. (See also [327].)

[314] A review of I. Steedman, *Marx After Sraffa*, in *Journal of Contemporary Asia*, 8(3), November: 381-84. Reprinted in [317] as "Formalism versus Dogma."

Siding with Steedman by writing that "Sraffa provides an illumination of Marx, rather than a critique," Robinson chastises dogmatic Marxists for "refusing to understand Sraffa and Kalecki." She maintains here and elsewhere [268] that Marxian analysis would be richer if the contributions of Post-Keynesians were appreciated.

[315] "Understanding the Economic Crises," *New York Review of Books*, 25(20), December 21: 33-34.

Ostensibly a review of R. Heilbroner's *Beyond Boom and Crash*, this essay is mostly about the Kaleckian principle of effective demand. Robinson maintains that Heilbroner's work--wide, sweeping, eloquent, and sharp as it is--would be much better if he had incorporated Keynesian/Kaleckian analysis into his own.

[316] "The Organic Composition of Capital: A Reply," *Kyklos*, 31(Fasc. 4): 692.

Referring to the comment that immediately precedes her reply, Robinson says the author of that comment is confused in his taking too literally the artificial world she constructed in her original article [309].

1979

[317] *Collected Economic Papers*, Volume 5, Oxford: Basil Blackwell, Republished by the MIT Press (Cambridge) in 1980.

This volume of Robinson's papers contains five sections, three of which stand out from the others. Sections 1 and 3 contain 17 essays which lay out the epistemology of Post-Keynesian economics. After reading these essays, one comes to a clear understanding of why Joan Robinson is the mother of this school of economic thought.

Section 5 of this volume--the last six essays, all written in the 1970s--calls for a nondogmatic reassessment of Marxian economic analysis. The criticism of Marxian thought embodied in this section of the book, coupled with the criticism of Neoclassical orthodoxy long associated with Robinson, vividly illustrates why she had to invent Post-Keynesian economics.

[317a] "Preface"

A narrative table of contents

"What Are the Questions?" [306]

"The Abdication of Neoclassical Economics" [278]

"Morality and Economics" [311]

"History versus Equilibrium" [276]

"The Meaning of Capital" [301]

"Growth and the Theory of Distribution" [218]

"The Unimportance of Reswitching" [282]

("Steady-State and Transient Relations: A Reply on Switching" by Paul A. Samuelson)

"Reply" (to Samuelson) [283]

[317b] "The Disintegration of Economics" (Reprinted in [334]).

In this original essay, Robinson lays out in straightforward terms the Post-Keynesian view of the evolution of economic thought. Laced with her usual digs--she characterizes academic economic teaching as bankrupt--Robinson spells out in simple English what is wrong with modern economics. Here is an essay that anyone with even a passing interest in economics can understand.

"Value Before Capitalism" [281]

"Gunnar Myrdal" [274]

[317c] "Thinking about Thinking" (Reprinted in [334]).

In one of her very first publications, the pamphlet *Economics Is a Serious Subject* [002], published in 1932, Robinson observed that "a serious subject ... is neither more nor less than its own technique." Forty-seven years later, in this original essay she returns to the same theme. After heaping criticism on neo-Neoclassical theory for its obsession with mathematical methodology, Robinson challenges economists to analyze economic systems from a variety of perspectives and not just that of econometrics.

"The Age of Growth" [291]

"Reflections on the Theory of International Trade" [277]

"Markets" [318]

"What Has Become of the Keynesian Revolution?" [266a]

"Smoothing Out Keynes" [215]

"Michal Kalecki" [299]

"What has Become of Employment Policy?" [300]

"Keynes and Ricardo" [312]

"Inflation West and East" [280]

"The Guidelines of Orthodox Economics" [298]

"Employment and the Choice of Technique" [296]

"Formalistic Marxism and Ecology without Classes" [273]

[317d] "Who is a Marxist?"

In this original essay, Robinson is critical of "verbal Marxists" for rejecting Sraffa's *Production of Commodities by Means of Commodities*. She argues that Sraffa's analysis can, when combined with Kalecki's work, make Marxism intelligible and so elevate it from mere ideology to a rigorous paradigm every bit as sophisticated as orthodox economic theory.

"Ideology and Analysis" [268]

"The Organic Composition of Capital" [309]

"Formalism versus Dogma" [314]

"The Labour Theory of Value" [305]

"The Labour Theory of Value as an Analytical System" [297]

[318] "Markets," *Enclyclopaedia Britannica*, Volume 11, 15th edition, Chicago: Benton Publisher: 511-15. Reprinted in [317].

Written from the Post-Keynesian perspective, this essay reviews the definition, development, benefits, and shortcomings of markets and the market system economy. Special attention is given to types of markets (perfect and imperfect), the origin and development of markets, and the welfare problems associated with markets.

[319] *Aspects of Development and Underdevelopment*, Cambridge: Cambridge University Press.

To orthodox economists, this slim volume in the Modern Cambridge Series is neither modern nor economics. It is, instead, the standard Marxian interpretation of third-world economics: "The third-world countries of today were drawn into the capitalist world market, under regimes of formal and informal colonialism, as appendages of the metropolitan nations to supply raw materials and exotic commodities to the industrial centre."

By contrast, this analysis is right on target for Post-Keynesian economists who see Robinson's book as the story of third-world economic development from the perspective of those countries, not that of the industrial nations.

Whichever view one subscribes to, one thing is evident in this book: Robinson's pessimism concerning the likelihood of genuine economic development in the third world.

[320] *Generalization of the General Theory and Other Essays*, London: Macmillan.

This is a republication of Robinson's 1952 book *The Rate of Interest and Other Essays* [089]. The two books are identical save that the order of the essays in the 1979 version differs from that of 1952.

[321] "Foreword" to K. Kuhne, *Economics and Marxism*, (two volumes), London: Macmillan: vii-xv.

Robinson maintains that Kuhne's book reiterates a point she has been making since her 1942 publication *An Essay on Marxian Economics* [049], namely, that mainstream, static-equilibrium economics "can find in Marx the basis for dynamic analysis of the development of capitalism." With that as her premise, she devotes this "Foreword" to an updated review of the ideas she first expounded nearly forty years earlier.

[322] "Commento all'Articolo di Garegnani," in P. A. Garegnani, *Capitale e domanda effettiva*, Turin: Einaudi. Appendix A. Reprinted in English in G. R. Feiwel, editor, *Joan Robinson and Modern Economic Theory* [480], New York: New York University Press, 1989: 360-61.

While claiming that "Garegnani and I have been on the same side in the 'capital' controversy," Robinson takes exception to his interpretation of her views. She is especially put off by Garegnani's suggestion that Robinson's position on capital agrees with Samuelson's.

[323] "Un Ulteriore Commento," in P. A. Garegnani, *Capitale e domanda effettiva*, Turin: Einaudi. Appendix C. Reprinted in English in G. R. Feiwel, editor, *Joan Robinson and Modern Economic Theory* [480], New York: New York University Press, 1989: 361.

Robinson reiterates an earlier point, namely, her basic disagreement with Samuelson over capital theory. She believes her views on this topic are close to Garegnani and cannot understand "why he wants to disallow mine."

[324] "Mao Tse-tung on Soviet Economics," *Monthly Review*, (30) January: 52-53.

Mao Tse-tung was always suspicious of Stalin's brand of socialism, and this is readily apparent in Mao's *A Critique of Soviet Economics*, which Robinson reviews in this essay.

[325] "Has Keynes Failed?", *Annals of Public and Co-operative Economy*, (50), March 27-29.

In this bittersweet essay, Robinson describes what Keynes's *General Theory* was supposed to do--precipitate "a radical reconsideration of the whole corpus of orthodox doctrine" and what actually happened: It became the new orthodoxy, and in the process, Keynes's vision of a rational economic policy "was muffled and distorted."

[326] A review of D. Patinkin and J. C. Leith, editors, *Keynes, Cambridge and the General Theory*, in the *Canadian Journal of Economics* (New Series), 12(1), February: 118-20.

The book Robinson reviews is the outgrowth of a conference held at the University of Western Ontario involving, among others, "three trans-Atlantic students ... who participated in the Keynesian Revolution." The most prominent of the three was Don Patinkin, who, like Robinson, was part of the Cambridge "Circus," the term used to describe the circle of economists and students working at Cambridge with Keynes during the 1930s.

While Patinkin was an active participant of the Circus, Robinson believes that he really didn't get it. That is, Robinson thinks that Patinkin's interpretation of Keynes as reflected in the proceedings of the conference is not an accurate reflection of the intellectual environment that nurtured the *General Theory*.

[327] "Comment on China since Mao," *Monthly Review*, (31) May: 48-56.

Reacting to C. Bettelheim's *China Since Mao*, Robinson says the author put too much stock in Chinese slogans that are primarily internal propaganda, and thus has missed the real changes occurring in China since Mao. (See also [313].)

[328] "Garegnani on Effective Demand," *Cambridge Journal of Economics*, (3), June: 179-80. Reprinted in J. Eatwell and M. Milgate, editors, *Keynes's Economics and the Theory of Value and Distribution*, New York: Oxford University Press, 1983: 70-71.

This short note is difficult to understand unless one is familiar with Garegnani's original article on effective demand (*Cambridge Journal of Economics*, 1978) and Keynes's concepts of consumption, savings, and investment. Basically, Robinson has mixed feelings about Garegnani's work, believing it both clarifies and muddles Keynes's views on effective demand.

[329] "Misunderstandings in the Theory of Production," *Greek Economic Review*, 1(1), August: 1-7. Reprinted in [334].

This article is a reiteration of the long-running debate about production theory that Robinson had with the American Keynesians, especially Robert Solow and Paul Samuelson.

[330] "Keynes Today," (with Francis Cripps), *Journal of Post Keynesian Economics*, 2(1), Fall: 139-44.

In a rather bland review of macroeconomics pre-Keynes, during Keynes, and post-Keynes, Robinson and her co-author argue that since Keynesian policies are so ingrained in Western societies, the basic question confronting economists today "is not whether intervention is necessary but what kind of intervention will be effective and consistent with a democratic society."

[331] "Surplus Value and Profits: The Rectification of Names," *Development and Change*, (10), October 693-95.

In this short article--really a note--Robinson makes two points: (1) The Marxian concept of surplus value "is a metaphor not an analytical proposition," and (2) Marx's idea that production prices yield a uniform profit rate over the monetary value of the stock of capital employed is impossible to measure precisely, because of continuous technological change.

[332] "Employment and Inflation," *Quarterly Review of Economics and Business*, 19(3), Autumn: 7-16. Combined with [333] and reprinted in [334] as "Stagflation."

Given as the David Kinley Lecture at the University of Illinois-Urbana/Champaign on March 28, 1979, this essay is Robinson's admission that Keynesian fiscal policy, so effective in economic slumps associated with deficient aggregate demand, may not be useful in controlling stagflation.

[333] "Solving the Stagflation Puzzle," *Challenge*, (22), November-December: 40-46. Combined with [332] and reprinted in [334] as "Stagflation."

Stagflation occurs when high unemployment and high inflation persist simultaneously, something that is not supposed to happen in a Neoclassical world. Robinson says the two can coexist because inflation is caused by the ability of firms to control price and not, as is commonly believed, by the supply of money. Effective policies for dealing with inflation must recognize this reality.

1980

[334] *Further Contributions to Modern Economics*, Oxford: Basil Blackwell. Also published by M. E. Sharpe (Armonk, NY) in 1981 as *What are the Questions? And Other Essays: Further Contributions to Modern Economics*.

In this sequel to *Contributions to Modern Economics* [308], Robinson has bundled together twenty-one essays, of which three are original to this book and two are amended versions of previously published works. The essays are clustered into four groups: Analysis--discussions of methodology; Controversy--attacks on equilibrium and Neoclassical production analyses; Tributes--valentines to Joseph Schumpeter, Piero Sraffa, and Gunnar Myrdal; Aspects of Marxism--"an appeal to contemporary Marxists to eschew dogmatism."

[334a] "Introduction"

Robinson identifies and reviews the four major areas or clusters of essays contained in the book.

"What are the Questions?" [306]

"The Age of Growth" [291]

"Stagflation" [332 and 333]

"Thinking about Thinking" [317c]

"Accumulation and Exploitation: An Analysis in the Tradition of Marx, Sraffa, and Kalecki" [338]. (Reprinted without original mathematical appendix.)

"Keynes and Ricardo" [312]

"Time in Economic Theory" [336]

"The Disintegration of Economics" [317b]

[334b] "Survey: 1950s"

In this amended version of the Introduction to volume 2 of the *Collected Economic Papers* (Second edition, 1975) [143b], Robinson argues for a dynamic economic analysis that considers history and the context of the culture in which events transpire. This amended introduction can be found in the 1980 MIT Press republication of volume 2 of Robinson's *Collected Economic Papers* [143].

[334c] "Survey: 1960s"

In this amended version of the Introduction to Volume 3 of her *Collected Economic Papers* (Second edition, 1975) [195b], Robinson reviews her criticisms of neo-Neoclassical economics, focusing on the debates involving capital, the rate of return, and the pseudo-production function. This amended introduction can be found in the 1980 MIT Press republication of volume 3 of Robinson's *Collected Economic Papers* [195].

[334d] "Debate: 1970s"

The emergence of the Post-Keynesian movement was not without internal strife. In this essay, Robinson addresses two issues about which Post-Keynesians of the 1970s were at odds: "the meaning and status of a pseudo-production function and the use of the concept of long-period equilibrium in historical analysis."

[334e] "Retrospect: 1980"

In this continuation of the discussion developed in [151] and [336], Robinson reexamines Sraffa's long-period analysis, concluding that his theory, though fundamentally sound, is flawed when dealing with switch points.

"Misunderstandings in the Theory of Production" [329]

"Joseph Schumpeter: *Capitalism, Socialism and Democracy*" [063]

"Piero Sraffa: *Production of Commodities by Means of Commodities*" [151]

"Gunnar Myrdal: *Against the Stream*" [274]

"Marxism: Religion and Science" [167]

"An Open Letter from a Keynesian to a Marxist" [097]

"The Organic Composition of Capital" [309]

"The Labour Theory of Value" [305]

[334f] "Marxism and Modern Economics"

In the late 1970s, Robinson published a number of articles critical of what she called "dogmatic Marxism." This essay is the most comprehensive of those articles. It deals with effective demand theory and the marginal productivity of capital, two concepts that Robinson believes Neoclassicalists and Marxists got wrong. On another level, this essay captures Robinson's disenchantment with Marxism as that school of thought evolved in the 1960s and 1970s.

[335] *Collected Economic Papers*: General Index, MIT Press Edition: Cambridge. Also published by Basil Blackwell (London) in 1980.

This sixty-page index completes Robinson's *Collected Economic Papers*.

[335a] "Preface"

Robinson thanks Murray Milgate and Prue Kerr for compiling the index and preparing it for publication.

[335b] "Foreword" (by M. Milgate and P. Kerr)

The foreword offers a brief description of how to use the index.

[336] "Time in Economic Theory," *Kyklos*, 33(Fasc.2): 219-29. Reprinted in [334].

True to the title, Robinson examines the meaning of logical time and historical time as each relates to economic theory. She claims that economics will advance only if less emphasis is placed on logical time and more on historical time when analyzing the world in which we live.

[337] A review of J. F. Becker, *Marxian Political Economy: An Outline*, in *American Journal of Sociology*, 85(6), May: 1474-76.

Characterizing Becker as one of those Marxists opposed to the Post-Keynesian school because he will "not allow anything to be said except in Marx's own words," Robinson is extremely critical of this book, which she sees as long on rhetoric but short on substance.

[338] "Accumulation and Exploitation: An Analysis in the Tradition of Marx, Sraffa, and Kalecki," (with A. Bhaduri), *Cambridge Journal of Economics*, 4(2), June: 103-15. Reprinted in [334].

Contrary to the title, this essay is a Post-Keynesian review and elaboration of Sraffa's economic model as presented in his book *Production of Commodities by Means of Commodities*.

[339] A review of D. Moggridge, editor, *The Collected Writings of John Maynard Keynes. Volume XXIV. The General Theory and After--A Supplement*, in *Economic Journal*, 90(358), June: 391-93.

In addition to reviewing this compilation of Keynes's work, Robinson reminisces over the intellectual environment of the early 1930s, the period in which Keynes's greatest work, *The General Theory*, was taking shape.

[340] A review of H. Chenery, et al., *Structural Change and Development Policy*, in *The Journal of Developing Areas*, 15(1), October: 131-32.

Robinson is critical of this book because she things it reflects mainly a pre-Keynesian perspective. The book is, in her estimation, too focused on Neoclassical (technical) issues at the expense of the real human problems confronting the third world.

1982

[341] "The Arms Race," in S. M. McMurrin, editor, *The Tanner Lectures on Human Values*, Volume 3, Salt Lake City: University of Utah Press and Cambridge: Cambridge University Press: 255-89.

Near the end of her life, Robinson published a number of papers that centered on one theme: "Unless mankind can give up the habit of making national wars, it seems that sooner or later it will destroy itself." This essay deals exclusively with that issue.

As she sees it, the arms race is fueled by three phenomena: "the Cold War, the momentum of research and development, and the connection of armaments with the problems of employment." She takes up the first two topics in a lecture delivered at the University of Utah on April 14, 1981, and the last topic in the sequel lecture given two days later.

The first lecture is a review of how the arms race got started and where it is headed. The lecture has almost nothing to do with economics. The second lecture discusses the Keynesian idea of managing aggregate demand to avoid economic slumps and describes the role of the arms race in implementing that policy.

[342] "The Current State of Economics," *Contributions to Political Economy*, (1), March: 47-49.

Robinson finds the state of economics in the early 1980s wanting. She laments the rising popularity of supply-side economics and is particularly disturbed by the policies of Margaret Thatcher, policies which Robinson sees as an intellectual affront to the great advances in economic understanding achieved in Keynesian and Post-Keynesian analyses.

[343] "Shedding Darkness," (a review of A. Leijonhufvud, *Information and Coordination: Essays in Macroeconomic Theory*), in *Cambridge Journal of Economics*, (6), September: 295-96.

Robinson has little praise for this collection of previously published papers combined with one long, new essay. She finds Leijonhufvud's thinking and writing confusing. For her, "The arguments all seems to be chopped up into short lengths then stirred together as though to make soup." Obviously, Robinson did not find the results very appetizing.

1983

[344] "Logica e Ideologica" (with F. Wilkinson), in F. Vicarelli, editor, *Attualita di Keynes*, Bari: Laterza (in Italian). Reprinted in English as "Ideology and Logic" in [347].

Robinson begins this essay by observing that "it was a serious misfortune that religion came to the West in the form of an implausible piece of history, for this created a clash between the requirements for the development of spiritual life and the requirements of intellectual honesty. At a lower level--the sphere of economic theory--there is a similar conflict between ideology and logic." She then proceeds to identify such conflicts in Marxian and Neoclassical analyses, and concludes that Keynesian theory as seen through Post-Keynesian lenses is largely, but not completely, free of this problem.

[345] "The Economics of Destruction," *Monthly Review*, 935), October: 15-17.

Despite the title, there is almost no economics in this essay. Instead, Robinson questions the value of discussing such meaningless topics as whether the rate of inflation is high or low, especially when the survival of the world in the age of weapons of mass destruction is so problematic. Published posthumously, this short article is based on a talk Robinson gave in Montreal on May 9, 1980.

1985

[346] "The Theory of Normal Prices and Reconstruction of Economic Theory," in G. R. Feiwel, editor, *Issues in Contemporary Macroeconomics and Distribution*, Albany, NY: State University of New York Press: 157-65.

Originally published in mimeograph in 1983 under the title "Spring Cleaning," this essay is probably Joan Robinson's last writing on economics. In what seems at times a work in progress, she laments the rise of American economics after WWII. She is distressed by the American split of economics into micro and macro branches. This regrettable division is among her prime candidates for "spring cleaning," as are the usual vestiges of Neoclassical economics such as the concept of long-term equilibrium.

[347] "Ideology and Logic" (with F. Wilkinson), in F. Vicarelli, editor, *Keynes's Relevance Today*, Philadelphia: University of Pennsylvania Press and London: Macmillan: 73-98. For annotation see [344].

Chapter 3
Works about Joan Robinson and Her Writings

This portion of the bibliography is comparable in format to the previous section but different in scope. To the best of our knowledge, the annotated bibliography of works by Joan Robinson is complete, in that it covers all the publicly available publications Joan Robinson authored or co-authored. The annotated bibliography of the works about Joan Robinson is selective and with good reason. Because she is such a major figure in the history of Western economic thought, Joan Robinson is mentioned in numerous articles and books. Often these references cite one of her publications or discuss briefly her contribution to the development of some aspect of economic theory. Annotating all these citations would be physically impossible and relatively unproductive. We have opted instead to annotate a select listing of works about Joan Robinson, focusing our efforts on those books, articles, and essays of consequence and substance. Naturally, this selection process involves an element of judgement, and although we tried to be representative in the nearly 140 works we did annotate, we readily concede that our annotated bibliography of works about Joan Robinson and her writings is not exhaustive.

1930s

[348] A. C. Pigou, "A Note on Imperfect Competition," *Economic Journal*, 43(169), March, 1933: 108-12.

Calling Robinson's first major publication [004] "a very suggestive and admirably lucid article," Pigou uses this note to confirm and generalize her conclusions.

[349] G. F. Shove, "The Imperfection of the Market," *Economic Journal*, 43(169), March, 1933: 113-25.

While generally supportive of the results in Robinson's first major article [004], Shove takes her to task on a number of specific, highly technical points, some of which, he argues, misrepresent his own work on these very issues.

[350] R. F. Harrod, "A Further Note on Decreasing Costs," *Economic Journal*, 43(170), June, 1933: 337-41.

Building on Robinson's [004] and Shove's [349] works, Harrod seeks to refine their analyses while making sure that the reader is introduced to his own, which, he repeatedly points out, predates the others.

[351] "Imperfect Competition," *The Times* (London), Literary Supplement, October 5, 1933: 660.

In this critique of Robinson's *The Economics of Imperfect Competition* [005], the writer notes that, "though severely academic in tone and method," the book is an important contribution to practical economics because it makes imperfect competition the general rule and not the exception, showing how output, price, and costs can be rationally explained in markets where competition is less than perfect.

[352] G. F. Shove, a review of *The Economics of Imperfect Competition* [005], in *Economic Journal*, 43(172), December, 1933: 657-61.

Although Shove observes that, in producing "an interesting and stimulating book," Robinson has defined terms and assumptions "more fully and clearly than is common in treatises on economic theory," he still considers the work disappointingly conservative, especially considering the youth of the author.

[353] C. D. Edwards, a review of *The Economics of Imperfect Competition* [005] and E. H. Chamberlin's *The Theory of Monopolistic Competition*, in *American Economic Review*, 23(4), December, 1933: 683-85.

Showing no clear preference for either book, Edwards sees value in each and notes that together these two works mark "the maturity of a new approach to value theory."

[354] J. A. Schumpeter, "Robinson's Economics of Imperfect Competition," *Journal of Political Economy*, 42(2), April, 1934: 249-57.

Schumpeter gives Robinson's classic [005] a glowing review, calling the book "an admirable performance, both by virtue of its pioneer achievements and by the energy and straight-forwardness of its exposition." Citing the concept of marginal revenue as Robinson's most significant contribution, Schumpeter believes that the science of economics owes much to the theorists of imperfect competition, "among whom Mrs. Robinson in this book established a claim, certainly to a leading, and perhaps to the first place."

[355] A. J. Nichols, a review of *The Economics of Imperfect Competition*, in *Journal of Political Economy*, 42(2), April, 1934: 257-9.

A counterpoint to Schumpeter's favorable review, Nichols thinks that the title of Robinson's book [005] is misleading because more space is devoted to monopoly and perfect competition than to imperfect competition. Robinson's failure to reference either Cournot or Edgeworth, also noted by Schumpeter in his review, is seen as a serious flaw, as is the avoidance of simple mathematics in favor of the "excessive" use of geometry.

[356] N. Kaldor, "Mrs. Robinson's 'Economics of Imperfect Competition,'" *Economica*, 1(3), August, 1934: 335-41.

There is much praise for *The Economics of Imperfect Competition* [005], and also much criticism, although Kaldor writes that such criticism "is not meant as a criticism of the book itself" but more as "a criticism of its title." In fact, Kaldor is critical of the book, specifically Robinson's orthodox approach to the subject.

[357] H. Barger, "Disguised Unemployment: A Comment," *Economic Journal*, 46(184), December, 1936: 756-59.

Barger elaborates on several points that Robinson overlooked in her "extremely interesting article" [024] on disguised unemployment.

[358] A review of *Essays in the Theory of Employment*, in *The New Statesman*, (13), May 8, 1937: 786.

Characterizing Keynes as the generalissimo in the campaign against Classical economics and Robinson as an able lieutenant, this review sees Robinson's book [032] as extending Keynesian methods with "bewildering virtuosity" and conviction.

[359] C. O. Hardy, a review of *Essays in the Theory of Employment*, in *American Economic Review*, 27(3), September, 1937: 529-32.

After outlining Robinson's book [032], Hardy devotes the bulk of his comments to her essay on "The Long-Period Theory of Employment" [021]. As Hardy sees it, this essay "brings out clearly the difference between generally accepted economic theories and Mr. Keynes's doctrine as it is understood by one of his most competent followers."

[360] "Employment Explained," *The Economist*, September 18, 1937: 567.

Calling her work "always forceful, lucid and original,"this review describes Robinson's book [032] as a guide to practical policy based on Keynes's *General Theory.*

[361] R. G. Hawtrey, "Essays in the Theory of Employment," *Economica*, 4(16), November, 1937: 455-60.

More than a review of Robinson's book [032] of the same title, this is a comment on the work, and not a favorable one at that. Hawtrey is especially critical of Robinson's rejection of monetary policy and her support for fiscal policy as a means of stabilizing aggregate economic activity.

[362] C. O. Hardy, a review of *Introduction to the Theory of Employment*, in *American Economic Review*, 28(3), September, 1938: 528-29.

Robinson's little book [033] is seen as a well-written guide to Keynesian economics, interpreting difficulty points and concepts of that theory with such clarity that professional economists and interested amateurs alike will benefit from reading it.

[363] P. T. Ellsworth, a review of *Introduction to the Theory of Employment*, in *Journal of Political Economy*, 46(5), October, 1938: 730.

While critical of Keynesian thought, Ellsworth finds this book [033] "a masterpiece of verse and vivid exposition" that "should be extremely useful as a prolegomena and companion piece to the *General Theory*."

1940s

[364] "Marxian Theory," *The Times* (London), Literary Supplement, August 29, 1942: 430.

In this review of *An Essay on Marxian Economics* [049], the author comments on the interesting connections Robinson draws between Marxian analysis and modern economic theory as embodied in Keynesian doctrine and her own theory of imperfect competition.

[365] H. Mager, "Marx Without Incense," *New Republic*, (107), October 12, 1942: 473-74.

A well-written and thoughtful review of *An Essay on Marxian Economics* [049] that commends Robinson for treating Marx as a serious thinker and not the "son of Satan" or "an embalmed saint."

[366] E. M. Chossudowsky, a review of *An Essay on Marxian Economics* [049], in *Economica*, 9(36), November, 1942: 389-92.

While full of praise for Robinson's "serious and honest attempt to consider the relationship between recent 'unorthodox' trends in economics and Marxian teachings," Chossudowsky still has reservations about this work. Particular exception is taken to Robinson's claim that Marx's analysis clearly leads to the conclusion that maldistribution of consuming power is the root cause of much of what is wrong with capitalism.

[367] C. W. Guillebaud, a review of *Private Enterprise or Public Control* [050], in *Economica*, 10(39), August, 1943: 265.

Guillebaud questions the wisdom of Robinson's support of "full-bodied socialism" in a world trying to restore freedom and "not merely to exchange one form of tyranny for another."

[368] G. F. Shove, "Mrs. Robinson on Marxian Economics," (a review of *An Essay on Marxian Economics* [049]) *Economic Journal*, 54(213), April, 1944: 47-61.

This comment approaches being a point-by-point discussion of what Marx meant and how Robinson interpreted it, often incorrectly according to Shove. Writing that Robinson's political "sympathies are with Marx," Shove has several specific criticisms of Robinson's views of Marx, including her claim that he anticipated "the modern ideas about the nature and significance of 'effective demand.'"

1950s

[369] E. H. Chamberlin, "'Full Cost' and Monopolistic Competition," *Economic Journal*, 62(246), June, 1952: 318-25.

Not directly aimed at Joan Robinson or her work on imperfect competition, this comment is meant to correct some misimpressions raised by certain economists during the "full cost" debate. Robinson is referenced as one of several who have contributed to the discussion.

[370] R. M. Goodwin, a review of *The Rate of Interest and Other Essays* [089], in *Economic Journal*, 62(248), December, 1952: 930-35.

Goodwin considers Robinson's work a "stimulating little book" that extends Harrod's dynamic economics by skipping over Neoclassical methods "to state the problem in social aggregates and in terms of simple proportionalities, in a word, to return to Ricardian and Marxian types of thinking."

[371] G. L. S. Shackle, a review of *Collected Economic Papers*, Volume 1 [086], in *Economica*, 20(77), February, 1953: 73-74.

Calling Robinson "a notable iconoclast, a strong exemplar of self-determination in economic thought, one of the most ingenious and subtle thinkers that our discipline has produced in modern times," Shackle expresses concern for the unevenness of essays in this volume: Some are "brilliant pieces of clarification and exposition," but others are polemical stories "where every character is either deepest black or purest white, a wicked apologist of laissez faire or a noble victim of it."

[372] A. D. Knox, a review of *The Rate of Interest and Other Essays* [089], in *Economica*, 20(78), May, 1953: 170-71.

A short review in which Knox describes Robinson's work as a "stimulating book of essays," especially the one on "The Generalization of the General Theory."

[373] A. Smithies, a review of *The Rate of Interest and Other Essays* [089], in *American Economic Review*, 43(4), September, 1953: 636-41.

Saying that "this book lacks the crisp lucidity of Joan Robinson's earlier work," Smithies takes issue with a number of propositions Robinson puts forth, including but not limited to her "lack of a theory of the mechanism of the business cycle."

[374] K. J. Arrow, a review of *Collected Economic Papers*, Volume 1 [086], in *Econometrica*, (21), October, 1953: 621-23.

Arrow begins his review by writing, "Any publication of Mrs. Robinson's is a happy event, and this is no exception." One would think that this is going to be a glowing review, a conclusion supported by Arrow's further remark "I do not wish my remarks to be taken as criticism." But critical they are, nonetheless. Arrow, ever the econometrician, is particularly upset with "Mrs. Robinson's antagonistic attitude toward rigorous theoretical analysis."

[375] S. Tsuru, "Keynes versus Marx: The Methodology of Aggregates," in K. K. Kurihara, editor, *Post Keynesian Economics*, New Brunswick: Rutgers University Press, 1954: 320-44.

Inspired by the work of Joan Robinson, this essay looks for similarities between Marx and Keynes while openly admitting to the obvious differences between the two.

[376] R. Solow, "The Production Function and the Theory of Capital," *Review of Economic Studies*, (23), 1955-1956: 101-8.

Responding to a paper by Robinson [099] of the same title, Solow takes exception to Robinson's idea that capital cannot be measured, at least not in the way Neoclassical economists go about it.

[377] R. Solow, "A Contribution to the Theory of Economic Growth," *Quarterly Journal of Economics*, 70(1), February, 1956: 65-94.

In relaxing the Harrod-Domar assumption of fixed proportions of labor to capital, Solow is able to develop a more generalized model of growth, a feat that eventually won him a Nobel Prize and instantly drew the wrath of Joan Robinson.

[378] T. W. Swan, "Economic Growth and Capital Accumulation," *Economic Record*, (32), November, 1956: 334-61.

In an appendix to an article that traces the connection between capital accumulation and the changing productivity of the labor force, Swan devotes a major section to "Joan Robinson's Puzzle." Swan defends the Neoclassical approach to the analysis of economic growth while recognizing the value of Robinson's criticism as expressed in [099] and [111]. For Robinson's reply to Swan's criticism, see [124].

[379] B. S. Keirstead, "The Structure and Accumulation of Capital," *Canadian Journal of Economics and Political Science*, 23(4), November, 1957: 555-59.

In a review of two books on capital theory, including *The Accumulation of Capital* [111], Keirstead summarizes Robinson's work without characterizing it except to say that the time was ripe for a reappraisal of capital theory.

[380] T. Barna, a review of *The Accumulation of Capital* [111], in *Economic Journal*, 67(267), September, 1957: 490-93.

In this favorable review, Barna lays out the basic question Robinson addresses in her book: "What are the conditions for the achievement of a cumulative long-term growth of wealth and what is the outcome for the relation between wages and profits?" Barna then describes the methods by which Robinson answers this and related questions concerning the measurability of capital and the validity of the concept of the marginal productivity of capital.

[381] A. P. Lerner, a review of *The Accumulation of Capital* [111], in *American Economic Review*, 47(5), September, 1957: 693-99.

Despite the book's flaws, Lerner writes that "the volume is not only a work by a distinguished economist on a most important subject, but it is an important book." Lerner's review focuses on the big picture, the gestalt of Robinson's idea, and not on the intricate particulars. Although noting that the book is more complex and abstract than it needs to be--and noting "the tough cuteness of Mrs. Robinson's style"--Lerner still believes that there is much of substance here.

[382] L. R. Klein, a review of *The Accumulation of Capital* [111], in *Econometrica*, (26), October, 1958: 622-24.

Like most critics of Robinson, Klein begins this review with kind words: "We know that when she has concentrated her great intellectual powers on a subject for some time, a resulting book is certain to be important." The facade is then quickly dropped, and the criticism of Robinson--"being insular in her intellectual outlook and horizon"--begins in earnest.

[383] G. D. N. Worswick, "Mrs. Robinson on Simple Accumulation: A Comment with Algebra," *Oxford Economic Papers*, (11), January, 1959: 125-41.

Worswick delivers what is promised: "The main purpose of this paper is to translate into algebra Mrs. Robinson's model of simple accumulation with constant technique, which is described in her book *The Accumulation of Capital* ..." [111]. The purpose is to clarify, correct, and embellish a model for which Worswick has high regard; the goal is achieved. For Robinson's comment on Worswick's paper, see [136].

1960s

[384] K. Lancaster, "Mrs. Robinson's Dynamics," *Economica*, 27(105), February, 1960: 63-70.

In what is basically a review of *The Accumulation of Capital* [111], Lancaster writes:

> Any work by Mrs. Robinson must command respect, and when she writes a book which seems intended to be as important a contribution to the theory of growth and economic dynamics as her *Imperfect Competition* was to the theory of price, then such a book can be judged only by the highest standards. ... The book must be judged as a whole, in terms of its fabric, its method and its general sweep. ...

Evaluating the book in these terms, Lancaster concludes that it does not succeed, principally because the static technique that worked so well in *Imperfect Competition* is ill suited to handle "the dynamic problems of capital."

[385] M. Bronfenbrenner, a review of *Collected Economic Papers*, Volume 2 [143], in *American Economic Review*, 51(3), June 1961: 413-14.

Bronfenbrenner believes that this volume of the *Collected Economic Papers* reflects much of Robinson's long-running battle with orthodox economics and "her intolerance of opposition, particularly from academic sources."

[386] R. Clower, a review of *Exercises in Economic Analysis* [144], in *American Economic Review*, 51(4), September, 1961: 701-2.

Although Clower writes that this book is "a charming and provocative introduction to economic theory--original in outlook, full of pithy comments about every subject on which it touches," he does chastise Robinson for failing to take seriously the writings of "Continental and American scholars."

[387] G. C. Harcourt, a review of *Exercises in Economic Analysis* [144], in *Economic Record*, (37), September, 1961: 393-95.

Despite noting "a number of omissions, errors and misprints," Harcourt finds the book useful "not only because of the witty, illuminating and stimulating passages of many of its pages, but also for its (in the main) clarity of exposition and wide coverage."

[388] H. Minsky, a review of *Collected Economic Papers*, Volume 2 [143], in *Journal of Political Economy*, 69(5), October, 1961: 497-98.

Claiming that none of the essays is a "time-tested classic," Minsky focuses more on reporting the book's content than on reviewing its contributions or shortcomings. (Note that the volume being reviewed is mislabled "Vol. I.")

[389] "Analysis of Growth," a review of *Essays in the Theory of Economic Growth* [159], in *The Economist*, (206), January 12, 1963: 123.

Classifying this work [159] as an introduction to her earlier and extremely difficult *The Accumulation of Capital* [111], this review says that the differences between Robinson's model of growth and those of other authors--e.g., Harrod and Kaldor--"will be apparent only to the cognoscenti." Aimed at those well-versed in the esoteric branch of economic theory, the book is seen as easy to read but deceptively abstract and academic.

[390] R. Findlay, "The Robinson Model of Accumulation," *Economica*, 30(117), February, 1963: 1-12.

In this lengthy, mathematical review of *The Accumulation of Capital*

[111], Findlay compares and contrasts Robinson's model with those of several neoclassical economists and concludes, "Behind Harrod and Domar there is Keynes; beyond Solow and Swan there is Wicksell; and behind Mrs. Robinson there is Marx."

[391] G. J. Stigler, a review of *Economic Philosophy* [158], in *Journal of Political Economy,* 71(2), April, 1963: 192-193.

In a critical review, Stigler sees this small volume as tracing familiar territory and accepting some old errors of Marxian thought while adding new ones, so that the end result is a book that reflects Robinson's philosophy, not that of economics or economists.

[392] G. D. N. Worswick, a review of *Essays in the Theory of Economic Growth* [159], in *Economic Journal*, 73(290), June, 1963: 295-97.

Saying that Mrs. Robinson's main concern in these essays is to get economics "off the mud of static equilibrium," Worswick discusses the six principal determinants--technical conditions, competitive conditions, wage bargaining, finance, investment policy, and thriftiness--that Robinson believes are the keys to economic growth.

[393] P. A. Baran, a review of *Economic Philosophy* [158], in *American Economic Review*, 53(3), June, 1963: 455-58.

In this dark, almost brooding review, Baran is sympathetic with Robinson's purpose, which is to demonstrate "the persistent bias in favor of the status quo which has vitiated the work of most economists." He takes exception, however, to the exaggerated significance Robinson gives economic ideas over the importance of vested interest in shaping history.

[394] W. Jaffe, a review of *Economic Philosophy* [158], in *Annals of the American Academy of Political and Social Sciences*, (348), July, 1963: 164-65.

Jaffe writes that the "main purpose of this book is to sort out the mixture of ideology and science in economics, without prejudice to either ingredient." Having no strong feelings about whether Robinson succeeds, Jaffe is content to contrast Robinson's view that economics and political economy are inseparable with that of Milton Friedman, who holds that one can have a positive economics free of any particular ethical position or set of value judgements.

[395] "Economics and Growth," a review of two books including *Essays in the Theory of Economic Growth* [159], in *The Times* (London), Literary Supplement, July 5, 1963: 495.

Calling the book "a needlessly opaque and inelegant one," this review chastises Robinson for failing to square her theory with the facts or at least to indicate how one would go about testing the hypotheses presented. Avoiding equations by putting them into words, Robinson has written a book that this review says is lacking the economy of mathematical rigor and the clarity needed for practical application.

[396] K. Klappholz, a review of *Economic Philosophy* [158], in *Economica*, 30(119), August, 1963: 321-22.

Klappholz writes that Robinson's main theme is the idea that economic theory is used "to bolster the 'ideology' of laissez-faire." Klappholz is not convinced that Robinson has made her case in this book.

[397] K. E. Boulding, a review of *Economic Philosophy* [158], in *American Sociological Review*, 28(4), August, 1963: 657-58.

Praising Robinson as "one of the greatest economists of our day," Boulding finds the book so crammed with "wit, wisdom, and error that it is impossible to do justice to it in a brief review." Although in agreement with much of Robinson's critique, Boulding feels "that Mrs. Robinson is selling economics too short and giving up her own profession too easily."

[398] J. W. Nevile, a review of *Essays in the Theory of Economic Growth* [159], in *Economic Record*, (39), September, 1963: 385-86.

Nevile writes that this book "will be widely welcomed by all those who have found Mrs. Robinson's *Accumulation of Capital* difficult." Nevile believes Robinson has succeeded in achieving her purpose: to make lucid and thus accessible many of the ideas first presented in *Accumulation*.

[399] R. Findlay, "A Reply," *Economica*, 30(117), November, 1963: 411-12.

In his rebuttal to Robinson's response [176], Findlay claims that his interpretation of accumulation models, including Robinson's, allows for feedback between key variables, something lacking in Robinson's "uni-linear conception of causation."

[400] D. Hamberg, a review of *Essays in the Theory of Economic Growth* [159], in *American Economic Review*, 53(5), December, 1963: 1109-14.

Saying that the book is uneven and suffering "from the typical Robinson defect of shabby treatment of whatever does not conform with her own preconceptions," Hamberg finds little of value in these essays. Believing that there is no significant difference between Robinson's growth model, first described in *The Accumulation of Capital* [111], and that of Kaldor, Hamberg thinks that the book tries to create a distinction where none exists.

[401] S. P. (S. Plastrik), "In the Eye of the Beholder," *Dissent*, 12(2), Spring, 1965: 250-51.

This review of *Notes from China* [178] finds Robinson too eager to accept the Chinese version of the history of such events as the Sino-Indian border dispute of 1962, the Tibet problem, and the reorganization of the commune system in the early 1960s.

[402] P. Samuelson and F. Modigliani, "Reply to Pasinetti and Robinson," *Review of Economic Studies*, (33), October, 1966: 321-30.

Less than one page of this article is devoted to Robinson's comment [213] on Samuelson and Modigliani's original paper. The bulk of Samuelson and Modigliani's remarks are aimed at Pasinetti and his model of golden-age equilibrium, which the two Nobel Laureates find inferior to their work on growth and accumulation.

[403] "Light Blue and Scarlet," a review of *Economics: An Awkward Corner* [204], in *The Economist*, 221(6432), December 3, 1966: 1032, 1037.

In reviewing what is called an "only half-brilliant little book on Britain's current ... economic crisis," three kinds of Robinsonian analyses are discussed. The first is the old-fashioned radicalism of the 1920s; the second, Keynesian theory; and the third, a superficial review of postwar economics. The reviewer finds Robinson's recommendation that Britain "settle down to being a small country devoted to neutrality and peace" and disassociate itself from the American crusade against communism, "an oddly irrelevant flourish with which to end an otherwise often-stimulating book."

[404] H. D. Marshall, *The Great Economists: A History of Economic Thought*, New York: Pitman, 1967: 318-23.

Unlike the essay by Gram and Walsh [463] which describes Robinson's macroeconomics to the near exclusion of her other contributions, Marshall trains his summary of Robinsonian economics on her theory of imperfect competition. The analysis focuses on a comparison of her view of imperfect competition with that of Edward Chamberlin, the American economist who published *The Theory of Monopolistic Competition* in 1933, the same year Robinson's *The Economics of Imperfect Competition* [005] appeared. Marshall notes that although similar to Chamberlin's work, Robinson's book is more inclusive, discussing monopsony, discriminating monopolists, and the implications of imperfect competition for productivity, issues Chamberlin largely ignored.

[405] R. Lekachman, Introduction to the American edition of *Economics: An Awkward Corner* [204], New York: Random House, 1967: v-xiii.

More than a foreword to the book, Lekachman's introduction is a snapshot of Robinson's thinking (circa 1966) on equality, free markets versus planning, foreign policy, and the state of the British economy.

[406] G. L. S. Shackle, *The Years of High Theory: Invention and Tradition in Economic Thought*, 1926-1939, Cambridge, Cambridge University Press, 1967.

Chapter 5 of this book--"The New Establishment in Value Theory: (I) Joan Robinson"--is a detailed review of Robinson's *The Economics of Imperfect Competition* [005]. The sixth chapter of the book is a comparison of Edward Chamberlin's *The Theory of Monopolistic Competition* with Robinson's work on imperfect competition.

[407] H. Johnson, "Civic Virtue," a review of two books including *Economics: An Awkward Corner* [204], in *New Statesman*, (73), January 6, 1967: 15-16.

Johnson describes Robinson's book as uneven--sometimes shrewd and perceptive, and other times muddled with unfounded assertions passed off as established facts. He believes that Robinson's solution to contemporary British economic problems is not really a solution per se but "only rationalizing a position reached on a prime ideological ground."

[408] E. Eschag, a review of *Collected Economic Papers*, Volume 3 [195], in *Economic Journal*, 77(306), June, 1967: 351-54.

According to Eschag, the common theme of the articles in this volume is "criticism of orthodox, respectable and generally accepted opinions." Because of this, Eschag considers the book "intellectually stimulating," and the articles therein, or at least most of them, "provide much food for thought."

[409] J. Corina, a review of *Economics: An Awkward Corner* [204], in *Cambridge Quarterly*, 2(3), Summer, 1967: 290-91.

This favorable review characterizes Robinson's book as "a concise and well-written account of the current British plight." Corina notes that Robinson avoids the pitfalls that seem to trap most authors of popular books on economics: "How often has one picked up a paperback where Britain's economic dilemma is served as a brew of value judgements topped by the froth of economic jargon. This book is a brilliant exception."

[410] H. Uzawa, a review of *Collected Economic Papers*, Volume 3 [195], in *American Economic Review*, 58(1), March, 1968: 204-6.

After summarizing the table of contents, Uzawa trains his comments on the first two parts of the book, which contain essays that shed light on and aid in the understanding of *The Accumulation of Capital* [111]. Uzawa concludes that this volume of Robinson's collected papers makes "the conceptual basis of her capital theory ... more readily comprehensible" and so increases the attractiveness of that theory compared with the more orthodox version, even though the two are not appreciably different.

[411] E. T. Chase, "Radical Wisdom," a review of *Economics: An Awkward Corner* [204], in *The Newleader*, (51), March 11, 1968: 21-23.

This glowing review has high praise for Robinson ("the ... doyenne of British economists and quite possibly the greatest women economist ever") and her book, which describes the plight of a Great Britain saddled with the anachronistic habits of nineteenth-century laissez-faire doctrine.

[412] O. Lattimore, "Chinese Bells," a review of several books including *The Cultural Revolution in China* [235], in *New Statesman*, (77), March 14, 1969: 364-65.

This reviewer accepts Robinson's judgements on China and considers the book a reliable, "quick-read" account of the Cultural Revolution.

[413] "Parables of Never-Never Land," a review of *The Cultural Revolution in China* [235], in *The Times* (London), Literary Supplement, May 29, 1969: 579.

The title of this review reflects succinctly the attitude of the author toward Robinson's book. While commending Robinson for assembling a useful collection of source material, the reviewer takes her to task for accepting without question the official version of the causes and consequences of the Cultural Revolution.

[414] G. C. Harcourt, "Some Cambridge Controversies in the Theory of Capital," *Journal of Economic Literature*, 7(2), June, 1969: 369-405.

An excellent summary of the debate sparked by Robinson's "The Production Function and the Theory of Capital" [099], and similar essays, e.g., [108] and [110]. This article is a chronological discussion of the points Robinson raised and the many responses--some sympathetic and some critical--to her thesis.

[415] M. E. Sharpe, a review of *Economics: An Awkward Corner* [204], in *Science and Society*, 33(1), Winter, 1969: 99-100.

Ostensibly a "catalogue of the economic woes that beset Britain during the balance of payments crisis of 1966," this book applies to any developed capitalist country, or so Sharpe believes. Like Robinson, Sharpe thinks that the Keynesian fixation on the overall level of employment is too narrow, and that we need to be sensitive "to what the employment should be for."

1970s

[416] "A Gallop Round the Globe," a review of *Freedom and Necessity* [241], in *The Times* (London), Literary Supplement, April 16, 1970: 60.

Calling the book "slight and hasty," the reviewer admonishes Robinson for trying to do so much--an economic interpretation of history--in just 124 small pages. This "breathless chase through the millennia" stimulates but does not satisfy.

[417] A review of *Freedom and Necessity* [241], in *Publisher's Weekly*, 197(60), May 4, 1970: 60.

A short review full of high praise for a stimulating, witty, and barbed interpretation of economic history as seen "through the corrective lens of social practice, with an assist from Darwinian biology."

[418] F. Copper, a review of *The Cultural Revolution in China* [235], in *Pacific Affairs*, (43), Fall, 1970: 438-39.

One of the few reviewers of this book to praise the work, Cooper finds real value in Robinson's "analysis of the theory behind the Cultural Revolution and its relevance to Marxist ideology."

[419] A review of *Freedom and Necessity* [241], in *The New Republic*, (163), October 3, 1970: 28.

A favorable review that sees in this short book (124 pages) the "distillation of much hard thought and very wide reading." Though believing that the general public will find much of value in the book, the reviewer thinks that economists and sociologists may find the work disconcerting because Robinson sides "with Norbert Wiener, who accused economists of dressing up impressive ideas in calculus language," while she herself "sees sociologists aping economists who are aping physicists."

[420] A review of *Freedom and Necessity* [241], in *Choice*, February, 1971: 1704.

This review finds provocative Robinson's conclusion about the difference between natural and social sciences, and considers the breadth of the book ambitious, touching as it does on a number of larger questions in the development of human society such as the emergence of races, classes, commerce, capitalism, and socialism.

[421] J. Gurley, "The State of Political Economics," *American Economic Review*, 61(2), May, 1971: 53-62.

In the mid-1960s, a group of economists dissatisfied with the conventional core of the discipline formed an association called the Union for Radical Political Economics. The views of this left-wing group were reflected to a large degree in N. D. Ruggle's *Economics* (1970), which Gurley reviews in this essay. While not directly related to Joan Robinson or her works, this review is noteworthy because the author expresses the belief that Robinsonian economics was not part of the radical movement, a proposition many radicals would take exception to.

[422] C. E. Ferguson, "Capital Theory Up-To-Date: A Comment on Mrs. Robinson's Article," *Canadian Journal of Economics* (Revue canadienne d'Economique), 4(2), May, 1971: 250-54.

"I feel distinctly honoured that Mrs. Robinson read my recent book and wrote a review article on one-half of one chapter of it. One could not hope for a more distinguised or less unbiased reviewer." After opening with that broadside, C. E. Ferguson launches into a rebuttal of Robinson's analysis of his book *The Neoclassical Theory of Production and Distribution*, reviewed in [245] and [255]. Ferguson challenges Robinson's capital theory and that of other "Cambridge Critics," as he calls them. The depth of Ferguson's discontent with Robinson and those of her ilk is revealed in a paraphrase of Robert Solow: "Some of the critics appear to write their comments just as oysters make pearls--out of sheer irritation."

[423] P. Wasserman, a review of *Economic Heresies* [251], in *Library Journal*, (96), June 15, 1971: 2078.

The reviewer describes Robinson's probing of the philosophical and intellectual contributions of the major theorists as "an original and thought-provoking monograph" about the alleged inherent incongruities in orthodox economic thinking.

[424] "In Theory," a review of *Economic Heresies* [251], in *The Economist*, 240(57), July 24, 1971: 57-58.

The reviewer criticizes Robinson for focusing her comments on the shortcomings of theory while ignoring the accomplishments of applied economics--the "patient accumulation of empirical knowledge, statistical testing"--where contributions are important but not grand.

[425] M. Moszer, "Mene mene....," a review of *Economic Heresies* [251], in *Monthly Labor Review*, 95(3), March, 1972: 69-70.

Moszer finds these eight essays right on target in terms of identifying the inability of orthodox economics to come to grips with "today's poverty of ill-used resources." The basic problem as Moszer sees it is that mainstream economics "has assumed away the problem," a sentiment Robinson often expressed in her writings.

[426] A. Asimakopulos, a review of *Economic Heresies* [251], in *Canadian Journal of Economics*, 5(2), May, 1972: 314-16.

Calling the book "a basic critique of neo-classical and neo-neoclassical approaches to economic theory," Asimakopulos praises Robinson for "her ability to concentrate on fundamental issues in economic analysis," especially the role of capital in aggregate production functions, the orthodox treatment of time and expectations, and the roles of interest and profit in a market economy.

[427] F. H. Hahn, a review of *Economic Heresies* [251], in *Economica*, 39(154), May, 1972: 205-6.

Hahn takes pity on Robinson, for as he sees it, "When Professor Robinson is not engaged in either fantasies about orthodoxy or in expounding once again the 'formula' of thrift and animal spirits or the 'pseudo-production function' she can be very stimulating."

[428] D. L. Thomson, *Adam Smith's Daughters*, New York: Exposition Press, 1973: 105-33.

In a book about the contributions of six noted women economists, there is an easy-to-read chapter summarizing Robinson's *The Economics of Imperfect Competition* [005], *The Accumulation of Capital* [111], and other major analytical works. Thomson also details Robinson's humanistic books such as *Economic Philosophy* [158], *Economics: An Awkward Corner* [204], *Freedom and Necessity: An Introduction to the Study of Society* [241], and *Economic Heresies* [251], works seldom referenced or reviewed by her Post-Keynesian followers.

[429] J. A. Kregel, *The Reconstruction of Political Economy: An Introduction to Post-Keynesian Economics*, New York: Wiley, 1973.

In a book devoted to the origins, theories, and policy implications of Post-Keynesian economics, Kregel repeatedly pays homage to Joan Robinson, author of the foreword [267] to the book.

[430] H. F. Breimyer, a review of two books including *Economic Heresies* [251], in *American Journal of Agriculture Economics*, (55), February, 1973: 130-31.

Noting that "depreciation of economic orthodoxy is in vogue," Breimyer considers Robinson one of the more distinguished and articulate critics of mainstream theory. He thinks that *Economic Heresies*, which "is never shrill, [and] by no means iconoclastic," accurately targets what is wrong with contemporary theory--the tendency to ignore institutional considerations in favor of a "behavior paradigm that is empirically invalid."

[431] S. A. Marglin, a review of *Economic Heresies* [251], in *Economic Journal*, 83(330), June, 1973: 535-38.

Admitting that he agreed to review this book because Joan Robinson "is one of the two members of her generation who helped me to see orthodox micro-economics theory ... for what it principally is, an ideological defense of capitalism," Marglin praises the work almost without exception.

[432] J. Tobin, "Cambridge (U.K.) vs. Cambridge (Mass)," *The Public Interest*, (31), Spring, 1973: 102-9.

In what is fundamentally a review of Robinson's *Economic Heresies* [251], Tobin writes that the book is "an illuminating, entertaining, and characteristically lucid account of the developments and controversies in economic theory over ... the past 40 years." Particular attention is given to the topic implied in the title of Tobin's review. There are also some harsh words: "Mrs. Robinson is just unaware of the volume of research over the past 10 years on poverty, inequality, pollution, conservation, externalities, and public goods. A theorist par excellence, she pays no attention to empirical studies and policy applications that constitute the great bulk of economists' output."

[433] "The Revolution Has Bored Its Children," a review of *After Keynes* [266], in *The Economist*, (248), August 25, 1973: 100.

Pictured as a book of "high-class intellectual fun," *After Keynes* is reviewed from *The Economist* perception of Robinson: a brilliant young economist who became a discontented battle-ax in her old age.

In the one essay Robinson contributed to the volume, her discontent spills over onto many topics, including her patron saint, John Maynard Keynes.

[434] "Big Questions," a review of *An Introduction to Modern Economics* [265], in *The Economist*, (249), October, 1973: 147-48.

Calling this text book exactly what one would expect--"idiosyncratic, left-wing, clear and brilliant"--this reviewer summarizes in a linear fashion the contents of the book. Big questions such as the distribution of income and the sources of economic growth are the major concerns of the text. The review of microeconomic theory is called "curiously patchy," and the final section of the book, an analysis of the problems in capitalist, socialist, and third-world countries, is deemed unsatisfactory. Still, the review is genuinely positive, predicting wide sales for the text, a forecast that may have proved accurate in England but did not hold up in the United States.

[435] "More To It Than Mathematics," a review of two books including *After Keynes* [266], in *The Times* (London), Literary Supplement, October 12, 1973: 1224.

In this potpourri of essays--over a third of which do not deal with economics per se but with such topics as air pollution, water pollution, and the environment--this reviewer finds redeeming value in the essay by E. F. Schumacher, who realizes that if economics is to help, it must shake the fascination with theory and embrace the contributions of related disciplines such as sociology and political science. Robinson's essay dealing with the betrayal of the Keynesian revolution by those who are supposed to interpret it has little appeal for the reviewer.

[436] J. Gurley, a review of *Introduction to Modern Economics* [265], in *Economic Journal*, 84(334), June, 1974: 447-50.

Noting that "this is a most unusual book for beginners in economics," Gurley is sad that its Post-Keynesian orientation will limit adoptions. He believes that that is too bad because "this type of economics can much better prepare the coming generation of students for understanding and solving the real problems of the world than neo-neoclassical economics. ..."

[437] P. A. Samuelson, "Steady State and Transient Relations: A Reply on Reswitching," *Quarterly Journal of Economics*, 89(1), February, 1975: 40-47.

Despite the high praise for Robinson--"Economics owes much to Joan Robinson for her many contributions across the whole spectrum of the subject" --Samuelson considers her input to the modern capital theory debate to be suboptimal.

[438] A review of *An Introduction to Modern Economics* [265], in *Journal of Business Education*, (50), February, 1975: 217.

This short review recommends the book for "the teacher of economics who feels the need for a change in vista," for although it covers conventional topics, the book does so from a historical perspective with more attention given to socialism than is typical of conventional American texts.

[439] D. Houston, a review of *Introduction to Modern Economics* [265], in *Sloan Management Review*, 16(3), Spring, 1975: 112-14.

Houston finds the book to be an exception to the mainstream principles texts, most of which seem to have been "composed in corporate board rooms." The one caveat he offers--the book is "less empirical and more terse and difficult than the typical American text"--could very well be considered a compliment.

[440] "A Socialist Who Sounds Like a Conservative," *Business Week*, (2403), October 20, 1975: 80+.

In 1975, the International Year of the Woman, everyone, including the editors of *Business Week*, expected Joan Robinson to win the Nobel Prize in economics. She didn't. That year the prize was shared by Tjalling Koopmans and Leonid Kantorovich.

Published in anticipation of Robinson's "Nobel," this essay notes that although she reigned as the titular head of British Keynesians, on the American side of the Atlantic she was "more ignored than adored." The article discusses the reasons for this, explaining the sharp differences between British and American Keynesians and why Robinson referred to the latter as "bastard Keynesians."

[441] A. S. Eichner and J. A. Kregel, "An Essay on Post-Keynesian Theory: A New Paradigm in Economics," *Journal of Economic Literature*, 13(4), December, 1975: 1293-1314.

A review article that compares and contrasts Post-Keynesian theory with Neoclassical theory, giving due recognition to the contributions of Joan Robinson, Luigi Pasinetti, Geoffrey Harcourt, Michal Kalecki, and others who forged the Post-Keynesian movement.

[442] F. Mahloudji, "A Critical Examination of the Economics of Joan Robinson," unpublished PhD thesis, Duke University, Durham, NC 1976.

Mahloudji traces Robinson's disenchantment with the mechanical determinatism of the Neoclassical tradition, beginning with her refinement of Marshallian statics in *The Economics of Imperfect Competition* [005], continuing with her discovery of historical time in *An Essay on Marxian Economics* [049] and her study of economic dynamics in *The Accumulation of Capital* [111], and culminating in her later works which characterize economic processes as irreversible, novel, and basically indeterminate.

[443] K. de Schweinitz, a review of *Introduction to Modern Economics* [265], in *Journal of Economic Issues*, (10), March, 1976: 176-79.

Believing the book is "best suited for students who already have a knowledge ... of contemporary economics," de Schweinitz lavishes considerable praise on the text and even more on Joan Robinson: "Unlike many economists ... in the autumnal years of their career, who devote their energies to the defense of their early successes, ... she is always on the attack." Curiously, de Schweinitz refers to Robinson as a "giant among neoclassical economists," a comment that would make most Post-Keynesians shudder.

[444] S. Weintraub, editor, *Modern Economic Thought*, Philadelphia: University of Pennsylvania Press, 1977.

While not singled out as the centerpiece in any of the book's twenty-eight essays, Robinson is mentioned, often extensively, in twelve of the essays in this anthology about modern economists and economics.

[445] J. Eatwell, "Joan Robinson: Portrait," *Challenge*, (20), March-April, 1977: 64-66.

A short but insightful analysis of Robinsonian economics. Eatwell argues that economists miss the point if they approach Robinson's work with "apprehension and ... bewilderment" because her exposition is literary and not mathematical. Robinson's "originality rests on intellectual foundations that are fundamentally different from those of orthodox economists, and no amount of formalization can squeeze her ideas back into the orthodox mold." To understand Robinson's economics, one must appreciate the two interrelated principles that are essential to her approach: "First, a prerequisite of any satisfactory economic theory is the specification of the relevant characteristics of the society, the economic life of which it purports to explain. ... Second, economic analysis must take time seriously."

[446] P. Deane, *The Evolution of Economic Ideas*, Cambridge: Cambridge University Press, 1978.

While citing Robinson frequently when discussing the evolution of many different ideas, Deane devotes most of her Robinsonian references to the development and impact of Robinson's theory of imperfect competition. Incidentally, this book is one of the volumes in the modern Cambridge Economics Series, of which Deane and Robinson served as editors and co-authors of the series preface (page v).

[447] P. Allen, *The Cambridge Apostles*, Cambridge: Cambridge University Press, 1978.

The title of this book refers to a secretive student society at Cambridge University, well known as a training ground for a long succession of gifted British thinkers. Among the society's members was Frederick Denison Maurice, Joan Robinson's great-grandfather and the primary focus of chapters 4 and 5 in this book. These chapters give a profile of the feisty F. D. Maurice and provide insights into the rich intellectual heritage that surrounded Robinson when she was growing up.

[448] "Ahead of Her Time," a review of *Contributions to Modern Economics* [308], in *The Economist*, (269), November 11, 1978: 124.

The book contains twenty-four essays, most written during what the reviewer believes was Robinson's heyday--the 1930s and 1940s. As the reviewer sees it, the essays, mostly of a nontechnical nature, "are written with a clarity and robustness of argument which will appeal to anyone interested in economics."

[449] G. C. Harcourt, "Joan Robinson," in D. S. Stills, editor, *International Encyclopedia of Social Sciences*, Biographical Supplement, New York: Free Press, 1979: 663-71.

"Joan Violet Robinson is the rebel with a cause par excellence." So begins Harcourt's biographical review of Robinson's life, works, and her many conflicts with mainstream economics and economists. A Post-Keynesian, Harcourt has produced a biographical sketch that is sympathetic but not saccharine.

[450] P. Garegnani, "Notes on Consumption, Investment, and Effective Demand: A Reply to Joan Robinson,"*Cambridge Journal of Economics*, (3), June, 1979: 181-87.

A tightly written, heavily footnoted, strictly academic reply to Robinson's earlier comments [322, 323, and 328] regarding Garegnani's original article. It seems to boil down to a disagreement between Post-Keynesian economists over what Keynes really meant when discussing the relationship between consumption, investment, and effective demand.

[451] K. Schott, "Crisis Points," a review of three books including *Collected Economic Papers*, Vol. 5 [317], in the *New Statesman*, (98), August 24, 1979: 275-76.

Schott poses the question "is steady growth with full employment and stable prices ever a long-term possibility in a capitalist society?" and then gives his answer, "Certainly Harrod, Keynes, Robinson and Kalecki did not seem to think so, but their message got lost in the actual economic success of the 1950s and 1960s." Schott agrees with Robinson that the only way to achieve stable growth over the long term is through planning, a theme alluded to throughout volume 5 of her *Collected Economic Papers* [317].

[452] M. Bronfenbrenner, a review of *Contributions to Modern Economics* [308], in *Economic Journal*, 89(354), June, 1979: 446-47.

Paraphrasing Voltaire, Bronfenbrenner writes, "Speaking as a 'bastard Keynesian' purveyor of 'rubbish' and 'stinking fish,' ... I do not agree with most of what Joan Robinson has been saying these past forty years, but hope she wins a Nobel Prize for saying it."

Noting that Joan Robinson "has done more than any other contemporary economist (Milton Friedman being her only rival) to save our discipline from ossified cut-and-driedness," Bronfenbrenner takes exception to many of her ideas, but reverently so.

1980s

[453] P. Davidson, "Post Keynesian Economics," *The Public Interest*, (Special Issue on "The Crisis of Economic Theory"), 1980: 151-73.

Davidson lays out three "fundamental characteristics of the historical and humanistic models employed by Post Keynesian[s] ...": (1) The economy is a historical process; (2) in an uncertain world, expectations play a significant role in the economic process; and (3) institutions, especially economic and political ones, are important in shaping real-world events. In identifying the three cornerstones of Post-Keynesian thought, Davidson reaffirms the basic tenets of Robinsonian economics.

[454] A review of *Aspects of Development and Underdevelopment* [319], in *Choice*, (16), February, 1980: 1624.

With no graphs and few statistical tables, the book is seen as a non-technical volume suitable for "the intelligent undergraduate and interested general reader." The reviewer believes that Robinson's criticism of orthodox development economics shows through, especially her skepticism about the alleged benefits of free trade for developing economies.

[455] E. Penrose, a review of *Aspects of Development and Underdevelopment* [319], in *Economic Journal*, 90(359), September, 1980: 623-25.

Although she thinks that Robinson's book is uneven, Penrose believes the insights are sound, and the presentation well written, "with a refreshing lack of the atrocious jargon which so often characterizes some development economists. ..."

[456] M. Bronfenbrenner, a review of *Aspects of Development and Underdevelopment* [319], in *Journal of Economic Literature*, 18(4), December, 1980: 1581-82.

Bronfenbrenner considers this book a good "third-world" point of view of development economics. As such, he welcomes it as a useful counterpoint to the "first-world" point-of-view texts customarily assigned intermediate students of economics studying development. As a standalone volume, however, Bronfenbrenner finds the book limited in scope, somewhat doctrinaire, and a bit preachy.

[457] M. Vandoorne, a review of *Collected Economic Papers*, Vol. 5 [317], in *Economic Journal*, 90(360), December, 1980: 929-30.

According to Vandoorne, the fifth and final volume of Robinson's collected papers has two thrusts: "a powerful attack on neoclassical orthodoxy" and a reaffirmation of the Keynesian revolution, with its theory and policy implications. Like other reviewers of Robinson's work, Vandoorne finds her short on specific reforms to deal with the dual problems of inflation and unemployment but full of sarcasm for mainstream economic theory and programs. In short, Robinson is unsatisfied with the present state of affairs but is apparently at a loss about how to make things better.

[458] T. Skouras, "The Economics of Joan Robinson," in J. R. Shackleton and G. Locksley, editors, *Twelve Contemporary Economists*, New York: Wiley & Sons, 1981: 199-218.

Claiming that "it is impossible, in a brief paper, properly to survey Joan Robinson's work," Skouras focuses on two broad themes of Robinsonian economics: the theory of value and the theory of accumulation. The review of the first theme begins with an analysis of *The Economics of Imperfect Competition* [005] and carries through the reswitching debate Robinson had with the Neoclassical School. The discussion of the second theme traces the Robinson/Kalecki/Keynes nexus. In so dividing Robinson's economics, Skouras has, probably inadvertently, segmented Robinson's work into the microeconomics-versus-macroeconomics dichotomy to which she strongly objected.

Those interested in the origins of the Post-Keynesian movement are encouraged to read the essay about Michal Kalecki, one of the other economists examined in this book.

[459] K. P. Jameson, a review of two books including *Aspects of Development and Underdevelopment* [319], in *Journal of Economic Issues*, (15), March, 1981: 264-67.

In comparing and contrasting two books on development theory, Jameson finds Robinson's work illuminating but pessimistic.

[460] J. Foster, a review of *Contributions to Modern Economics* [308] and *Generalization of the General Theory* [320], in *Economic Journal*, 91(364), December, 1981: 1041-43.

While noting that over the past twenty-five years "her allies have been few and temporary," Foster lauds Robinson's fighting spirit and "strength of character" as she takes on, simultaneously, Neoclassical orthodoxy, bastard Keynesians, monetarists, and dogmatic Marxists. Foster believes that for the most part Robinson's views on economics and the economic process are valid, especially in light of the macroeconomic crisis that beset the Western world in the late 1970s and early 1980s.

[461] F. M. Fisher, *Disequilibrium Foundations of Equilibrium Economics*, Cambridge: Cambridge University Press, 1983.

In a mainstream book about disequilibrium analysis, Joan Robinson is conspicuous by her absence. Neither listed in the index nor included among the references, Robinson is not mentioned or cited once. In what is essentially a Neoclassical work--this is a volume in the Econometric Society Monographs in Pure Theory--one would hardly expect many references to Robinson. But none at all?

[462] E. K. Hunt, "Joan Robinson and the Labour Theory of Value," *Cambridge Journal of Economics*, (7), 1983: 331-42. Reprinted in [484].

Ostensibly about Robinson's profound ambiguity toward the labor theory of value as revealed in her writings, the essay is actually a lengthy argument that the labor theory is superior to the orthodox theory of value.

[463] H. Gram and V. Walsh, "Joan Robinson's Economics in Retrospective," *Journal of Economic Literature*, 21(2), June, 1983: 518-50.

Reprinted in [484].

Despite the title, this essay, occasioned by the republication of Robinson's Collected Economic papers (1980), is not an exhaustive survey of her economics. Instead, Gram and Walsh focus their analysis on her macroeconomics or what has come to be called Post-Keynesian economics. Considerable attention is given to Robinson's concepts of equilibrium and disequilibrium as developed in her essay "A Model of Accumulation" [159b]. And the authors discuss not only the influences of Marshall and Keynes on Robinson but also her theory of international trade and her interpretation of Marx. Noticeably absent is any serious analysis of her economics of imperfect competition. The survey ends with an extensive bibliography of writings about Robinson's works.

[464] S. Chakravarty, "Joan Robinson: An Appreciation," *Economic and Political Weekly* (Bombay), October 1, 1983: 1712-16.

More than an appreciation, this essay is a glowing tribute to Robinson. It also is a good, short biography of her intellectual life, beginning with Keynes's "Circus," passing through Robinson's interest in Marx, and ending with her critique of the production function and her ideas on historical time, capital, and accumulation.

[465] S. Narasimhan, "Joan Robinson: In the Radical Vein: A Laywoman's Homage," *Cambridge Journal of Economics*, (7), 1983: 213-19.

A brief history of Robinson's life and works, filled with many personal anecdotes.

[466] A. Klamer, *Conversations with Economists*, Totowa, NJ: Rowman and Allanheld, 1984.

Robinson is not one of the eleven economists--new Classical economists and their critics--with whom Klamer has a conversation. She is cited, however, by several of the economists interviewed and thus merits a listing in the "Glossary of Names," where she is described as a prominent English Post-Keynesian economist who "did not yet receive a Nobel prize."

[467] A. S. Eichner, "Joan Robinson's Legacy," *Challenge*, May-June, 1984: 42-46.

Consistent with his Post-Keynesian perspective, Eichner concentrates his tribute to Joan Robinson on the significance of her book *The Accumulation of Capital* [111], a work that "seeks nothing less than to replace the traditional static analysis with a dynamic theory rooted in historical time."

[468] G. C. Harcourt, "The End of an Era: Joan Robinson (1903-1983) and Piero Sraffa (1898-1983)," *Journal of Post Keynesian Economics*, 6(3), Spring, 1984: 466-69.

A short lament on the deaths of Joan Robinson (August 5, 1983) and Piero Sraffa (September 3, 1983), both of whom were professional and personal friends of the author.

[469] A. Asimakopulos, "Joan Robinson and Economic Theory," *Banca Nazionale Del Lavoro Quarterly Review*, (151), December, 1984: 381-409. Reprinted as Chapter 9 in A. Asimakopulos, *Investment, Employment, and Income Distribution*, Boulder, CO: Westview Press, 1988.

A thorough, balanced analysis of five important areas of Joan Robinson's economics: the economics of imperfect competition, the theory of employment, the theory of accumulation in the long run, the concept of capital and the production function, and the problem of time in economics. While acknowledging the impact Marshall, Keynes, Sraffa, Kahn, and other Cambridge economists had on Robinson's intellectual development, Asimakopulos pays particular attention to the contributions of Michal Kalecki and Karl Marx, "the most important 'outside' influences on her work."

[470] M. C. Marcuzzo, "Joan Violet Robinson (1903-1983)," *Materiali di discussions*, Dipartimento di economia Politica, Universita Delgi Studi: Modena, Italy, 1985: 135 pages. An updated version of the bibliographic portion of this working paper can be found in I. H. Rima, editor, *The Joan Robinson Legacy* [482], Armonk, NY: M. E. Sharpe, 1991: 250-75.

This mimeographed working paper is divided into two parts: a biographical essay that traces the intellectual development and contributions of Robinson in a chronological fashion, and a chronological bibliography of works Robinson published. The biographical essay relies on Robinson's published output but also makes extensive use of letters and other materials found in Robinson's papers deposited in the Library of King's College at Cambridge University.

The unannotated bibliography is exhaustive or nearly so, referencing all of Robinson's major books and articles and most of the minor and truly obscure ones. There are references to works by Robinsons whose first names are James, Jay, or John. Nonetheless, the bibliography is complete and as free of errors as a document involving so much detail can be.

[471] M. Blaug, *Great Economists Since Keynes*, Totawa, NJ: Barnes and

Noble, 1985: 207-9.

One of the best precis of Robinson's life and her place in twentieth-century economic thought. A black-and-white photo of a mature Joan Robinson accompanies this essay.

[472] A Lindbeck, "The Prize in Economic Science in Memory of Alfred Nobel," *Journal of Economic Literature*, 23(1), March, 1985: 37-56.

Technically, the "Nobel Prize in Economics" is not a Nobel Prize. In his will, Alfred Nobel designated five fields for prizes: physics, chemistry, medicine or physiology, literature, and peace. In 1968, the Central Bank of Sweden endowed a new prize--The Central Bank of Sweden Prize in Economic Science in Memory of Alfred Nobel--to be awarded at the same time as the five original Nobels, creating the illusion of a "Nobel Prize in Economics."

In this essay, Lindbeck, a member of the Economics Prize Committee since 1969, describes the background, past recipients, procedures, and criteria for the award in such detail that, after reading the article, one is left wondering, "Why didn't Joan Robinson get the prize?"

[473] G. C. Harcourt, "On the Influence of Piero Sraffa on the Contributions of Joan Robinson to Economic Theory," *Economic Journal*, 96 (Supplement), 1986: 96-108.

As Harcourt sees it, the primary influence of Sraffa on Robinson was the former's interest in reviving Classical political economy, a latent but nevertheless important aspect of the Post-Keynesian movement, the origins of which can arguably be traced to Robinson. Despite the title of the article, Harcourt does not limit his analysis to the influence of Sraffa on Robinson. He also considers the impact of Marshall, Keynes, Kahn, Kalecki, and several Post-Keynesian contemporaries on Robinsonian economics.

[474] G. C. Harcourt, "On the Contributions of Joan Robinson and Piero Sraffa to Economic Theory," in O. F. Hamouda, editor, *Controversies in Political Economy: Selected Essays of G. C. Harcourt*, New York: New York University Press, 1986: 90-110. This essay is reprinted in M. Berg, editor, *Political Economy in the Twentieth Century*, Savage, MD: Barnes and Noble, 1990: 35-67.

Written by a professional economist for professional economists, this essay is a longer version of [473]. Although Harcourt, who knew and worked with both Robinson and Sraffa, provides some insights into their personalities, he concentrates most of his analysis on Robinsonian economics, particularly the theories expounded in *The Accumulation of Capital* [111]. Considering that book to be Robinson's magnum opus,

Harcourt discusses the book's four major themes and how they relate to the works of Sraffa and other noted economists. This essay cites many works about Robinsonian economics. There are numerous references to Robinson throughout the other essays in the Hamouda-edited book as well.

[475] G. R. Feiwel, "Intellectual Revolutions in Modern Economic Theory: Joan Robinson's Contributions and Challenges," *Keio Economic Studies*, 24(2), 1987: 47-86.

This article is a precursor of Feiwel's two-volume effort [479 and 480] to describe Robinson and her contributions and significance to modern economics. Feiwel laces his presentation with many long passages from Robinson's works, and in so doing allows Joan Robinson to tell her story in her own words. The article is a comprehensive review of Robinsonian thought and well within the grasp of anyone interested in her economics.

[476] G. W. Danford, "The Economics of Joan Robinson: A Study in Comparative Value Theory and Methodology," unpublished PhD thesis, Washington State University, Pullman, WA, 1987.

Believing that Robinson's theory of value and methodology have been misunderstood, Danford tries to set the record straight by reviewing Robinson's positions on the analytic method and comparing her approach to John Dewey's instrumentalism, with a dash of Thorstein Veblen's institutionalism thrown in for good measure.

[477] L. L. Pasinetti, "Joan Violet Robinson," *The New Palgrave Dictionary of Economics*, J. Eatwell, M. Milgates, and P. Newman, editors, London: Macmillan Press, 1987: vol. 4, pages 212-17.

Written by a fellow Post-Keynesian and personal friend, this biographical sketch contains basic information about Robinson, a unique section on "Distinctive Traits of Her Intellectual Personality," and a summary of her scientific achievements. This essay is readily accessible to the interested reader.

[478] A. Asimakopulos, "Kalecki and Robinson: An 'Outsider's' Influence," *Journal of Post Keynesian Economics*, 11(2), Winter, 1988-89: 261-78.

A detailed account of Kalecki's influence on Robinson's economics and her extension of Keynes' *General Theory*. Asimakopulos shows that Robinson incorporated and made her own Kalecki's "theory of distribution, the double-sided relation between profits and investments, and the general features of his mark-up theory of pricing for manufactured goods, along with the way in which it could be integrated into a macroeconomic model." While Robinson occasionally recognized the influence of Kalecki--"it was Michal Kalecki rather than I who brought imperfect competition into touch with the theory of employment" [005, 1969 edition, p. viii]-- she often labels as Keynesian concepts clearly Kaleckian.

[479] G. R. Feiwel, editor, *The Economics of Imperfect Competition and Employment: Joan Robinson and Beyond*, New York: New York University Press, 1989. See annotation for [480].

[480] G. R. Feiwel, editor, *Joan Robinson and Modern Economic Theory*, New York: New York University Press, 1989.

This book and its companion volume [479] are advertised as being "about Joan Robinson, her impact on modern economics, her challenges and critiques, and the advances made in the science and art of economics." The two volumes are certainly that and much more.

One book [479] is a collection of essays about imperfect competition and Post-Keynesian economics and how Robinson was able to combine the two into a unique school of thought. In the other book [480], the essays focus on Robinson's influence on modern economic theory, especially in the areas of capital, growth, distribution, and develop - ment and trade. The sheer volume of material in the two books is imposing: seventy-seven essays covering more than 1,000 pages, produced by seventy-eight authors writing individually or in groups. The quality of the scholarship is equally impressive: Eight of the contributors are Nobel Laureates in economics, several others will probably become so in the near future, and almost every author is a recognized scholar.

In putting together what is arguably the consummate work about the significance of Joan Robinson, Feiwel thoughtfully includes material about Robinson the person as well as Robinson the economist. The final part of [480] is titled "Veteris Vestigia Flammae" and contains reminiscences and tributes penned by fourteen personal and professional acquaintances of Robinson. Each book has a photographic plate of Robinson. The familiar picture of a mature Robinson can be found in [480], while [479] features a rare photo of Robinson as a young woman.

[481] M. S. Turner, *Joan Robinson and the Americans*, Armonk, NY: M. E. Sharpe, 1989.

Not the official biography of Joan Robinson--that is to be written by G. C. Harcourt, who is steward of Robinson's papers kept at Cambridge

University--this book is the most comprehensive biography of Robinson that is available at this time. The book is a chronological blending of Robinson's life and works. It has extensive footnotes and references, and ten black-and-white photographs of Joan Robinson.

1990s

[482] I. H. Rima, editor, *The Joan Robinson Legacy*, Armonk, NY: M. E. Sharpe, 1991.

Nineteen contributions by friends and/or followers of Joan Robinson dealing with virtually every aspect of Robinsonian economics. Included in this anthology are a biographical memoir, an overview of Robinson's Post-Keynesian economics, and the essay "Joan Robinson: Why Not a Nobel Laureate?" The last chapter in this book is Maria Cristina Marcuzzo's comprehensive bibliography [470] of Robinson's published writings.

[483] G. C. Harcourt, "Joan Robinson (1903-1983)," in P. Aresti, editor, *A Biographical Dictionary of Dissenting Economists*, Brookfield, VT: Elgar, 1991: 454-63.

In what is almost certainly a preview of the definitive Robinson biography he has pledged to write but has yet to publish, Harcourt discusses Robinson's life and works, her contributions and blindspots, and he does so with objective compassion.

[484] M. Blaug, editor, *Joan Robinson (1903-1983) and George Shackle (1903-1992)*, Brookfield, VT: Elgar, 1992. This book is No. 45 in the series "Pioneers in Economics."

There are eleven reprinted essays in this book, and the two that deal with Robinson can be found elsewhere [462 and 463]. The real value of this book is Blaug's introduction (pages ix-xi), half of which is devoted to Joan Robinson. Blaug concludes his comments about Robinson with this telling observation: "She is one of the best counter-examples of the generalization that all economists write badly: her style, marked by the frequent use of colloquialisms, rhetorical barbs, and a peculiar but intoxicating type of verbal algebra is a sheer delight to read. On the other hand, her admiration of Mao's China and Kim-Sung's North Korea was a continual embarrassment to her friends and foes alike."

[485] Z. Emani, "History versus Equilibrium: Joan Robinson on Teaching Economics," *International Journal of Social Economics*, 19 (10,11,12), 1992: 83-94.

Emani examines three major elements of Robinsonian economics--history versus equilibrium, conflict versus harmony, and the present as history--and then considers the implications of each on Robinson's approach to teaching.

[486] J. A. T. R. Araujo and G. C. Harcourt, "Maurice Dobbs, Joan Robinson and Gerald Shove on Accumulation and the Rate of Profit," *Journal of the History of Economic Thought*, 15(1), Spring, 1993: 1-30.

In his review [368] of Robinson's *An Essay on Marxian Economics* [049], Shove made a comment that sparked an exchange of letters among Shove, Robinson, and Dobb. Araujo and Harcourt mine those letters for the contents of this article and the addendum to the article, which is itself based on another cache of letters discovered after the original article was in page proofs.

[487] J. Keppler, *Monopolistic Competition Theory: Origins, Results, and Implications*, Baltimore, MD: Johns Hopkins University Press, 1994.

This book is an intellectual history of monopolistic competition theory, which at the height of its influence "provided a unique combination of theoretical progress, practical relevance, and desirable policy prescriptions." Although favoring Chamberlin's term (monopolistic competition) over Robinson's (imperfect competition), Keppler devotes extensive coverage to *The Economics of Imperfect Competition* [005], Robinson's major contribution to this branch of economic theory. While imperfect competition theory is subsumed in Keppler's study of monopolistic competition theory, it is distinguished from the latter. In addition to recognizing Robinson, Keppler also pays homage to the other participants in the development of this theory, including Allyn Young, Piero Sraffa, Richard Kahn, Roy Harrod, and Heinrich von Stackelberg.

[488] M.C. Marcuzzo, L. L. Pasinetti, and A. Roncaglia, editors, *The Economics of Joan Robinson*, New York, NY: Routledge, 1996.

The 26 essays in this book were selected from papers presented at a conference held in Turin in 1993 in memory of Joan Robinson. The contributions are wide-ranging and address various aspects of Robinson's work including the economics of imperfect competition, technical innovation and capital theory, and her preference for history over equilibrium as a medium of analysis. The book concludes with the fifth version of Marcuzzo's detailed bibliography of Joan Robinson's writings. The book is by professional economists for professional economists.

Index

Note: All references to works annotated in this book are framed by brackets. Entries [001] through [347] refer to works by Joan Robinson, while entries [348] through [488] refer to works about Joan Robinson and/or her writings.

—A—

Accumulation. *See* Capital accumulation
Advertising ethics, 48
Allen, P., 31; *The Cambridge Apostles*, 154
American Economics Association, xix, 23
An Essay on Marxian Economics [049], xviii, 11, 47, 124, 153
An Introduction to Modern Economics [265], 107
Araujo, J. A. T. R., "Maurice Dobbs, Joan Robinson and Gerald Shove on Accumulation and the Rate of Profit," 164
Aresti, P., (editor) *A Biographical Dictionary of Dissenting Economists*, 163
Arms race, 130
Arrow, Kenneth J., 83; criticism by Joan Robinson, 83; review [374] of *Collected Economic Papers*, Volume 1 [086], 138
Asimakopulos, A., xiv; "Joan Robinson and Economic Theory," 159; review [426] of *Economic Heresies: Some Old-Fashioned Questions in Economic Theory* [251], 149
Association for Education in Citizenship, 48

—B—

Balance of payments, 52, 53, 62, 78, 80, 92
Balance of trade, 68
Bancor plan, 50
Baran, P. A., review [393] of *Economic Philosophy* [158], 142
Barger, H., "Disguised Unemployment: A Comment," 135
Barna, T., review of [380] *The Accumulation of Capital* [111], 139
Barnard College, xix, 113
Baumol, William, 99
Becker, J. F., *Marxian Political Economy: An Outline*, 129
Bensusan-Butt, D., *Pre-Keynesian Theory: A Modest Defence*, 92
Berg, M., (editor) *Political Economy in the Twentieth Century*, 160
Bettelheim, C., *China Since Mao*, 125; *Problèmes Théoriques et Pratiques de*

la Planification, 61; *Questions sur la chine aprés la mort de Mao Tse-tung*, 120
Bharadwaj, K., xiii
Birth control, 70
Blaug, M., (editor) *Joan Robinson (1903-1983) and George Shackle (1903-1992)*, 163; *Great Economists Since Keynes*, 159
Borden, N. H., *The Economic Effects of Advertising*, 48
Boulding, K. E., xiv; review [397] of *Economic Philosophy* [158], 143
Breimyer, H. F., review [430] of *Economic Heresies* [251], 150
Bretherton, R. F., F. A. Burchardt, and R. S. G. Rutherford, *Public Investment and the Trade Cycle in Great Britain*, 47
Bretton Woods, 10, 57
Britain, and European Economic Community, 103; and laissez-faire economics, 146; crisis of 1966, 147; economic crisis, 144; trade with Soviet Union, 67
British Association for the Advancement of Science, 107
British Chancellor of the Exchequer, 50
British Oxygen Company, 68
Bronfenbrenner, M., 32; review [385] of *Collected Economic Papers,* Volume 2 [143], 141; review [452] of *Contributions to Modern Economics* [308], 155; review [456] of *Aspects of Development and Underdevelopment* [319], 156
Brun, E. and J. Hersh, *Socialist Korea: A Case Study in the Strategy of Economic Development*, 117
Brus, W., *The Market in a Socialist Economy*, 109
Buck, J. L., *Food and Agriculture in Communist China*, 94
Business Week, ix, 30, 152

—C—

Cairncross, A. K., *Factors in Economic Development*, 82
Cambridge (MA), xi, 12, 14, 15, 20; debate with Cambridge (UK), 74
Cambridge (UK), xi, 12, 13, 14, 15; debate with Cambridge (MA), 74
Cambridge Apostles, 154
Cambridge Economics Series, 154
Cambridge School of Anglo-Italian theory, 111
Cambridge University, xviii, 5, 7, 10, 12, 28, 29; Circus, xvii; secret society, 154
Capital, 15; accumulation, 8, 15, 72, 80, 98; and household savings, 112; and labor productivity, 139; and socialist economies, 98; problems of, 108; translation into algebra, 72; composition, 119; difficulties of concept, 72; definition, 73; marginal productivity, 15, 139; meaning and measurement, 100, 104; measurement, 15, 73, 102, 103, 139; socialization, 50; theory, 105, 110, 124, 146; value of, 73
Capitalism, British, 41; conditions necessary for growth, 68; government assisted, 86; health, 80; versus socialism, 82
Caste system, 35
Castro, Fidel, 78
Central Bank of Sweden, ix, 160
Ceylon. *See* Sri Lanka
Chakravarty, S., "Joan Robinson: An Appreciation," 158
Chamberlin, Edward H., 6; "'Full Cost' and Monopolistic Competition," 61, 137; compared to Joan Robinson, 145; imperfect competition, 144; *The Theory of Monopolistic Competition*, 6, 134, 144, 145
Chase, E. T., review [411] of *Economics: An Awkward Corner* [204], 146
Chaudhuri, Sachin, memorial to, 94
Cheng, C., *Communist China Economy*, 86
Chicago School, 101
China, x, xviii, 21, 30, 81, 83, 87, 89, 108; agriculture, 92, 93; and socialism, 90; and Western Press, 83; birth control, 70; changes since Mao, 125; commune system, 84, 86, 100, 114; development of, 92; role in Great Leap Forward, 92; structure of, 85; commune system, reorganization, 144; compared to India, 87, 97; conditions, 95; criticism of, 84; Cultural Revolution, 86, 97, 98, 114,

146, 147; economic condition, 86, 104; economic development, 83; 1840-1937, 95; 1933-1959, 90; 1949-1958, 76; economic policy, 100; economic system, 90, 104; educational system, 116; foreign investment, 1840-1937, 95; historical background, 95; hyper-inflationary period, 95; impressions and insights, 114; inflation 1937-1949, 86; wartime, 95; minorities in Yunnan, 111; observations by Joan Robinson, 69; point of view, 84; portrayal of life in, 96; relations with the West, 95; Sino-Indian border dispute, 144; steel industry, 93; the 1960s, 100; threats to India, 83; views of Bettelheim, 120; visits by Joan Robinson, 84, 104
Chi-Yi, C., *La Reforme Agraire en China Populaire*, 93
Chossudowsky, E. M., review [366] of *An Essay on Marxian Economics* [049], 136
Chou, S. H., *The Chinese Inflation, 1937-1949*, 86
Christian Socialist, 2
Circus, 7, 112, 125
Clower, R., review [386] of *Exercises in Economic Analysis* [144], 141
Cohen, Ruth, 16
Cold war, 70, 130; masking of problems, 80; politics, 67
Cole, G. D. H., *The Means to Full Employment*, 51
Collier, E. and J., *China's Socialist Revolution*, 113
Colonialism, 123
Commission on Monopolies and Restrictive Practices, 10
Committee on Resale Price Maintenance, 85
Consumption, 80
Cooperative farm, model, 94
Copper, F., review [418] of *The Cultural Revolution in China* [235], 147
Corina, J., review [409] of *Economics: An Awkward Corner* [204], 145
Crook, I. and D., *First Years of Yangyi Commune*, 92
Crowther, G., *Ways and Means of War*, 46
Cuba, 21, 78, 90
Cultural Revolution, 86, 114; causes and meaning, 97; description, 113; firsthand account by Joan Robinson, 100; impact on economic system, 104; perspective of Mao Tse-tung's supporters, 98
Czechoslovakia, 93, 97

—D—

da Empoli, A., *Theory of Equilibrium*, 38
Dalton, Hugh, collaborated with Joan Robinson, 4
Danford, Gerald W., xiv; "The Economics of Joan Robinson: A Study in Comparative Value Theory and Methodology," 161
Das-Gupta, A. K., *Planning and Economic Growth*, 92
David Kinley Lecture at University of Illinois, xix, 126
Davidson, P., xiv; "Post Keynesian Economics," 155
de Schweinitz, K., review [443] of *Introduction to Modern Economics* [265], 153
de Vere, Edward, 37
Deane, P., xiv; *The Evolution of Economic Ideas*, 153
Defense spending, 70
Demand curve, discontinuous, 6, 36
Demand theory, effective, 128
Demand, aggregate, 126; and full employment, 55; avoidance of economic slumps, 130
Demand, law of, 16
Determinacy, 43
Development theory, 65, 157
Dewey, John, 161
Disequilibrium, 11, 57, 157
Disinvestment, 43
Distribution of income, 74, 76, 83, 95, 112
Distribution, problems of, 108
Distribution, theory of, 69, 94, 98, 102
Dobb, M., *Soviet Economic Development Since 1917*, 56; *Soviet Economy and the War*, 47
Domar, Evsey, model of cooperative farm, 94
Double switching. *See* Reswitching

Duopoly, 38
Dynamic economics, 11, 74

—E—

Eatwell, J., "Joan Robinson: Portrait," 153
Eatwell, John, co-author of *An Introduction to Modern Economics*, 107
Economic accumulation and production function, 73
Economic analysis using history and culture, 127
Economic growth, 14, 142
Economic Heresies: Some Old-Fashioned Questions in Economic Theory [251], 102, 148, 149, 150
Economic Philosophy [158], xviii, 22, 79, 142, 143, 149
Economic theory, 67; and equilibrium, 77; and time, logical and historical, 129; classical focus, 110; philosophical basis, 79; shortcomings, 62; conflicts with religion, 131; derivation of, 76; evolution, 121
Economics of naivete, 71
Economics Tripos, 3
Economists, classical, 25, 158; Continental, 35; English, 35; Soviet, treatment of Keynes and Kalecki, 101
Edwards, C. D., review [352] of *The Economics of Imperfect Competition* [005], 134
Effective demand, 120; and Keynes, 125
Eichner, Alfred S., 28; "Joan Robinson's Legacy," 158; and Post-Keynesian economics, 29
Eichner, Alfred S. and J. A. Kregel, "An Essay on Post-Keynesian Theory: A New Paradigm in Economics," 152
Elasticity of substitution, 40
Ellis, H. S., *German Monetary Theory*, 39
Ellsworth, P. T., review [363] of *Introduction to the Theory of Employment* [033], 136
Emani, Z., "History versus Equilibrium: Joan Robinson on Teaching Economics," 163
Emmanuel, A., *Unequal Exchange: A Study of the Imperialism of Trade*, 109
Employment, 105, 115; theory, 8, 17, 18, 90, 105, 159
Environmental economics, 108
Equilibrium, 11, 14, 15, 27, 43, 108; growth models, 78; in historical analysis, 128; irrelevancy, 78; Pasinetti's model, 144
Eschag, E., review [408] of *Collected Economic Papers,* Volume 3 [195], 145
Euler's Theorem, 15, 38
European Economic Community, 26, 103
Exchange depreciation, 45
Exchange economy, 70
Exchange rates, 40, 43
Exercises in Economic Analysis, 76

—F—

Fairbank, J. K., E. O. Reischauer, and A. M. Craig, *East Asia: Tradition and Transformation*, 113
Federation of British Industries, 49, 50
Feinstein, C. H., (editor) *Socialism, Capitalism and Economic Growth: Essays in Honor of Maurice Dobb*, 93
Feiwel, George R., xiv; (editor) *Joan Robinson and Modern Economic Theory*, 162; (editor) *The Economics of Imperfect Competition and Employment: Joan Robinson and Beyond*, 162; *The Intellectual Capital of Michal Kalecki*, 113
Ferguson, C. E., "Capital Theory Up-To-Date: A Comment on Mrs. Robinson's Article," 148; rebuttal to Robinson, 102, 148; *The Neoclassical Theory of Production and Distribution*, 100, 148
Findlay, R., xiv; "A Reply," 143; mathematical model, 83
Fiscal policy, Keynesian, 126
Fisher, Franklin M., 103; "The Existence of Aggregate Producton Functions," 102; *Disequilibrium Foundations of Equilibrium Economics*, 157; praise by Joan Robinson, 30
Foster, J., review [460] of *Contributions to Modern Economics* [308], 157; review [460] of *Generalization of the General Theory* [320], 157

Free trade, 92, 156
Friedman, Milton, 155; compared to Joan Robinson, 142; Nobel Prize, 32
Frisch, R., co-author of "Draft of a Multilateral Trade Clearing Agency," 80; *Planning for India*, 81
Full employment, 15, 42, 48, 50, 51, 155; and balance of payments, 78; and inflation, 68, 78; effects of, 110; obstacles, 53; post-WWII, 68

—G—

Galbraith, John Kenneth, xix, 21, 30; *American Capitalism: The Concept of Countervailing Power*, 62; relationship with Joan Robinson, 23
Garegnani, P., "Notes on Consumption, Investment, and Effective Demand: A Reply to Joan Robinson," 154
General Theory, 77, 78, 103, 108, 124
George, Lloyd, 1
Germany, post-WWI hyperinflation, 45
Giffen paradox, 16
Gildersleeve Lecture, 113
Gillman, Dr., *The Falling Rate of Profit*, 72
Girton College, xvii, 2, 3
Gold standard, 50, 62
Goodwin, R. M., review [370] of *The Rate of Interest and Other Essays* [089], 137
Gottheil, F. M., *Marx Economic Predictions*, 97
Graham, F. D., (editor) *Planning and Paying for Full Employment*, 55
Gram, H., xiv
Gram, H. and V. Walsh, "Joan Robinson's Economics in Retrospective," 157
Great Depression, 5, 6, 40, 52, 71, 79, 91, 104, 116
Great Leap Forward of 1958, 84, 86, 92
Gross Domestic Product, 15
Grossman, G., *Economic Systems*, 96
Growth, 56; criticism of models, 81; Harrod's model, 65; purpose, 117; unbalanced, 99
Guidelines of Project Evaluation, 115
Guillebaud, C. W., review [367] of *Private Enterprise or Public Control* [050], 137
Gurley, J., xiv; "The State of Political Economics," 148; review [436] of *Introduction to Modern Economics* [265], 151

—H—

Haavelmo, T., 77
Hahn, F. H., review [477] of *Economic Heresies: Some Old-Fashioned Questions in Economic Theory* [251], 149
Hall, R. L., *The Economic System in a Socialist State*, 44
Hamberg, D., review [400] of *Essays in the Theory of Economic Growth* [159], 143
Hamouda, O. F., (editor) *Controversies in Political Economy: Selected Essays of G. C. Harcourt*, 160
Hansen, Alvin, 93; *A Guide to Keynes*, 44
Harcourt, G. C., 20, 31, 162, 164; "Joan Robinson," 154; "Joan Robinson (1903-1983)," 163; "On the Contribution of Joan Robinson and Pierro Sraffa to Economic Theory," 160; "On the Influence of Pierro Sraffa on the Contributions of Joan Robinson to Economic Theory," 160; "Some Cambridge Controversies in the Theory of Capital," 146; "The End of an Era: Joan Robinson (1903-1983) and Pierro Sraffa (1898-1983)," 159; review [387] of *Exercises in Economic Analysis* [144], 141
Hardy, C. O., review [359] of *Essays in the Theory of Employment* [032], 135; review [362] of *Introduction to the Theory of Employment* [033], 136
Harris, S. E., *Economics of Social Security*, 48; *Exchange Depreciation*, 45
Harrod's knife-edge, 88
Harrod, R. F., "A Further Note on Decreasing Costs," 134; dynamic analysis, 101; growth model, 101; link between Keynes and Hobson, 56; response to his criticism, 37; *The Trade Cycle*, 41; *Toward a Dynamic Economics*, 55
Harrod-Domar assumption, 139
Harvard University, xix, 6, 10, 23

Hawtrey, R. G., review [361] of *Essays in the Theory of Employment* [032], 136
Hayek, controversy with Keynes, 36
Heilbroner, R., *Beyond Boom and Crash*, 120
Hicks, John, 40
Hicks, Marshall, 50
Hilferding, R., *Bohm-Bawerk's Criticism of Marx*, 57
Hoarding, 45
Horsefield, J. K., *The Real Cost of the War*, 46
Houston, D., review [439] of *Introduction to Modern Economics* [265], 152
Hughes, T. J. and D. E. T. Luard, *The Economic Development of Communist China 1949-1958*, 76
Hunt, E. K., "Joan Robinson and the Labour Theory of Value," 157
Hyperinflation, 58; China, 95; post-WWI Germany, 45

—I—

Imperfect competition, 6, 7, 17, 36, 38, 48, 71, 74, 95, 112, 134, 136, 137, 140, 144, 145, 154, 158, 159, 164; and effective demand analysis, 115; and Keynesian theory, 92; and Post-Keynesian economics, 162
Income distribution. *See* Distribution of income
Increasing returns, 39
India, 3, 87; and orthodox economics, 76; compared to China, 87; economic development, compared to China, 97; economic planning, 81; five-year plans, 66, 67; military and economic threats, 83; planning, mathematical, 112; stagnation, 1949-1964, 87; threats from China, 83
Induced investment, 77
Inflation, and full employment, 68, 78, 110; and unemployment, 70, 126; inability to control, 91; post-WWII, 54; rate of, 131; stages of, 58; wartime, 46
Input/output analysis, 96
Interest rates, determinants, 59; determination of time-shape, 75
International Monetary Fund, 52
International trade, and orthodox economics, 107; classical model, 54; development of theory, 110
International Year of the Woman, ix, 152
Introduction to the Theory of Employment [033], xviii, 8, 44, 136
Investment, 8, 36, 46

—J—

Jaffe, W., review [394] of *Economic Philosophy* [158], 142
Jameson, K. P., review [459] of *Aspects of Development and Underdevelopment* [319], 157
Jensen, H. E., xiii, 4
Johnson, H. G., 13, 81; *Money, Trade and Economic Growth*, 81; review [407] of *Economics: An Awkward Corner* [204], 145
Johnson, Lyndon B., and Keynesian economics, 20
Jones, G. T., *Increasing Returns*, 39
Journal of Post Keynesian Economics, xix

—K—

Kahn, Richard F., 36; and Circus, 7; *L'occupazione e la Crescita*, 112
Kaldor, Nicholas, 69, 98; "Mrs. Robinson's 'Economics of Imperfect Competition'," 135
Kalecki, Michal, xviii, 26, 69, 71, 112, 157; and WWII, 46; anticipation of Keynesian revolution, 91; compared to Keynes, 112, 115; employment theory, 90; *Essays in the Theory of Economic Fluctuations*, 48; *Essays on Developing Economies*, 112; general theory, 117; influence on Joan Robinson, 17, 159, 161; Memorial Lecture, 115; Rockefeller Scholarship, 17; *Selected Esssays in the Dynamics of a Capitalist Economy*, 103; theory of unemployment, 17
Kantorovich, Leonid, ix
Keirstead, B. S., *Capital, Interest and Profits*, 77; review [379] of *The Accumulation of Capital* [111], 139;

"The Structure and Accumulation of Capital," 139
Kennedy, John F., and Keynesian economics, 20
Keppler, J., 4, 7; *Monopolistic Competition Theory: Origins, Results, and Implications*, 164
Keynes, John Maynard, xvii, xviii, 3, 7, 10, 12, 14, 23, 151; and WWII, 46; compared to Kalecki, 112, 115; compared to Marshall, 64; compared to Marx, 55, 64, 138; controversy with Hayek, 36; influence on Joan Robinson, 17; praise by Joan Robinson, 35; *The General Theory of Employment, Interest and Money*, 7, 38, 42; *The Treatise on Money*, 7, 38; understanding of Marx and Kalecki, 47
Keynesian economic theory, philosophical basis, 79; shortcomings, 62
Keynesians, "bastard," 11, 14, 20, 21, 32, 91, 108, 113, 152
Kirby, E. S., (editor) *Contemporary China*, 81
Klamer, A., *Conversations with Economists*, 158
Klappholz, K., review [396] of *Economic Philosophy* [158], 143
Klein, L. R., criticism of Joan Robinson, 140; review [382] of *The Accumulation of Capital* [111], 73, 140
Knight, A. W., *Abolish Slumps: A Diagnosis of the Trade Cycle*, 44
Knox, A. D., review [372] of *The Rate of Interest and Other Essays* [089], 138
Koopmans, Tjalling C., ix
Korea, North, x, 21, 30, 87, 117; admiration by Joan Robinson, 163; economic miracle, 21, 89; visit in 1964, 89
Korea, South, 89, 117
Kregel, J. A., xiv; *The Reconstruction of Political Economy: An Introduction to Post-Keynesian Economics*, 108, 150
Kurihara, K. K., (editor) *Post Keynesian Economics*, 138; *The Keynesian Theory of Economic Development*, 72

—L—

Labor theory of value, 14, 64, 117, 157
Laissez-faire economics, 9, 39, 41, 71, 86; shortcomings, 87
Lancaster, K., review [384] of *The Accumulation* of *Capital* [111], 140
Lange, Oskar, 89; criticism by Joan Robinson, 91
Larry, H. B. and Associates, (editors) *The United States in the World Economy*, 52
Lattimore, O., review [412] of *The Cultural Revolution in China* [235], 146
League of Nations, International Currency Experience, 53
Leijonhufvud, A., *Information and Coordination: Essays in Macroeconomic Theory*, 130; *On Keynesian Economics and the Economics of Keynes*, 99
Lekachman, Robert, 91; "Introduction" to *Economics: An Awkward Corner*, 145; *The Age of Keynes*, 93
Leontief, Wassily, *Essays in Economics: Theories and Theorizing*, 96; *Input-Output Economics*, 97; *The Structure of American Economy, 1919-1929: An Empirical Application*, 11
Lerner, A. P., (editor) *Planning and Paying for Full Employment*, 55; review [381] of *The Accumulation of Capital* [111], 139
Lindbeck, A., "The Prize in Economic Science in Memory of Alfred Nobel," 160
Liquidity, general, 77
Liquidity preference, 78
Lloyd Jacob Committee on Resale Price Maintenance, 85
London Conference of Town Planning, 52
Long-period analysis, 128
Luxemburg, Rosa, *The Accumulation of Capital* [087], 59
Lynch, D., *The Concentration of Economic Power*, 56

—M—

Macroeconomics, 7; equilibrium, 108; history, 126
Mager, H., review [365] of *An Essay on Marxian Economics* [049], 136
Maharajah of Gwailor, xvii, 3

Mahloudji, F., xiv; "A Critical Examination of the Economics of Joan Robinson," 152
Mainstream economics, 13, 14; and *The Accumulation of Capital*, 18
Mao Tse-tung, 111, 114, 124, 125
Marchant, L. R., *The Phoenix Seat: An Introductory Study of Maoism and the Chinese Communist Quest for a Paradise on Earth*, 111
Marcuzzo, M. C., xiii, 18, 163; "Joan Violet Robinson (1903-1983)," 159; unannotated listings, 33
Marginal productivity, 14, 15, 30, 87, 95, 128
Marginal revenue, 6, 36
Marglin, S. A., review [431] of *Economic Heresies* [251], 150
Market system, 88, 123
Marsh, Frederick Howard, 2
Marsh, Helen Margaret, 1
Marsh, Jane Perceval, 2
Marshall, Alfred, xvii, 3, 14, 36; compared to Keynes and Marx, 64; dynamics of Marshallian economics, 60; influence on Joan Robinson, 17; short-period analysis, 60; theory of value, 6
Marshall, H. D., *The Great Economists: A History of Economic Thought*, 144
Marshallian economics, 5, 60
Marx, Karl, x, 9, 14, 138; analysis of unemployment, 47; as prophet, 81; compared to Keynes, 138; compared to Marshall and Keynes, 64; comparison with Samuelson, 26; dynamics of Marxism, 60; influence on Joan Robinson, 17, 159; labor theory of value, 57, 97; *The Poverty of Philosophy*, 66
Marxian economic theory, 121; capital accumulation, 67; combined with Sraffa and Kalecki, 122; composition of capital, 119; criticism by Joan Robinson, 128; economic interpretation of history, 67; idealogical contamination, 108; interplay of class interests and technology, 67; religious aspects, 81; review of, 48; shortcomings, 62; stages of history, 67
Massachusetts Institute of Technology, 10
Maurice debate, 1
Maurice, Frederick D., 1, 2, 154
Maurice, Joan Violet. *See* Robinson, Joan
Maynard, G., *Economic Development and the Price Level*, 82
Meade, J. E., 7; *A Neo-Classical Theory of Economic Growth*, 78
Meek, R. L., *Studies in the Theory of Value*, 117
Michal Kalecki Memorial lecture, 115
Microeconomic theory, 6, 8, 36
Minhas, B. S., *An International Comparison of Factor Costs and Factor Use*, 85
Minsky, H., review [388] of *Collected Economic Papers*, Volume 2 [143], 141
Mirrlees-Kaldor model, 98
Monetarists, 39
Monetary policy, 62, 77
Monopolistic competition, 7, 164
Monopoly, 7, 18, 67, 68
Monopsony, 144
Montias, J. M., *Central Planning in Poland*, 82
Morgan, E. V., *The Conquest of Unemployment*, 55
Morgan, T., *Income and Employment*, 55
Morison, Dorothea, coauthor of "Beauty and the Beast," 59
Moscow Economic Conference, 13
Moscow University, 71
Moszer, M., review [425] of *Economic Heresies* [251], 149
Moussa, P., *The Underprivileged Nations*, 82
Multiplier-accelerator interaction, 41
Myrdal, Gunnar, *Against the Stream*, 109; *Asian Drama: An Inquiry into the Poverty of Nations*, 97; *Report from a Chinese Village*, 96

—N—

Narasimhan, S., "Joan Robinson: In the Radical Vein: A Laywoman's Homage," 158
National Economic Committee, 56
National Peace Council, 51
National Planning Council, xviii, 71
Nemmers, E. E., *Hobson and Under Consumption*, 69

Neoclassical economic theory, 11, 14, 92, 101, 110; compared to Neoclassical theory, 152; criticism, 102; fusion with Keynes, 10; philosophical basis, 79; real agenda, 103; shortcomings, 100
Neoclassical production function, 16; application to third-world economies, 115; limitations, 63; shortcomings, 115
Neo-Neoclassical economic theory, 93, 127
Netherlands School of Economics, 86
Nevile, J. W., review [398] of *Essays in the Theory of Economic Growth* [159], 143
New Deal, 50
Newman, P., 161
New mercantilism, 92
Nichols, A. J., review [355] of *The Economics of Imperfect Competition* [005], 135
Nobel Prize, Economics, ix, 12, 15, 20, 30, 32, 160
Nobel, Alfred, ix
Norris, R. T., *The Theory of Consumers' Demand*, 50

—O—

O'Malley, L. S. S., *Indian Caste Customs*, 35
Oligopoly, 67
Orthodox economics, 6, 9, 13, 14, 16, 41, 44, 78, 85, 95, 102, 149; and international trade, 107; and *The Accumulation of Capital*, 18; criticism of, 107, 115; irrelevance, 110; shortcomings, 117; value to India, 76

—P—

Paish, F. W., "Reducing Internal Demand," 54
Pasinetti, Luigi L., ix, 102, 161; *Growth and Income Distribution: Essays in Economic Theory*, 111
Patinkin, D., 125
Patinkin, D. and J. C. Leith, (editors) *Keynes, Cambridge and the General Theory*, 125
Peace Aims Conference, 51
Pelissier, R., *The Awakening of China, 1793-1949*, 95
Penrose, E., review [455] of *Aspects of Development and Underdevelopment* [319], 156
Perceval, Spencer, 2
Perfect competition, 6, 39, 64
Perkins, D. H., *Market Control and Planning in Communist China*, 94
Pigou, A. C., 36; "A Note on Imperfect Competition," 133; praise by Joan Robinson, 35; theory of value, 35
Planned economies, 89
Plastrik, S., review [401] of *Notes from China* [178], 144
Poland, central planning, 82
Political trade cycle, 81, 103, 113, 117. *See* Kalecki, Michal
Population growth and economic prosperity, 71
Portisch, H., *Eyewitness in China*, 95
Post-Keynesian economics, 12, 26, 28, 74, 76, 110; and Kalecki, Michal, 17; compared to Neoclassical economics, 152; epistemology, 121; origins, 16, 26, 60
Prices, competition, 85; demand and supply, 80; determination, 76; function, 66; philosophy, 70, 74; theory, 36; under capitalism, 74; under planned economy, 74
Private enterprises, 82
Production function, 15, 60, 73, 81, 87, 146, 159; aggregate, 14, 16, 21, 30, 102, 104; and economic accumulation, 73; and historical data, 75; and nature of time, 77; Cobb/Douglas, 80; criticism, 81; problem of measuring capital, 65; pseudo, 16, 128, 149; validity, 65
Production theory, 100, 125
Profits, 15, 61, 80
Public enterprises, 82

—Q—

Quantity theory of money, 38, 73, 101

—R—

Radcliffe Report, 77

Radford, A., *Patterns of Economic Activity*, 41
Reagan, Ronald, 27
Resale maintenance, 85
Reswitching, 16, 95, 100, 111, 116, 151, 156
Returns to scale, 37
Review [358] of *Essays in the Theory of Employment* [032], 135
Review [360] of *Essays in the Theory of Employment* [032], 136
Review [364] of *An Essay on Marxian Economics* [049], 136
Review [389] of *Essays in the Theory of Economic Growth* [159], 141
Review [395] of *Essays in the Theory of Economic Growth* [159], 142
Review [403] of *Economics: An Awkward Corner* [204], 144
Review [416] of *Freedom and Necessity* [241], 147
Review [417] of *Freedom and Necessity* [241], 147
Review [419] of *Freedom and Necessity* [241], 147
Review [420] of *Freedom and Necessity* [241], 148
Review [424] of *Economic Heresies: Some Old-Fashioned Questions in Economic Theory* [251], 149
Review [433] of *After Keynes* [266], 150
Review [434] of *An Introduction to Modern Economics* [265], 151
Review [435] of *After Keynes* [266], 151
Review [438] of *An Introduction to Modern Economics* [265], 152
Review [448] of *Contributions to Modern Economics* [308], 154
Review [454] of *Aspects of Development and Underdevelopment* [319], 155
Reviewed by Joan Robinson, Angell, N., *The Money Mystery*, 41; Becker, J. F., *Marxian Political Economy*, 129; Bettelheim, C., J. Charriere, and H. Marchisto, *La Construction du Socialisme en China*, 90; Bettelheim, Charles, *China Since Mao*, 125; Bettelheim, Charles, *Problèmes Théoriques et Pratiques de la Planification*, 61; Bettelheim, Charles, *Questions sur la chine aprés la mort de Mao Tse-tung*, 120; Borden, N. H., *The Economic Effects of Advertising*, 48; Bresciani-Turroni, C., *The Economics of Inflation*, 45; Bretherton, R. F., F. A. Burchardt, and R. S. G. Rutherford, *Public Investment and the Trade Cycle in Great Britain*, 47; *Britain Without Capitalists*, 41; Brun, E. and J. Hersh, *Socialist Korea: A Case Study in the Strategy of Economic Development*, 117; Brus, W., *The Market in a Socialist Economy*, 109; Buck, J. L., *Food and Agriculture in Communist China*, 94; Cairncross, A. K., *Factors in Economic Development*, 82; Chenery, H., et al., *Structural Change and Development Policy*, 130; Cheng, C., *Communist China Economy*, 86; Chi-Yi, C., *La Réforme Agraire en Chine Populaire*, 93; Chou, S. H., *The Chinese Inflation, 1937-1949*, 86; Clay, H., *The Problem of Industrial Relations*, 34; Cole, G. D. H., *The Means to Full Employment*, 51; Collier, E. and J., *China's Socialist Revolution*, 113; Crook, I. and D., *First Years of Yangyi Commune*, 92; Crowther, G., *Ways and Means of War*, 46; da Empoli, A., *Theory of Equilibrium*, 38; Das-Gupta, A. K., *Planning and Economic Growth*, 92; Dobb, M., *Soviet Economic Development Since 1917*, 56; Dobb, M., *Soviet Economy and the War*, 47; Einzig, P., *Bankers, Statesmen and Economist*, 40; Ellis, H. S., *German Monetary Theory*, 39; Emmanuel, A., *Unequal Exchange: A Study of the Imperialism of Trade*, 109; Fairbank, J. K., E. O. Reischauer, and A. M. Craig, *East Asia: Tradition and Transformation*, 114; Ferguson, C. E., *The Neoclassical Theory of Production and Distribution*, 101; Frisch, R., *Planning for India*, 81; Galbraith, J. K., *American Capitalism: The Concept of Countervailing Power*, 62; Gjottheil, F. M., *Marx Economic Predictions*, 97; Grossman, G., *Economic Systems*, 96; Hall, R. L., *The Economic System in a*

Socialist State, 44; Harris, S. E., *Economics of Social Security*, 48; Harris, S. E., *Exchange Depreciation*, 45; Harrod, R. F., *The Trade Cycle*, 41; Harrod, R. F., *Toward a Dynamic Economics*, 55; Heilbroner, R., *Beyond Boom and Crash*, 120; Hilferding, R., *Bohm-Bawerk's Criticism of Marx*, 57; Horsefield, J. K., *The Real Cost of the War*, 46; Hou, C. M., *Foreign Investment and Economic Development in China, 1840-1937*, 94; Hughes, T. J. and D. E. T. Luard, *The Economic Development of Communist China 1949-1958*, 76; Johnson, H. G., *Money, Trade and Economic Growth*, 81; Jones, G. T., *Increasing Returns*, 39; Kalecki, M., *Selected Essays in the Dynamics of a Capitalist Economy*, 103; Keirstead, B. S., *Capital, Interest and Profits*, 77; Kirby, E. S., *Contemporary China*, 81; Knight, A. W., *Abolish Slumps: A Diagnosis of the Trade Cycle*, 44; Kurihara, K. K., *The Keynesian Theory of Economic Development*, 72; Larry, H. B. and Associates, (editors) *The United States in the World Economy*, 52; League of Nations, International Currency Experience, 53; Leijonhufvud, A., *Information and Coordination: Essays in Macroeconomic Theory*, 130; Leijonhufvud, A., *On Keynesian Economics and the Economics of Keynes*, 99; Lekachman, R., *The Age of Keynes*, 93; Leontief, W., *Essays in Economics: Theories and Theorizing*, 96; Leontief, W., *Input-Output Economics*, 97; Lerner, A. P. and F. D. Graham, (editors) *Planning and Paying for Full Employment*, 55; Lester, R. A., *Monetary Experiments*, 46; Liu, T. C. and K. C. Yeh, *The Economy of the Chinese Mainland: National Income and Economic Development, 1933-1959*, 90; Lynch, D., *The Concentration of Economic Power*, 56; Mao Tse-tung, *A Critique of Soviet Economics*, 124; Marchant, L.R., *The Phoenix Seat: An Introductory Study of Maosim and the Chinese Communist Quest for a Paradise on Earth*, 111; Marx, Karl, *The Poverty of Philosophy*, 67; Maynard, G., *Economic Development and the Price Level*, 82; Meade, J. E., *The Rate of Interest in a Progressive State*, 38; Meek, R. L., *Studies in the Theory of Value*, 117; Minhas, B. S., *An International Comparison of Factor Costs and Factor Use*, 85; Moggridge, D. (editor), *The Collected Writings of John Maynard Keynes. Volume XXIV. The General Theory and After--A Supplement*, 129; Montias, J. M., *Central Planning in Poland*, 82; Morgan, E.V., *The Conquest of Unemployment*, 55; Morgan, T., *Income and Employment*, 55; Moussa, P., *The Underprivileged Nations*, 82; Myrdal, G., *Against the Stream*, 109; Myrdal, G., *An Inquiry into the Poverty of Nations*, 97; Myrdal, G., *Monetary Equilibrium*, 45; Myrdal, G., *Report from a Chinese Village*, 96; Nemmers, E. E., *Hobson and Under Consumption*, 69; Norris, R. T., *The Theory of Consumers' Demand*, 50; O'Malley, L. S. S., *Indian Caste Customs*, 35; Oxford Institute of Statistics, *The Economics of Full Employment*, 53; Pasinetti, L. L., *Growth and Income Distribution: Essays in Economic Theory*, 111; Patinkin, D. and J. C. Leith, (editors) *Keynes, Cambridge and the General Theory*, 125; Pelissier, R., *The Awakening of China, 1793-1949*, 95; Perkins, D. H., *Market Control and Planning in Communist China*, 94; Pierson, J. H. G., *Full Employment*, 48; Portisch, H., *Eyewitness in China*, 95; Radford, A., *Patterns of Economic Activity*, 41; Reynolds, L. G., *The Three Worlds of Economics*, 109; Rowse, A. L., *Mr. Keynes and the Labor Movement*, 42; Rudra, A., *Indian Plan Models*, 112; Rymes, T. K., *On Concepts of Capital and Technical Change*, 104; Schlesinger, R., *Changing Attitudes in Soviet Russia:*

The Family, 56; Schumpeter, Joseph A., *Capitalism, Socialism and Democracy*, 51; Shaffery, H. G., *The Soviet Economy: A Collection of Western and Soviet Views*, 86; Shivji, I. G., *Class Struggles in Tanzania*, 113; Solow, Robert, *Growth Theory, An Exposition*, 104; Sraffa, P., *Production of Commodities by Means of Commodities*, 77; Steedman, I., *Marx after Sraffa*, 120; Strachey, J., *Contemporary Capitalism*, 67; Strachey, John, *The Nature of Capitalistic Crisis*, 40; Tsuru, S., *Has Capitalism Changed?*, 79; Turner, C. B., *An Analysis of Soviet Views on John Maynard Keynes*, 101; von Bohm-Bawerk, *Karl Marx and the Close of his System*, 57; von Bortkiewecz, L., *On the Correction of Marx's Fundamental Theoretical Construction in the Third Volume of Capital*, 57; Walker, K. R., *Planning in Chinese Agriculture*, 92; Wicksteed, P. H., *The Coordination of the Laws of Distribution*, 37; Wiles, P. J. D., *The Political Economy of Communism*, 91; Wilkinson, R. G., *Poverty and Progress*, 109; Wilson, T., *Fluctations in Income and Employment*, 49; Wolfson, M., *A Reappraisal of Marxian Economics*, 96; Wootton, B., *Freedom Under Planning*, 52; Wu, Y. L., *The Steel Industry in Communist China*, 93; Wu, Y. L., *The Economy of Communist China*, 94; Young, A. N., *China's Wartime Finance and Inflation, 1937-1945*, 94; Zeitlin, L., *Life's Value in Cash*, 84

Reynolds, L. G., *The Three Worlds of Economics*, 109

Ricardian rent, 74

Richard T. Ely Lecture, xix, 23, 104

Rima, I. H., xiii; (editor) *The Joan Robinson Legacy*, 159, 163

Robertson, Dennis, 12

Robinson, Austin, xvii, 3, 7, 29

Robinson, Joan, "Theory of Long-Run Development," 65; 1930-1939, 9; 1940-1949, 9; academic progression, 29; admiration of North Korea, 163; alternative to monopolistic capitalism, 49; *An Essay on Marxian Economics*, 11; and Garegnani, 124; and Keynesian movement, 8; and mainstream economics, 13; and male chauvinism, 29; and purpose of employment, 24; and Rosa Luxemburg, 59; and the gold standard, 50; approach to teaching, 164; approaches to economics, 35; as publisher, 98; biases, 48; bibliography, 159; biography, 154, 158, 159, 160, 162; book reviews, 34; Christian Socialist, 4; comment on *Pre-Keynesian Theory: A Modest Defence*, 92; compared to Chamberlin, 144, 145; compared to Harrod and Kaldor, 141; compared to Hicks and Harrod, 45; compared to Kaldor, 143; compared to Milton Friedman, 142; compared to neoclassical economists, 142; consumer behavior and modern psychology, 50; consummate society, 4; criticism of American Keynesian economists, 93; criticism of China, 84; criticism of Kenneth Arrow, 83; criticism of Marxism, 68, 128; criticism of neoclassical economics, 102; criticism of neo-Neoclassical economics, 93; criticism of orthodox economics, 14, 16; criticism of Oskar Lange, 91; criticism of P. J. D. Wiles, 91; criticism of Robert Solow, 65, 85; criticism of T. W. Swan, 69; debates with Paul Samuelson, 15, 30; debates with Robert Solow, 15, 30; defense of Keynes, 57; defense of Marx, 97; disdain for Americans, 30; economic theoretician, 28; empirical research, 31; employment and interest rates, 55; explanation of Keynes, 44; first major article, 36; focus of scholarship, 8; honorary Doctor of Laws, xix; impressions of Soviet Union, 61; India, 3; infatuation with China, 21; influence of Sraffa, 57; influences on economics, 162; inspiration to read Marx, 11; intellectual acknowledgments, 28; intellectual development, 108, 118, 159; interest in Marx, 11; international currency, 50, 52; international trade,

54, 158; interpretation of Marx, 137, 158; last economic writing, 131; letters, 159; major influences on, 17; marginal revenue, 134; Marxian phase, 108; means to full employment, 52; meeting Mao Tse-tung, 114; model of accumulation, 60; Nobel Prize, ix, 21; non-economic writing, 37; obstacles to full employment, 53; on determinacy, 43; on determination of foreign exchange rates, 43; on equality, 145; on foreign policy, 145; on the state of the British economy, 145; orthodox economics, battle with, 141; popularity, 20, 23; post-Keynesian-movement, 12; post-WWII inflation, 54; predictions, 27; productivity in the 1960s, 21; profile in *Applied Economics*, 29; rejection of monetary policy, 136; relationship with John Kenneth Galbraith, 23; relationship with Keynes, 7; relationship with students, 31; remedies for unemployment, 49; reply to Willett, 97; response to L. R. Klein, 73; review (condensed) of *Has Capitalism Changed?*, 79; reviews, (*See* Reviewed by Joan Robinson); shortcomings of modern economics, 116; similarity to Frederick D. Maurice, 2; socialism, 13; and capitalism, 79; and planning, 50; support for, 21, 137; sources of controversy, 30; space and time, 11; stages of inflation, 58; suggestions for Sri Lanka (Ceylon), 71; summary of economic philosophy, 104; summary of Keynesian economics, 116; textbook, 107; *The Accumulation of Capital* [111], 16, 65; theory of technical progress, 60; theory of the firm, 6; transformation of value into price, 89; travels in Asia, 87; unnecessary poverty, 51; view of Kuhne, 124; view of life, 99; view of Marx, 57; views on monopoly, 68; vision of society, 4; visit to Soviet Union, 13; visit to Sri Lanka (Ceylon), xviii; visit to United States, 21; visits to China, 13, 63, 104; work after 1970, 26

Rockefeller Scholarship, and Kalecki, Michal, 17

Rudra, A., *Indian Plan Models*, 112

Ruggle, N. D., *Economics*, 148

Russia. *See* Soviet Union

Rymes, T. K., *On Concepts of Capital and Technical Change*, 104

—S—

Samuelson, Paul, 10, 15, 124, 125, 151; "bastard" Keynesian, 30; "Exact Consumption-Loan Model of Interest," 75; analytical methodology, 111; comparison with Marx, 26; criticism by Joan Robinson, 81, 109, 119; debates with Joan Robinson, 15, 16, 30; *Foundations of Economic Analysis*, 11; theory of capital, 16

Samuelson, Paul and F. Modigliani, "Reply to Pasinetti and Robinson," 144

Savings theory, 8, 36

Say's Law, "dynamic" version, 24

Scandinavia, 46

Schlesinger, R., *Changing Attitudes in Soviet Russia: The Family*, 56

Schott, K., review [451] of *Collected Economic Papers*, Vol. 5 [317], 155

Schumpeter, Joseph A., 13, 81; *Capitalism, Socialism and Democracy*, 115; positive vision, 4; praise of Joan Robinson, 134; review [354] of *The Economics of Imperfect Competition* [005], 134

Shackle, G. L. S., xiv; review [371] of *Collected Economic Papers*, Volume 1 [086], 138; review [406] of *The Economics of Imperfect Competition* [005], 145

Shackleton, J. R. And G. Locksley, (editors) *Twelve Contemporary Economists*, 156

Shaffery, H. G., (editor) *The Soviet Economy: A Collection of Western and Soviet Views*, 86

Shakespeare, "real" identity, 37

Sharpe, M. E., review [415] of *Economics: An Awkward Corner* [204], 147

Shivji, I. G., *Class Struggle in Tanzania*, 113

Shove, G. F., xiv; "The Imperfection of the Market," 133; critique of Robinson, Joan, 37; review [352] of *The*

Economics of Imperfect Competition [005], 134; review [368] of *An Essay on Marxian Economics* [049], 137, 164
Simon, Herbert, 31
Skouras, T., "The Economics of Joan Robinson," 156
Smithies, A., review [373] of *The Rate of Interest and Other Essays* [089], 138
Social welfare, 38
Socialism, 44, 70; Chinese, 87, 99; Cuban, 90; European, defects of, 93; shortcomings, 93
Socialist economies, and capital accumulation, 98; westernization, 96
Solow, Robert, 15, 16, 73, 81, 102, 125, 142, 148; "A Contribution to the Theory of Economic Growth," 139; "bastard" Keynesian, 30; "The Production Function and the Theory of Capital," 138; *Capital Theory and the Rate of Return*, 85; criticism by Joan Robinson, 65, 81; debates with Joan Robinson, 15, 30; *Growth Theory, An Exposition*, 103; lectures in 1969 and 1970, 103; model of growth, 139; Nobel Prize, 139; production and distribution, 85
Soviet Union, xviii, 21, 61; collective farms, 94; command economy, 96; conference on Soviet Life, 61; consumers, 96; economic development, 56; economic success, 91; economic system, essays, 86; socialism, view of Mao Tse-tung, 124; trade with Britain, 67
Space and time, 11
Sraffa, Piero, 6, 7, 89, 159; economic model, 129; influence on Joan Robinson, 160; praise by Joan Robinson, 119; *Production of Commodities by Means of Commodities*, 77, 97, 119, 122, 129
Sri Lanka, suggestions for economic growth, 71; visit by Joan Robinson, xviii
St. Paul's School for Girls, 2
Stagflation, 81, 126
Steedman, I., *Marx after Sraffa*, 120
Stigler, G. J., review [391] of *Economic Philosophy* [158], 142
Stiglitz, J. E., model of accumulation, 98
Strachey, John, collaborated with Joan Robinson, 4; *Contemporary Capitalism*, 67
Sung, Kim Il, 89
Supply curve of capital goods, 38
Supply-side economics, 130
Swan, T. W., "Economic Growth and Capital Accumulation," 139; model of economic growth, 68
Swedish Academy of Science, x
Switching, 16, 65, 95

—T—

Tanner Lecture on Human Values. *See* University of Utah
Tanzania, class struggles, 113
Technical progress, 11, 65, 80, 87
Thatcher, Margaret, 27, 130
The Accumulation of Capital [111], xviii, 17, 18, 36, 68, 72, 79, 83, 139, 141, 144, 146, 149, 153, 158, 160; criticism, 18, 65; summary, 79
The Dictionary of National Biography, 2
The Economics of Imperfect Competition [005], ix, xviii, 6, 15, 36, 51, 63, 134, 135, 149, 153, 156, 164; and Nobel Prize, 32; masterpiece of modern economic thought, 28; shortcomings, 63; summary and analysis, 36
The General Theory of Employment, Interest and Money, 129
Third world, 123; economic development, 123; economics, Marxian interpretation, 123; problems of, 130
Thomson, D. L., *Adam Smith's Daughters*, 149
Tibet, 144
Time and space, 11
Tobin, J., xiv; review [432] of *Economic Heresies* [251], 150
Trade-cycle theories, 49
Trinity College, 7
Tsuru, S., "Keynes versus Marx," 138; *Has Capitalism Changed?*, 79
Turner, C. B., *An Analysis of Soviet Views on John Maynard Keynes*, 101
Turner, M. S., x, 2; biography of Joan Robinson, 31; *Joan Robinson and the Americans*, 162

—U—

Underdeveloped nations, 82
Unemployment, 8, 42, 43, 68, 95, 105; and inflation, 91, 126; disguised, 8, 40, 41, 42, 135; remedies, 42
Union for Radical Political Economics, 148
Unitas plan, 50
United Nations, 72, 115
United States, balance of payments, 52; economic activity, 1919-1937, 49; view of Cuba and Castro, 78
University of Basel, 100
University of Illinois, David Kinley Lecture, xix, 126
University of Maine, 119
University of Rennes, 70
University of Utah, 130. *See* Tanner Lecture
University of Western Ontario, 125
Utility theory, 50
Uzawa, H., review [410] of *Collected Economic Papers,* Volume 3 [195], 146

—V—

Value theory, 5, 35, 98, 111, 126, 161
Vandoorne, M., review [457] of *Collected Economic Papers*, Vol. 5 [317], 156
Veblen, Thorstein, 10, 161
von Bohm-Bawerk, E., *Karl Marx and the Close of his System*, 57
von Bortkiewecz, L., *On the Correction of Marx's Fundamental Theoretical Construction in the Third Volume of Capital*, 57

—W—

Wage economy, 70
Wage-price spiral, 70
Walker, K. R., *Planning in Chinese Agriculture*, 92
Walrasian accumulation, 87
Walsh, V., xiv
Wasserman, P., review [423] of *Economic Heresies* [251], 148
Weintraub, S., (editor) *Modern Economic Thought*, 153
Wicksell effect, pseudo, 70; real, 71, 75
Wicksteed, P. H., *The Coordination of the Laws of Distribution*, 37
Wiles, P. J. D., *Political Economy of Communism*, 91
Wilkinson, R. G., *Poverty and Progress*, 109
Wilson, Harold, 69
Wilson, T., *Fluctuations in Income and Employment*, 49
Wolfson, M., *A Reappraisal of Marxian Economics*, 96
World War II, 9, 46, 49
Worswick, G. D. N., "Mrs. Robinson on Simple Accumulation," 140; algebraic treatment of model of accumulation, 72; review [392] of *Essays in the Theory of Economic Growth* [159], 142
Wu, Y. L., *The Economy of Communist China*, 94; *The Steel Industry in Communist China*, 93

—Y—

Yugoslavia, 96
Yunnan, status of minorities, 111

—Z—

Zeitlin, L., *Life's Value in Cash*, 84
Zero savings, 43

About the Authors

JAMES CICARELLI, a PhD economist from the University of Connecticut, is the Dean of the Walter E. Heller College of Business Administration at Roosevelt University in Chicago.

JULIANNE CICARELLI holds a Master's degree from the State University of New York at Fredonia.

Together they have co-authored several publications including contributions to *Biographical Directory of the Council of Economic Advisers* (Greenwood Press, 1988).

ISBN 0-313-25844-9

90000>

EAN

9 780313 258442

HARDCOVER BAR CODE